Social Issues in Esports

This book provides important new insights into social issues in the rapidly growing field of esports, filling a gap in the literature that has, until now, been dominated by business and management perspectives.

Bringing together leading esports experts from Europe, North America, and Australia, the book provides new sociological analyses that define and locate esports in social studies. It explores key issues in esports and in the wider sociology of sport, including gender equity, diversity, cheating and doping, physical and mental health, and issues related to the governance of esports. Presenting new empirical research alongside critical, theoretical perspectives, the book addresses themes such as digitalisation, technology, equality, innovation, and welfare, suggesting directions for future research and highlighting implications for practice and development in the esports industry.

This is essential reading for advanced students, researchers, and practitioners working in esports, the sociology of sport, gaming studies, media studies, sociology, or the interaction of ICT and wider society.

Anne Tjønndal is Head of the Department of Leadership and Innovation and Head of RESPONSE – Research Group for Sport and Society at Nord University, Norway. She is also Visiting Professor at the Norwegian University of Science and Technology (NTNU).

Routledge Research in Sport, Culture and Society

Athlete Activism
Contemporary Perspectives
Edited by Rory Magrath

Training the Body
Perspectives from Religion, Physical Culture and Sport
Edited by David Torevell, Clive Palmer and Paul Rowan

Indigenous Sport and Nation Building
Interrogating Sámi Sport and Beyond
Eivind Å. Skille

Sport, Identity and Inclusion in Europe
The Experiences of LGBTQ People in Sport
Ilse Hartmann-Tews

Social Innovation, Entrepreneurship, and Sport for Development and Peace
Edited by Mitchell McSweeney, Per G. Svensson, Lyndsay M.C. Hayhurst and Parissa Safai

Sport and Physical Activity in Catastrophic Environments
Edited by Jack Black and Jim Cherrington

Social Issues in Esports
Edited by Anne Tjønndal

Sport, Physical Activity and Criminal Justice
Politics, Policy and Practice
Edited by Haydn Morgan and Andrew Parker

For more information about this series, please visit:
www.routledge.com/routledgeresearchinsportcultureandsociety/book-series/RRSCS

Social Issues in Esports

Edited by Anne Tjønndal

LONDON AND NEW YORK

First published 2023
by Routledge
4 Park Square, Milton Park, Abingdon, Oxon OX14 4RN

and by Routledge
605 Third Avenue, New York, NY 10158

Routledge is an imprint of the Taylor & Francis Group, an informa business

© 2023 selection and editorial matter, Anne Tjønndal; individual chapters, the contributors

The right of Anne Tjønndal to be identified as the author of the editorial material, and of the authors for their individual chapters, has been asserted in accordance with sections 77 and 78 of the Copyright, Designs and Patents Act 1988.

All rights reserved. No part of this book may be reprinted or reproduced or utilised in any form or by any electronic, mechanical, or other means, now known or hereafter invented, including photocopying and recording, or in any information storage or retrieval system, without permission in writing from the publishers.

Trademark notice: Product or corporate names may be trademarks or registered trademarks, and are used only for identification and explanation without intent to infringe.

British Library Cataloguing-in-Publication Data
A catalogue record for this book is available from the British Library

Library of Congress Cataloging-in-Publication Data
Names: Tjønndal, Anne, 1988-
Title: Social issues in Esports / edited by Anne Tjønndal.
Description: Abingdon, Oxon; New York, N.Y.: Routledge, 2023. | Series: Routledge research in sport, culture and society | Includes bibliographical references and index.
Identifiers: LCCN 2022025878 | ISBN 9781032193205 (hardback) | ISBN 9781032193212 (paperback) | ISBN 9781003258650 (ebook)
Subjects: LCSH: eSports (Contests)–Social aspects. | eSports (Contests)–Management.
Classification: LCC GV1469.34.E86 S64 2023 | DDC794.8–dc23/eng/20220713
LC record available at https://lccn.loc.gov/2022025878

ISBN: 978-1-032-19320-5 (hbk)
ISBN: 978-1-032-19321-2 (pbk)
ISBN: 978-1-003-25865-0 (ebk)

DOI: 10.4324/9781003258650

Typeset in Goudy
by Deanta Global Publishing Services, Chennai, India

Contents

List of figures vii
List of tables viii
List of contributors ix
Acknowledgements xi
Abbreviations xii

PART I
Setting the scene 1

1 Introduction to social issues in esports 3
 ANNE TJØNNDAL

2 Social issues in esports: Current and emerging trends in research 11
 ANNE TJØNNDAL, FRIDA AUSTMO WÅGAN, AND STIAN RØSTEN

PART II
Gender 29

3 The representation of women in *Hearthstone* esports 31
 ESPEN SJOBERG AND RAQUEL WILNER

4 Leadership and gender inclusion in esports organisations 46
 LUCY PIGGOTT, ANNE TJØNNDAL, AND JORID HOVDEN

5 The importance of female characters in esports: A quantitative analysis of players' perceptions of gendered character representations in sports video games 65
 EGIL TRASTI ROGSTAD AND MADS SKAUGE

PART III
Mental health and integrity issues 81

6 Stress and coping in esports 83
DYLAN POULUS AND REMCO POLMAN

7 Doping in esports 101
JOANNA WALL TWEEDIE, REBECCA R. ROSENTHAL, AND JOHN T. HOLDEN

8 'Virtually cycling': The impact of technology, cheating, and
performance enhancement in bicycle e-racing 115
BRYCE DYER

PART IV
Diversity and inclusion 129

9 Understanding the potential for esports to support social
inclusion agendas 131
EMILY HAYDAY AND HOLLY COLLISON

10 The Olympic Movement and esports governance: Finding the
right way of cooperating for diversity, equity, and inclusion 148
CEM ABANAZIR

PART V
Conclusion 163

11 Conclusion: Moving forward in research on social issues in esports 165
ANNE TJØNNDAL

Index 173

Figures

6.1	The cognitive-motivational-relational theory (CMRT) of emotion. (Lazarus, 1999.)	84
6.2	Diagram and conceptual framework of how situational aspects and personality could influence coping behaviour. (Adapted from DeLongis & Holtzman, 2005, p. 3.)	94
8.1	e-cycling app example	116
8.2	The goals of performance enhancement	118

Tables

2.1	Research papers on social issues in esports by publication year	21
4.1	Description of the participants	52
5.1a	Descriptive statistics of dependent variables	70
5.1b	Descriptive statistics of explanatory variables and respondents' locations	71
5.2a	Logistic regressions for 'I believe most sports video games portray women poorly' (1 = Agree) (N = 289)	72
5.2b	Logistic regressions for 'Being able to play characters of the same gender as myself is important to me' (1 = Agree) (N = 376)	73
5.2c	Logistic regressions for 'I feel that there are too few female characters in sports video games' (1 = Agree) (N = 372)	75
5.2d	Logistic regressions for 'I believe more girls and women would engage in sports video games if there were more female characters in the games' (1 = Agree) (N = 405)	76
6.1	Stressors experienced by e-athletes	88
11.1	Sociological work on esports	169

Contributors

Cem Abanazir is an independent researcher and was formerly Legal Counsel at the Turkish Football Federation.

Holly Collison is Senior Lecturer in the Institute for Sport Business at Loughborough University London, UK.

Bryce Dyer is Deputy Head of the Design and Engineering Department at Bournemouth University, UK, and Visiting Professor of Assistive Technology at the University of Bolton, UK.

Emily Hayday is Sport Business Lecturer at Loughborough University London, UK.

John T. Holden is Assistant Professor in the Spears School of Business at Oklahoma State University, OK.

Jorid Hovden is Professor Emerita of Sociology of Sport at the Norwegian University of Science and Technology (NTNU), Norway.

Lucy Piggott is Postdoctoral Fellow at the Norwegian University of Science and Technology (NTNU), Norway.

Remco Polman is Head of School Exercise and Nutrition Sciences at the Queensland University of Technology in Brisbane, Australia.

Dylan Poulus is Lecturer in the School of Health and Human Sciences at the Southern Cross University on the Gold Coast, Australia.

Egil Trasti Rogstad is a doctoral student and a member of the Sport and Society Research Group at Nord University in Bodø, Norway.

Rebecca R. Rosenthal is Litigation Associate at Paduano & Weintraub LLP in New York City, NY.

Stian Røsten is Research Assistant at Nord University and a member of the Sport and Society Research Group at Nord University in Bodø, Norway.

Espen Sjoberg is Associate Professor of Psychology at Kristiania University College, Norway.

Mads Skauge is Assistant Professor and a member of the Sport and Society Research Group at Nord University in Bodø, Norway.

Joanna Wall Tweedie is a visiting scholar in the Department of Sport Management at Florida State University, FL.

Frida Austmo Wågan is a doctoral student and a member of the Sport and Society Research Group at Nord University in Bodø, Norway.

Raquel Wilner is an independent art history scholar and founder of the Cognition & Art research group in Norway.

Acknowledgements

I would like to thank the 17 chapter authors who contributed to this book with their empirical and theoretical analyses of social issues in esports. Secondly, I would also like to say thank you to all the members of the RESPONSE Research Group at Nord University. Several research group members have contributed to the chapters in this book and others have contributed by providing feedback on early drafts of chapter manuscripts. A special thanks to research assistants Stian Røsten and Frida Austmo Wågan for their support with reference checks and formatting before submission of the manuscript.

Thank you to the Faculty of Social Sciences at Nord University for funding the language editing of the book manuscript. I would like to thank Sue Glover Frykman for her thorough work proofreading and language editing the book. Finally, many thanks to senior publisher Simon Whitmore at the Sport and Leisure section of Routledge for supporting me during the time it took to write and put together *Social Issues in Esports*.

Abbreviations

DOTA 2	*Defence of the Ancients 2*
EJSS	*European Journal for Sport and Society*
IOC	International Olympic Committee
IRSS	*International Review for the Sociology of Sport*
NIF	Norwegian Olympic and Paralympic Committee and Confederation of Sports
OM	Olympic Movement
MOBA	Multiplayer online battle arena
PUBG	*PlayerUnknown's Battlegrounds*
SDP	Sport for Development and Peace
SVGS	Sports video games

Part I

Setting the scene

Chapter 1

Introduction to social issues in esports

Anne Tjønndal

Technology and digitalisation are the main drivers for change in sport today. For instance, technological innovations have had – and continue to have – significant impacts on athletic performance in elite sport (Miah, 2014; Lippi et al., 2008). Some would even argue that in the absence of technological innovation no general improvement in global elite sport performance should be expected (Balmer et al., 2012). However, it is not just sport performance that is impacted by technology and digitalisation. Digitalisation changes the way sport is mediatised, officiated, and organised. In other words, no aspects of sport escape the influence of technology and digitalisation. As a form of sport that is facilitated by electronic systems in every aspect of its practices, esports is perhaps the most visible example of how technology and digitalisation impact all areas of sport development. Esports demonstrates how media and digital communication technologies contribute to the creation of new sports (Frandsen, 2020). Therefore, esports represents a particularly relevant type of digital development in sport. As the digital development in sport continues to grow, it also changes the social role that sport plays in Western societies. While in many cases sport can be a force for social inclusion and social change, decades of critical sociology of sport investigations have documented that deeply embedded historical roots and ideas mean that this is not always the case. Like any other part of social life, sport is riddled with social issues relating to integrity, health, exclusion, maltreatment, and harassment in various forms and contexts.

This book focuses on how social issues relating to gender, integrity and fairness, health, diversity, and social inclusion shape esports. Specifically, it addresses how social issues commonly found in sport impact digitally mediated esports. The book is not meant to be an introduction to esports as a phenomenon, because several books and articles have already been written for that specific purpose (Billings & Hou, 2019; Rogers, 2020; Hayday et al., 2022; Jonasson & Thiborg, 2010; Hallmann & Giel, 2018; Tjønndal, 2020). There is therefore no need for another academic text to introduce esports and why it is important for sports scholars to study the phenomenon. For the same reason, this introduction does not devote time or attention to the presentation of statistics to show how vastly popular esports has become globally, how many spectators are drawn to it, or how many billions of pounds in revenue the esports industry generates annually. The main thing to note is that esports is here to stay and is increasingly being integrated into sport organisations.

It would be naïve to suppose that none of the social issues plaguing sport is to be found in esports. There is a need to investigate the issues that the people who are engaged in esports actually experience, and for this, critical social scientific lenses are needed. Against this background, the intention of the book is to provide empirical and theoretical explorations of social issues in esports. A mapping such as this is a necessary first step towards combating social issues in esports to ensure the diversity and inclusion of athletes, coaches, and managers in digitally played sport.

Sport organisations are becoming increasingly digitalised (Scholz, 2019; Jacobsen, 2021) and the increased use of costly digital technologies in the management and practices of sport may in some cases contribute to the reinforcement of social issues in sport. For instance, studies have documented how digital technologies can fortify the maltreatment and bullying of athletes in youth sport (Kavanagh et al., 2020; Kavanagh et al., 2022), contribute to increased gender inequality in elite sport (Tjønndal, 2022; Toffoletti et al., 2022), and reproduce racist stereotypes (Oates, 2014). While research has begun to investigate the impact of digitalisation on various social issues in sport, limited scholarly attention has been devoted to empirical examinations of social issues in esports. Studies that examine how social issues transpire, and the impact they have on the people involved in esports, are needed to ensure that inclusive digital sporting spaces become the norm in esports. As esports as a phenomenon is integrated into organised sports and perhaps at some point is also included in the Olympic Movement, knowledge like this becomes increasingly important.

Social issues in esports

Across academic disciplines, a significant proportion of the current esports research has been devoted to debates about the definition of esports (Zhang et al., 2007; Wagner, 2006; Hamari & Sjöblom, 2017; Taylor, 2016). This research is an important first step in the production of scientific knowledge about esports, especially as the definition of esports is part of the scholarly framework (Reitman et al., 2020). Beyond the discussion related to how esports is defined, analyses are situated in a variety of academic fields, such as business, law, sport science, sociology, psychology, informatics, and media studies. For business researchers, exploring the motivation for esports consumption and the design of effective marketing techniques is common (Hamari & Sjöblom, 2017; Seo & Jung, 2014; Weiss, 2011). In sport science, most publications aim to evaluate the potential and pitfalls of esports as a sport (Hemphill, 2005; Parry, 2019; Hallman & Giel, 2018). Research in psychology has focused on player performance and cognitive and behavioural differences between esports novices and experts (Reitman et al., 2020). In the field of informatics, studies have used user-generated play data to analyse team performances (Kim et al., 2016) and social interactions between players (Freeman & Wohn, 2017). Law studies mainly examine copyright and intellectual property in the digital spaces of esports (Holden et al., 2017). Research in media studies has investigated the relationships between esports, the media, and sport (Holt, 2016; Taylor, 2012). Here, live streaming and interactions between audiences and streamers appear to be a major research subject (Reitman et al., 2020). Finally, the work on the sociology of esports has analysed esports as a vehicle for and a result of cultural change and looked at issues of gender equality and the representations of women in esports (Ruvalcaba et al., 2018; Rogstad, 2021). However, across the scholarly disciplines, research on social issues in esports appears to be almost non-existent. Research that does examine social issues is mainly related to the marginalisation of women in esports (Taylor et al., 2009; Darvin et al., 2020), or mental health issues in esports athletes (Leis & Lautenbach, 2020; Poulus et al., 2021).

Social issues in esports include contemporary sport issues such as race, media, gender, ethics, integrity, economics, drugs, recruiting, injuries, and youth sports. Overall, these issues relate to people's experiences with organised competitive gaming. In their work on the societal impact of esports, Riatti and Thiel (2021) distinguish between social impact and societal impact and explain that

> social impact refers to positive effects being triggered directly or indirectly on a personal level by an intervention or an entity. Societal impact includes all effects on several areas of society, understanding how an entity is rooted in society, with both positive, therefore including social impact, and negative consequences.
>
> (p. 2)

Regarding social issues in esports, the starting point of this book is that such issues impact both the individual and societal levels. This is reflected in the chapters included in the book, where some contributions examine social issues at an individual level, while others analyse the negative consequences of social issues for esports more broadly.

Overview of the book

This book brings together empirical and theoretical analyses of social issues in esports. The main purpose of the book is to provide an explorative contribution to the much-needed knowledge production of issues related to gender, ethics and integrity, drugs, racism, social inclusion, and exclusion in esports. Further examination into such issues is needed in order to combat exclusionary practices, discrimination, and harassment in digitally played sport. This book should be read as a collection of early and exploratory studies of some of the social issues found in the esports landscape. It does not aim to provide a comprehensive overview of 'all' the social issues that are prevalent in esports, nor does it aim to be a handbook of social issues in esports. As highlighted in this chapter, research on social issues in esports is still in its infancy. Therefore, the book is meant to be a collection of studies of some of the social issues that are currently being examined by scholars. The 11 chapters of the book are in many cases both context and game genre specific.

The book is divided into five parts. Part I is entitled 'Setting the Scene' and consists of this introduction (Chapter 1) and Chapter 2, 'Social Issues in Esports: Current and Emerging Trends in Research', written by the editor in collaboration with colleagues Frida Austmo Wågan and Stian Røsten. This section provides the reader with the necessary background information for understanding the context of the research contributions included in the book. Specifically, Chapter 2 presents a review and mapping of extant scholarship on social issues in esports. The chapter provides insights into which topics are prioritised in research on social issues in esports and identifies some of the current and emerging thematic trends in the field. Through this review, it is found that two topics stand out in terms of scholarly attention: (1) gender and discrimination in esports and (2) mental health issues in esports. Other emerging trends in academic explorations of esports are issues related to integrity and cheating, violence, racism, and social inequality. The attention to gender in esports is also apparent in this book, in that three out of the 12 chapters focus on social issues related to gender.

Part II revolves around 'Gender' and consists of Chapters 3–5, all of which examine social issues related to gender in esports. In Chapter 3, 'The Representation of Women in *Hearthstone* Esports', Espen Sjoberg and Raquel Wilner outline the gender controversies that have occurred in the popular esports title *Hearthstone*. They do this by means of an overview of the four women who competed in the game at world-class levels between 2014 and 2021 and the gendered issues they faced in their esports careers. A main point is how these women had to manage media focus directed towards their gender, rather than their skill, and how they often felt that they were tokens in a male-dominated sporting landscape. Through their analyses the authors show how the *Hearthstone* esports scene has seen its fair share of controversy related to gender discrimination.

Following this, in Chapter 4, 'Leadership and Gender Inclusion in Esports Organisations', Lucy Piggott, Anne Tjønndal, and Jorid Hovden present their study of how organisational structures, processes, and practices influence the gendering of power in leadership and governance positions in esports organisations. They do this based on qualitative data derived from interviews with leaders in Norwegian esports organisations. Their findings show how women are underrepresented across all levels and positions in esports organisations. There is also evidence of gender segregation in leadership roles, with women tending to be absent in roles with the highest volume of symbolic capital. Additionally, their analyses show that recruitment is an example of an organisational process rooted in the structure and culture of the esports industry that produces gender inequality in esports organisations. This is through problematic informal recruitment processes in which male-dominated networks are highly influential.

A gender perspective on social issues in esports is continued in Chapter 5, 'The Importance of Female Characters in Esports: A Quantitative Analysis of Players' Perceptions of Gendered Character Representations in Sports Video Games', written by Egil Trasti Rogstad and Mads Skauge. Using quantitative survey data of esports players, they examine how representations of women as playable game characters in sports video games (SVGs) are perceived by players. The results of their logistic regression analyses reveal a clear gendered pattern, indicating that women have clearer and stronger opinions about female characters in SVGs than men. The players feel that female character options are too limited and that being able to play female characters is important to them. Moreover, the female respondents included in the study feel that SVGs portray women poorly and that more girls and women would engage in SVGs if more female characters were included.

Part III, 'Mental Health and Integrity Issues', consists of Chapters 6–8 and includes empirical and conceptual work relating to mental health in esports athletes, as well as issues associated with doping and cheating in esports. Chapter 6, 'Stress and Coping in Esports', by Dylan Poulus and Remco Polman, outlines the sources of stress, stress appraisals, coping, and coping effectiveness experienced by athletes in esports. They review the progress and prospects for stress and coping esports research, outline new areas for investigation, and discuss potential interventions for athletes that could improve their well-being. Their findings show that experiencing stress appears to be an inherent part of competitive and elite esports performance. Therefore, a main point from their analyses is the lack of research into the potential gender and age differences in esports athletes' stress and coping mechanisms, thus demonstrating the limited knowledge about how to improve different groups of athletes' well-being through stress coping mechanisms.

Chapter 7 changes the focus from mental health to integrity issues in esports. 'Doping in Esports', written by Joanna Wall Tweedie, Rebecca R. Rosenthal, and John T. Holden, describes the emergence of doping concerns in the esports industry. The authors demonstrate how the anti-doping battle in esports is mainly against cognition-enhancing stimulants like Adderall and Vyvanse. Tweedie, Rosenthal, and Holden argue that although various organisations have implemented policies to eradicate the pervasive doping culture present in the professional esports industry, the majority of leagues have shied away from enacting such regulations. The chapter concludes by offering doping policy recommendations for esports leagues that are designed to lessen player drug abuse and protect the legitimacy of the burgeoning esports industry.

Continuing the topic of integrity issues in esports, Chapter 8, '"Virtually Cycling": The Impact of Technology, Cheating, and Performance Enhancement in Bicycle e-Racing', by Bryce Dyer, explores the technology that is used to facilitate e-Cycling and categorises the legal and illegal ergogenics that can occur as a result of it. Using e-Cycling as an empirical case, Dyer discusses the various ways in which athletes may cyber-dope to win competitions, including methods such as avatar misrepresentation, in-game deception, data manipulation, and hardware manipulation. Overall, the analyses presented in Dyer's chapter illustrate how cheating, a well-known issue in competitive sports, has extended from the real world to the virtual domain.

Part IV, 'Diversity and Inclusion', consists of Chapters 9–10, both of which present theoretical perspectives on esports, sport policy, and social inclusion. Chapter 9, 'Understanding the Potential for Esports to Support Social Inclusion Agendas', by Emily Hayday and Holly Collison, explores how esports, through its unique characteristics and commercial positioning, can act as a new strategy to enhance social inclusion and social development outcomes, especially for youth populations that are often the target of SDP programmes. They argue that there is a need, justification, and space for esports within the SDP landscape. Specifically, Hayday and Collison highlight that esports's primary attraction to SDP is the enhanced opportunities it offers to interact with marginalised populations and those who shy away from traditional sporting spaces. In this way, esports can construct an inclusive bridging mechanism that does not discriminate by virtue of physicality, masculinity, or mainstream sporting cultures.

Following this, in Chapter 10, 'The Olympic Movement and Esports Governance: Finding the Right Way of Cooperating for Diversity, Equity, and Inclusion', Cem Abanazir explores the relationship between the Olympic Movement (OM) and SVGs esports to describe the major implications of the interplay between sport, esports, and social issues. In his chapter, Abanazir argues that the differences between the methods of production and governance of the OM and the esports industry give the OM more control over the production process of the Olympic Games that would better suit the interests of the esports industry. However, the inter-relationship between these forces could either create conflict or harmony on social issues, particularly regarding inclusion. Here, Abanazir highlights potential inclusion issues related to gender and transgender women in particular.

Part V, 'Conclusion', consists of the book's eleventh and final chapter, entitled 'Conclusion: Moving Forward in Research on Social Issues in Esports'. This chapter, written by the editor, summarises some of the overarching analytical points and findings across the individual chapters, with a focus on the current challenges related to social issues in esports and the consequences of these for athletes, coaches, and leaders.

References

Balmer, N., Pleasence, P., & Nevill, A. (2012). Evolution and revolution: Gauging the impact of technological and technical innovation on Olympic performance. *Journal of Sports Sciences*, 30(11), 1075–1083. https://doi.org/10.1080/02640414.2011.587018

Billings, A., & Hou, J. (2019). The origins of eSport: Half a century history of 'overnight' success. In R. Rogers (Ed.), *Understanding eSports – An introduction to a global phenomenon* (pp. 31–44). Lexington Books.

Darvin, L., Vooris, R., & Mahoney, T. (2020). The playing experiences of eSports participants: An analysis of treatment discrimination and hostility in eSports environments. *Journal of Athlete Development and Experience*, 2(1), 36–50.

Frandsen, K. (2020). *Sport and mediatization*. Routledge.

Freeman, G., & Wohn, D. Y. (2017a). eSports as an emerging research context at CHI: Diverse perspectives on definitions. In *Proceedings of the 2017 CHI Conference Extended Abstracts on Human Factors in Computing Systems (CHI EA'17)*, pp. 1601–1608. https://doi.org/10.1145/3027063.3053158

Hallmann, K., & Giel, T. (2018). eSports—Competitive sports or recreational activity? *Sport Management Review*, 21, 14–20. https://doi.org/10.1016/j.smr.2017.07.011

Hamari, J., & Sjöblom, M. (2017). What is eSports and why do people watch it? *Internet Research*, 27(2), 211–232. https://doi.org/10.1108/IntR-04-2016-0085

Hayday, E., Collison-Randall, H., & Kelly, S. (2022). *eSports insights*. Routledge.

Hemphill, D. (2005). Cybersport. *Journal of the Philosophy of Sport*, 32, 195–207. https://doi.org/10.1080/00948705.2005.9714682

Holden, J. T., Kaburakis, A., & Rodenberg, R. M. (2017). The future is now: Esports policy considerations and potential litigation. *Journal of Legal Aspects of Sport*, 27, 46–78. https://doi.org/10.1123/jlas.2016-0018

Holt, J. (2016). Virtual domains for sports and games. *Sport, Ethics and Philosophy*, 10, 5–13. https://doi.org/10.1080/17511321.2016.1163729

Jacobsen, J. M. (2021). *The essential guide to the business & law of eSports & professional video gaming*. Routledge.

Jonasson, K., & Thiborg, J. (2010). Electronic sport and its impact on future sport. *Sport in Society*, 13(2), 287–299. https://doi.org/10.1080/17430430903522996

Kavanagh, E., Litchfield, C., & Osborne, J. (2022). Social media, digital technology and athlete abuse. In J. Sanderson (Ed.), *Sport, social media, and digital technology: Sociological approaches* (pp. 185–204). Emerland Publishing.

Kavanagh, E., Litchfield, C., & Osborne, J. (2020). Virtual technologies as tools of maltreatment: Safeguarding in digital spaces. In M. Lang (Ed.), *Routledge handbook of athlete welfare* (pp. 221–230). Routledge.

Kim, J., Keegan, B. C., Park, S., & Oh, A. (2016). The proficiency-congruency dilemma: Virtual team design and performance in multiplayer online games. In *CHI'16 Proceedings of the 2016 CHI Conference on Human Factors in Computing Systems*, pp. 4351–4365. https://doi.org/10.1145/2858036.2858464

Leis, O., & Lautenbach, F. (2020). Psychological and physiological stress in non-competitive and competitive eSports settings: A systematic review. *Psychology of Sport and Exercise*, 101738. https://doi.org/10.1016/j.psychsport.2020.101738

Lippi, G., Banfi, G., Favaloro, E. J., Rittweger, J., & Muffalli, N. (2008). Updates on improvement of human athletic performance: Focus on world records in athletics. *British Medical Bulletin*, 87, 7–15.

Miah, A. (2014). The cybersport nexus. In A. Billings & M. Hardin (Eds.), *The Routledge handbook of sport and new media* (pp. 76–86). Routledge.

Oates, T. P. (2014). Madden men: Masculinity, race, and the marketing of a video game franchise. In R. A. Brookey & T. P. Oates (Eds.), *Playing to win: Sports video games, and the culture of play* (pp. 45–62). Indiana University Press.

Parry, J. (2019). E-sports are not sports. *Sports, Ethics and Philosophy* 13(1), 3–18. https://doi.org/10.1080/17511321.2018.1489419

Poulus, D., Coulter, T., Trotter, M., & Polman, R. (2021). Perceived stressors experienced by competitive eSports athletes. *International Journal of Esports.* https://www.ijesports.org/article/73/html.

Reitman, J. G., Anderson-Coto, M. J., Wu, M., Lee, J. S., & Steinkuehler, C. (2020). Esports research: A literature review. *Games and Culture 15*(1), 32–50. https://journals.sagepub.com/doi/pdf/10.1177/1555412019840892

Riatti, P., & Thiel, A. (2021). The societal impact of electronic sport: A scoping review. *German Journal of Exercise and Sport Research.* https://doi.org/10.1007/s12662-021-00784-w

Rogers, R. (2020). *Understanding eSports - An Introduction to the Global Phenomenon.* Rowman & Littlefield.

Rogstad, E. T. (2021). Gender in eSports research: A literature review. *European Journal for Sport and Society,* 1–19. https://doi.org/10.1080/16138171.2021.1930941

Ruvalcaba, O., Shulze, J., Kim, A., Berzenski, S. R., & Otten, M. P. (2018). Women's experiences in eSports: Gendered differences in peer and spectator feedback during competitive video game play. *Journal of Sport and Social Issues, 42,* 295–311. https://doi.org/10.1177/0193723518773287

Scholz, T. (2019). *eSports is Business - Management in the World of Competitive Gaming.* Palgrave Macmillan.

Seo, Y., & Jung, S.-U. (2014). Beyond solitary play in computer games: The social practices of eSports. *Journal of Consumer Care, 16,* 635–655. doi:10.1177/1469540514553711

Taylor, N. (2016). Play to the camera: Video ethnography, spectatorship, and e-sports. *Convergence, 22,* 115–130. https://doi.org/10.1177/1354856515580282

Taylor, N., Jenson, J., & de Castell, S. (2009). Cheerleaders/booth babes/Halo hoes: Progaming, gender and jobs for the boys. *Digital Creativity, 20,* 239–252. https://doi.org/10.1080/14626260903290323

Taylor, T. L. (2012). *Raising the stakes, E-sports and the professionalization of computer gaming.* MIT Press.

Tjønndal, A. (2020). "What's next? Calling beer-drinking a sport?!": Virtual resistance to considering eSport as sport. *Sport, Business and Management.* https://doi.org/10.1108/SBM-10-2019-0085

Tjønndal, A. (2022). *Idrettsteknologi.* Fagbokforlaget.

Toffoletti, K., Ahmad, N., & Thorpe, H. (2022). Critical encounters with social media in women's sport and physical culture. In J. Sanderson (Ed.), *Sport, social media, and digital technology: Sociological approaches* (pp 29–47). Emerland Publishing.

Wagner, M. (2006). On the scientific relevance of eSports. In *Proceedings of the 2006 International Conference on Internet Computing & Conference on Computer Games Development,* ICOMP 2006. https://www.researchgate.net/publication/220968200_On_the_Scientific_Relevance_of_eSports

Weiss, T. (2011). Fulfilling the needs of eSports consumers: A uses and gratifications perspective. In *BLED 2011 Proceedings, 30.* http://aisel.aisnet.org/bled2011/30

Zang, L., Wu, J., & Li, Y. (2007). Research on current situation of E-sports in Urumqi, Xinjiang. *International Journal of Sports Science and Engineering, 2,* 57–61. http://www.worldacademicunion.com/journal/SSCI/SSCIvol02no01paper08.pdf

Chapter 2

Social issues in esports
Current and emerging trends in research

Anne Tjønndal, Frida Austmo Wågan, and Stian Røsten

Social issues in esports encompass a variety of problems and challenges related to people's experiences with organised competitive gaming. In some instances, these issues also relate to esports interactions with society at large. This means that the topic of social issues in esports covers many different sub-fields of research. In the sociology of sport, common topics that are often discussed under the umbrella of social issues in sport are: (1) sport participation and dropout patterns, (2) integrity, ethics and moral behaviour, (3) race and ethnicity, (4) gender, (5) social class, (6) disability, (7) religion, (8) health, (9) governance and politics, and (10) doping and violence (Sleap, 1998; Kew, 1997; Woods & Butler, 2020). As these topics are research fields in their own right, it is clear that comprehensively mapping the current knowledge about social issues in any type of sport will prove challenging. Added to these difficulties is the somewhat blurred line between what researchers often refer to as social issues and the social impact of sport, and what is referred to as societal issues and the societal impact of sport (Riatti & Thiel, 2021; Bornmann, 2013), where some scholars make a distinction between issues that affect individuals at a personal level (social issues) and issues that affect several areas of society (societal issues). In this chapter, we do not make such a strict distinction between the two because we believe that these issues are often intertwined in complex ways.

Despite the difficulties of mapping the field of social issues in esports, the purpose of this chapter is to examine the current knowledge and research trends in social issues in esports. Specifically, our aim is to say something about which topics are prioritised in research and to share our reflections on the current and emerging trends in the field. Our work to consolidate social issues in the esports field builds on recent literature reviews of relevant sub-fields, such as gender and esports (Rogstad, 2021), the societal impact of esports (Riatti & Thiel, 2021), well-being and gaming addiction (Shulze et al., 2021; Chung et al., 2019), and mental health (Palanichamy et al., 2020). We combine an analysis of these reviews with database searches for novel research contributions and an examination of work referenced in these contributions. Using the databases SPORTDiscus, PubMed, Scopus, and Web of Science, we searched for research on integrity issues, gender, race, social class, health, doping, and violence. In

DOI: 10.4324/9781003258650-3

other words, the methodological approach we have used to consolidate current literature on social issues in esports can best be described as a type of narrative literature review (Jesson et al., 2011). As our aim is not to narrowly and systematically review a specific sub-field of social issues in esports, we have not conducted a systematic literature review with strict searches, mesh terms, and exclusion criteria. Rather, we broadly map what research on different social issues tells us about the current and emerging trends in the esports industry.

Based on our analysis of 63 scholarly publications, the chapter is structured in six thematic parts according to the topics of social issues in esports that we have identified in current research. These themes are: (1) integrity issues in esports, (2) violence and stigma in esports, (3) mental health and gaming addiction in esports, (4) social inequality in esports, (5) racism and harassment in esports, and (6) gender and esports. The chapter ends with some concluding reflections on the current and emerging trends in the esports research field.

Integrity issues in esports

As esports is a global multi-billion industry, research has started to identify the legal and regulatory concerns resulting from its rapid growth (Holden et al., 2019). As found in the literature on social issues in other sports, esports also faces integrity issues, such as internal and external corruption-related threats (Brickel, 2017; Holden et al., 2017a; Holden et al., 2019; Murray et al., 2020; Papaloukas, 2018; Tjønndal, 2020). Examples of internal corruption-related threats are doping (Gupta et al., 2021; Rosenthal, 2020), the manipulation or hacking of games through the use of software (i.e. 'edoping') (Conroy et al., 2021; Gohshal, 2019) and match-fixing (Abarbanel & Johnson, 2018; Yan, 2018). External corruption-related threats in esports include pressure from international gambling industries, both regulated (Holden et al., 2017b) and illegal gambling (Freitas et al., 2021; Greer et al., 2021; Macey & Hamari, 2018), as well as issues relating to a lack of governance and anti-doping work (Holden et al., 2017b).

Performance-enhancing drugs and edoping in esports

There are ongoing debates in the esports industry about the widespread use of doping and performance-enhancing drugs (PEDs) (Holden et al., 2019) and the prevalence of edoping[1] (Papaloukas, 2018). While doping in esports typically involves players taking 'study drugs' (e.g. Adderall, Ritalin) to improve their cognitive focus, perception, and reaction times (Gupta et al., 2021; Ghoshal, 2019; Rosenthal, 2020), edoping refers to technological methods that give players advantages over their opponents. This can be done by inserting cheat software to manipulate the game, hacking, or tampering with internet connections (Esports Integrity Coalition, 2016). Although most gaming servers have developed advanced protection systems to prevent and detect forms of edoping (Conroy et al., 2021; Gupta et al., 2021), very little drug testing or monitoring of players for PEDs is done in international competitive esports settings (Rosenthal, 2020).

Esports Integrity Coalition (2016) defines doping as a moderate threat in esports.[2] Still, very few empirical studies have actually investigated issues of doping in esports competitions (Riatti & Thiel, 2021). Our mapping of the field indicates that the majority of academic publications on the topic stress the lack of an international body for the governance and regulation of doping and other legal issues in esports (Brickell, 2017; Murray et al., 2020; Rosenthal, 2020). However, the studies of Gupta et al. (2021) and Freitas et al. (2021) are two novel contributions to the doping issue that are important to note.

Gupta et al. (2021) interviewed 25 professionals from the Esports Federation of India to explore the doping issue in the industry. Their participants emphasised that doping is a viable means of cheating in esports because it is difficult to detect without the implementation of standardised protocols and tests on players. Thus, doping is considered an 'easy option' in terms of gaining an advantage over opponents, especially cognition-enhancing drugs that achieve better focus, pattern recognition, and faster reaction times. Participants also expressed a 'need' for doping in order to boost cognitive performance which is linked to factors such as peer pressure and psychological benefits. However, as doping has a negative impact on the overall perception of esports, the participants also highlight the importance of mitigating doping by means of proper rules, regulations, and codes of conduct. Like Rosenthal (2020), Gupta et al. (2021) conclude that doping acts 'as a barrier to the legitimization of esports as a viable global industry' (p. 16).

Frietas et al. (2021) investigated which type of disreputable behaviour posed the biggest threat to esports sponsors using a quantitative approach with a sample of 1,592 esports fans globally. The participants were recruited from popular esports online forums. Interestingly, their results showed that the majority (61%) of esports fans stated that they had never witnessed evidence of doping in esports. Therefore, the findings of Frietas et al. (2021) somewhat contradict the widespread consumption of PEDs across the esports industry as suggested by other scholarly examinations (e.g. Holden et al., 2019). However, this can be linked to the fact that drug testing and the monitoring of esports players seldom take place (Rosenthal, 2020; Gupta et al., 2021) and that it would be difficult for an esports fan to observe whether or not a player was under the influence of PEDs. Nevertheless, Freitas et al. (2021) argued that doping appeared to be a low-risk threat to esports sponsors and that 'Maybe most of this attention has emerged from the general media and not so much from the esports community' (p. 55).

Match-fixing and gambling in esports

Given the significant growth of the esports industry, there have been extensive speculations about match-fixing in recent years (Brickell, 2017). Match-fixing is identified as a major threat to the growth and legitimacy of esports (Esports Integrity Coalition, 2016). Since the first international match-fixing scandal was discovered in 2010, issues relating to the manipulation of the outcome of games have increased considerably (Yan, 2018). For instance, the number '322' became synonymous with match-fixing in esports after a *Defence of the Ancients 2* (DOTA 2) player bet against his own team to win 322 USD (Ghoshal, 2019). It has been emphasised that match-fixing could be a strong temptation for esports players due to unstable salaries, the guarantee to win money regardless of the results of tournaments, or even where match-fixing provides higher profits than a tournament's prize money (Freitas et al., 2021). In an article discussing the professional context of esports, Brock (2017) addressed the problem of treating esports as 'work' and argued that match-fixing emerged as a rational option for players to survive in this context: 'Under conditions of intense competition and financial insecurity, professional players will make instrumental choices to try and endure' (p. 16). Hence, if professional esports players do not earn enough to survive, match-fixing could become a rational choice (Brock, 2017).

Whilst most scholarly attention focuses on the legal ramifications and regulations of match-fixing (e.g. Brickell, 2017; Holden et al., 2017a), very little empirical research has been conducted on esports and match-fixing. However, two exceptions are Abarbanel and Johnson (2018) and Freitas et al. (2021). Abarbanel and Johnson (2018) explored esports fans' (N = 1,321) perspectives on match-fixing in esports and found that esports fans were not unduly concerned about match-fixing yet at the same time thought that it was a difficult issue to govern and control. Similarly, Freitas et al. (2021) included esports fans' perspectives on match-fixing in their study and found that 64% of the fans included in their sample had seen some form of match-fixing and disliked the players, teams, or competitions associated with it.

Match-fixing is also closely linked to and has been exacerbated by the gambling market (Ghoshal, 2019). A prevalent theme in the media and public debate is esports gambling, where some contributions seek to warn parents about the high frequency of esports gambling amongst teenagers (Nairn, 2021), or that engagement in esports may contribute to gambling behaviour among youth (Rossi & Nairn, 2020). Others suggest that there is a double threat of developing addictive behaviour in terms of gambling addiction and gaming addiction in individuals engaging in esports (Kobek, 2019). Despite the interest of the media in gambling in esports, relatively few empirical studies have addressed it. However, some studies have explored the differences between esports gamblers and traditional gamblers (Peter et al., 2019; Greer et al., 2021). These studies indicate that socioeconomic and cultural backgrounds play a role in an individual's predisposition towards gambling, where unlike many traditional gamblers, esports gamblers tend to come from dual-income families, have a higher educational background, or a relatively high income (Choi et al., 2018; Peter et al., 2019). Further, these studies indicate that esports gamblers are younger, seem to gamble more frequently, and are more likely to experience at least one form of gambling-related harm than traditional gamblers (Greer et al., 2021; Gainsbury et al., 2017). Such gambling-related harm includes the overall consequences for the addicted individual, their family, and friends (Browne et al., 2018), such as economic problems due to betting or the neglect of school and work duties.

Overall, the current research on integrity issues in esports is in dire need of more empirical studies, particularly those that address the prevalence of and the mechanisms that contribute to such behaviour in esports. Here, empirical studies can make important knowledge contributions to the ongoing media and public debates.

Violence and stigma in esports

Violence and stigma in esports are, like several of the themes examined in this chapter, under-researched social issues. The studies that do address violence and stigma share a commonality in that they examine cultural concerns related to a correlation between engagement in esports and negative social impacts, such as addictive behaviour, gambling, aggressive behaviour, and violence (Peter et al., 2019; Freitas et al., 2021; Goh, 2021; Bascón-Seda & Macías, 2022). Interestingly, none of the articles addresses doping in relation to stigma, in contrast to traditional sports where doping is seen as one of the most stigmatised behaviours (Sefiha, 2017).

Stigmas associated with esports participation

Freitas et al. (2021) identified four main reasons why society had a negative perception of videogames: (1) gaming is an unproductive activity, (2) violent videogames incite aggressive behaviour, (3) videogames lead to gaming addiction, and (4) esports engagement leads to gambling addiction. Further, they concluded that these negative perceptions of esports may threaten future partnerships with sponsors and other stakeholders. On the other hand, based on their analysis of esports content, Bascón-Seda and Macías (2022) argued that this was not the case, and instead illustrated how esports could contribute to ethical development and individual learning. Specifically, Bascón-Seda and Macías (2022) argued that the virtualisation of the self through playing esports could enhance players' feelings of freedom, virtue, and self-knowledge.

A couple of empirical studies have identified stigmas related to different populations' engagement in esports (Peter et al., 2019; Zaho & Zhu, 2021). Using an experimental vignette study design, Peter et al. (2019) compared the degree of public stigma towards traditional casino gamblers, esports gamblers, and internet gamers using data from 822 Americans. Peter et al. (2019) found that all three types of addictions were heavily stigmatised, caused a significant amount of anger and blame and resulted in higher levels of desired social distance among the participants. Zaho and Zhu (2021) studied stigma and mental well-being among players, coaches, managers, and commentators working in 15 top esports clubs in the Chinese cities of Shanghai, Guangzhou, Suzhou, and Chengdu. They concluded that there was a societal perception of a correlation between esports and gaming addiction and that this social norm needed to be challenged in order for esports to be destigmatised and the mental well-being of esports players improved.

Esports athletes and aggressive behaviour

A few contributions examined aggressive behaviour among esports athletes (Butovskaya & Chargaziya, 2020; Ohno, 2021). Butovskaya and Chargaziya (2020) studied the potential risk factors of engaging in aggressive and violent behaviour among male esports players. Their findings indicated that inexperienced esports players were more likely to engage in aggressive behaviour and conflicts than experienced esports players (Butovskaya & Chargaziya, 2020). This suggests that the risk of engaging in violent behaviour decreases with the amount of time invested in playing esports.

In a study of Japanese students playing online games frequently (N = 874), Ohno (2021) determined that the only game genre associated with the development of aggressive feelings and violent outcomes was battle royale games such as *Fortnite* and *PUBG* (Ohno, 2021). From this finding, Ohno (2021) concluded that, as a gaming genre, battle royale games required more attention than other games in terms of the risk of developing aggressive feelings. On the other hand, the only identified risk factor for experiencing aggressive or violent behaviour was being a female player (Menti & de Araujo, 2017).

Gaming addiction and mental health in esports

Our efforts to map the social issues in the esports field indicate that mental health and gaming addiction is one of the sub-fields that has developed most academically. When searching the Scopus, SPORTDiscus, Web of Science, and PubMed databases, we identified 27 studies addressing mental health and gaming addiction in esports. Most of these studies gathered empirical data via internet surveys (Greer et al., 2021; Lelonek-Kuleta & Bartczuk, 2021; Macey & Hamari, 2018), although there are also examples of ethnographic studies (Fiskaali et al., 2020; Mao, 2021) and qualitative interviews (Zhao & Zhu, 2021). European, Asian, and North American studies were well represented in the literature, but no studies from African and South American countries were identified.

Gaming addiction in esports

A common finding in several of the studies is the notion that the risk of gaming addiction or other negative outcomes for mental well-being appears to be greater for individuals who spend a lot of time gaming (Macey & Hamari, 2019; Kelly et al., 2021; Baniày et al., 2019; Triberti et al., 2018; Macey & Hamari, 2018; Macey et al., 2020; Fiskaali et al., 2020). In a mixed-methods study combining a survey on well-being with participant observations in a school-related esports programme, Fiskaali et al. (2020) found that esports students who were highly involved in gaming had a lower score on mental health measurements and reported more loneliness than other students. The participant observations showed that inexperienced coaches and students hampered the establishment of a positive and nurturing training culture and that this could be a contributory factor to low scores on students' well-being. Other studies, such as those of Macey et al. (2020) and Kelly et al. (2021), have shown that there is a strong link between the time spent playing or watching esports and an increased risk of developing gaming addiction and negative mental health outcomes.

Some studies identified differences in the coping strategies and motivations for playing as possible explanations for differences in mental health outcomes and addiction scores (Lelonek-Kuleta & Bartczuk, 2021; Bànyai et al., 2021; Pereira et al., 2021). More specifically, motivations related to 'escapism' in terms of playing to escape from emotional problems in the real world were common for individuals with a high addiction score (Columb et al., 2020; Lelonek-Kuleta & Bartczuk, 2021). Other identified risk factors for developing a gaming addiction were found to be socioeconomic and cultural backgrounds, gender, and age, where the stereotypical esports addict seemed to be a young male (Macey & Hamari, 2019; Choi et al., 2018). Further, Choi et al. (2018) suggested that young males were at particular risk due to their flexible spare time and the fact that gaming and esports were important social arenas for young boys. This is in line with other studies on general gaming showing that female players, especially young girls, experience more adverse consequences, such as mental health and loneliness, because this is seen as a social arena for boys only (Talberg, 2019).

Mental health and well-being in esports

In addition to studies of esports and addictive behaviour, some research findings indicate that negative mental health outcomes like anxiety, depression, sleep disturbances, cognitive fatigue, and psychological distress are related to high involvement in esports (Palanichamy et al., 2020; Shulze et al., 2021). In their literature review, Palanichamy et al. (2020) noted that esports' excessive play and competitive nature seemed to increase the risk of experiencing a range of psychological problems, such as depression, anxiety, mental distress, distress in social life, and emotional disturbances. A review by Shulze et al. (2021) supported these findings.

However, the findings from a Chinese study suggest that when the cultural stigma associated with esports changes, athletes' mental health and well-being improve (Zhao & Zhu, 2021). A study based on in-depth interviews with Chinese esports athletes has shown that the positive changes in Chinese society in the last decade, with regard to cultural beliefs and social norms in relation to esports, have also had a positive impact on esports players' mental health and well-being (Zhao & Zhu, 2021). It is clear, though, that there is a need for more research on this topic (Chung et al., 2019). Also, more longitudinal research on the causal relationship between risk factors and negative health outcomes would deepen our understanding of the link between esports, addiction, and mental health.

Social inequality in esports

Many esports communities have shown an increased interest in structural and economic differences in the esports industry (Higgins, 2020). While this topic appears in many online opinion pieces, research on social inequality in esports is limited. The handful of studies that exist either look at the differences in how factors related to income and education influence youth participation in esports (Gainsbury et al., 2017; Choi et al., 2018), or the differences in income between professional esports players according to national or international wage statistics (McLeod et al., 2021; Parshakov et al., 2020).

Social inequality in esports players' earnings and youth participation

McLeod et al. (2021) used prize earnings data from 2005 to 2019 to examine inequality in earnings in the esports labour market and how these inequalities may have changed over the last 15 years. The authors based their analysis on data collected from the online database Esports Earnings[3] and found a simultaneous growth and inequality in esports earnings during the studied period. According to them, esports players can expect to earn more today than in 2005, although median incomes show inconsistent growth compared with top incomes. A main finding from their study is that most esports players still earn less than the USA poverty threshold. They also found gender inequalities when comparing the earnings of top female players with the labour market as a whole. That is, women esports players earn less than their male counterparts and are therefore at greater risk of falling below the USA poverty threshold. McLeod et al. (2021) concluded that the esports labour market provides opportunities for a few (primarily male) competitors and is supported by a growing class of poorly paid players.

Parshakov et al. (2020) examined the link between national unemployment figures and the popularity of esports games by comparing data from different countries with different income levels and labour productivity and found a positive link between increased popularity of video games and increasing unemployment rates amongst young people. Their results suggest that 'in countries in which playing video games is more popular, especially to the point of becoming a source of income for some participants, that unemployment is higher than in countries where gaming is less popular' (p. 830).

Although there seems to be a link between unemployment rates and the popularity of esports participation in young adults, it seems like youth from dual-income families spend more time playing esports games compared to youth from single-income families, at least in a Korean sample of esports participants (N = 246) (Choi et al. 2018). Choi et al. (2018) found that the motivation for playing was different for youth from multicultural families compared to youth from dual-income families; whereas adolescents from dual-income families were motivated to play in order to pass time, those who came from multicultural families reported playing online games to engage in social interaction. The adolescents from dual-income families also scored significantly higher than youth from single-income families on factors related to juvenile delinquency and addiction.

Racism and ethnicity in esports

Despite the image portrayed by many practitioners that esports is 'for everyone' (Cote, 2017), racism and discriminatory behaviour appear to be overarching issues in the esports landscape (Riatti & Thiel, 2021). As Chan (2005) has pointed out, race matters in esports. More specifically, race is visible in the environment around esports players with frequent instances of racial conduct and in games that reproduce common ideologies and narratives about race (Goh, 2021). An example of racial conduct in esports is the case of Terrence Miller, a former professional *Hearthstone* player. In 2016, Miller came second in an international tournament that was streamed on the Twitch platform and whenever he appeared on-screen viewers filled the chat box with slurs and racially coded emoticons (Winkie, 2021). Racial conduct is also apparent in the games themselves, where 'racialized ideas, bodies, and structures are constructed, mediated, and presented' (Leonard 2003, p. 3). However, race and ethnicity have been neglected in research on social issues in esports (Leonard, 2003; Shulze et al., 2021).

There are a few research contributions on the topic of racism and esports. For instance, Gray (2012) examined the social interactions of Xbox Live players and found that they were highly racialised. Specifically, non-white players were exposed to linguistic profiling and constructed as 'deviant' when they failed to conform to the white male as the default gamer. These findings indicate that, in general, people who differ from the majority are treated worse than their majority counterparts in esports (Cote, 2017). However, most studies do not clarify what demographic groups make up the majority in esports participation. In her study, Gray (2012) argued that much racism in esports stemmed from the myth that 'black people are not gamers', which has been perpetuated by the gaming industry, and concluded: 'This is a dangerous myth to disseminate because video games have the power to deploy stereotypical imagery and hegemonic ideologies and the virtual gaming communities have adopted these same exclusionary practices' (p. 274).

Two recently published literature reviews briefly discuss racism in esports (Riatti & Thiel, 2021; Shulze et al., 2021). Riatti and Thiel (2021) found that only a few programmes or approaches address discriminatory and exclusive issues. Due to the anonymity of players, and the fact that behaviour is barely regulated, they argue that esports can be abused as a platform for verbal discrimination based on ethnicity, gender, or other identity markers.

In another review, Shulze et al. (2021) summarised the different strategies that esports players could adopt to cope with racism and other forms of harassment. These included muting their microphones, masking their identities, avoiding randomised games, and playing with friends. However, both reviews emphasised that more research on the topic was required. Shulze et al. (2021) noted that as the environment around esports players has been less studied, very little is known about resilience and the outcomes of harassment in esports and that there was therefore a need for studies that included players from underrepresented identities (e.g. ethnicity, class, gender, and sexual identity), which would be an important step towards protecting and fostering esports players' well-being.

Gender and esports

Issues related to gender inclusion, and specifically the conditions for women, appear to have attracted the most scholarly attention in the broader research field of social issues in esports, alongside mental health. In a recent literature review, Rogstad (2021) analysed research on gender and esports published between 2006 and 2020. Using a narrative review strategy, he identified 21 contributions on gender and esports. On analysing these publications, Rogstad found that research on gender and esports revolved around three topics: (1) masculinities in esports (Jenson & Castell, 2018; Vermeulen et al., 2014), (2) online harassment (Ruvalcaba et al., 2018; Siutila and Havaste, 2019), and (3) gendered expectations (Cullen, 2018). From his analysis, Rogstad (2021) concluded that:

> Despite clear differences between traditional sports and esports, the reviewed literature suggests that many esports environments are shaped by the hegemonic masculinity dominating other sporting contexts. Some studies reviewed in this article argued that this is because the esports industry is organised by and for men, resulting in a highly masculine environment.
>
> (p. 15)

In short, Rogstad's (2021) review of gender and esports indicates that, despite the inclusive potential of esports, women face many of the same challenges as in other sports. Since the publication of his review, some novel research contributions have been made on this topic, especially with regard to women in non-playing roles (Darvin et al., 2021; McLeod et al., 2021; Yu et al., 2022).

Women and non-playing roles in esports

Whilst most of the current research on gender and esports has focused on esports athletes (Cullen, 2018; Taylor et al., 2009), Darvin et al. (2021) interviewed women players and managers from the USA, Canada, and England in their study. Their interview data supports previous research findings, namely that women and girls remain highly underrepresented throughout the esports industry. Hence, gender-based discrimination and harassment appear to affect women esports players and women in non-playing roles. Additionally, the authors showed how women who were employed in esports organisations encountered numerous gender barriers and obstacles that were similar to those of women esports players. They concluded that esports was a sexist and hostile sport environment for women that was plagued by harassment and where women needed to have strong resilience and coping strategies.

Similar to the work of Darvin et al. (2021), Taylor and Stout (2020) conducted a study in which they interviewed 21 collegiate esports leaders from the USA and Canada. Their study showed that there was greater gender diversity in leadership in student-run esports clubs, while well-funded varsity programmes remained male-dominated.

Yu et al. (2022) studied gender differences in another non-playing role in esports: the fans. Comparing men and women esports fans, they found that women watched esports for social opportunities and interest in the esports athletes, while men watched esports for entertainment and enjoyed watching aggression. Using social role theory, they further explored how perceived gender roles affected men's and women's attachment to esports athletes and found that female fans were more attached to esports players than men (Yu et al., 2022).

Overall, the current research on gender and esports appears to be dominated by qualitative approaches (Paaßen et al., 2017; Xue et al., 2019; Schelfhout et al., 2021). Furthermore, a main focus has been on women esports players' experiences as female athletes in a male-dominated sport. Less attention has been paid to gender discrimination, harassment, and inclusion in esports leadership and among fans (i.e. the experiences of women in non-playing roles).

Conclusion: current and emerging trends in research

Current research suggests that social issues are a notable part of the esports industry and represent challenges related to social inequality, gender, racism, mental health, ethics, and integrity issues. In this sense, esports is not unique, as these issues are common in other sports as well. Our review of the literature also indicates that social issues in esports is a young field of research. Forty-nine of the 63 analysed studies in this chapter have been published between 2018 and 2022 (see Table 2.1).

The aim of this chapter has been to map current and emerging research trends in the field of social issues in esports. As highlighted in the chapter, two topics

Table 2.1 Research papers on social issues in esports by publication year

Publication year	2000–2004	2005–2009	2010–2014	2015–2017	2018–2020	2021–2022
N =	1	2	2	9	29	20
Total N = 63						

stand out in terms of scholarly attention: (1) gender and esports and (2) gaming addiction and mental health in esports. Especially, mental health and gaming addiction was brought up across many of the other researched topics, such as gambling, violence, and social inequality. These two topics have developed the most and constitute current research priorities in the social issues in the esports field. There are certainly knowledge gaps in these two fields as well. In the case of gender and esports, there is a need for studies of women in non-playing roles and for studies of whether and how esports organisations promote gender equity. For gaming addiction and mental health in esports, there is a need for more longitudinal and causal research that addresses the potential contributions and factors in the development of gaming addiction and mental ill-health in esports athletes. In addition, more qualitative studies on mental health, addiction, and stigma are needed in order to better understand esports players' experiences related to these issues, since the majority of existing studies have taken a quantitative approach using online surveys. For gender and esports, the majority of research is conducted qualitatively. Hence, quantitative surveys could provide insight into the prevalence of gender-related issues in esports. There is also a need for greater diversity of theories used to examine social issues in esports related to mental health, as well as gender. In studies on mental health and gaming addiction, the most common perspectives were theories on cultural stigma and models of consumption, motivation, and self-regulation, while research on gender often relied on masculinity theories. In order to expand scientific knowledge of social issues related to both sub-fields, new theoretical perspectives should be applied in future research in the field.

Gender and esports as well as mental health and gaming addiction in esports also represent the sub-fields with the most empirical research conducted. In relation to the other sub-fields of social issues in esports, there is a dominance of theoretical and conceptual contributions. Hence, there is a need for more empirical studies on social issues in esports related to racism, integrity issues, social inequality, disability, religion, governance, and doping.

Furthermore, a common omission in the reviewed articles is related to descriptive clarity. For instance, many of the empirical papers do not provide a sufficient description of the study sample or report important variables such as demographic factors (e.g. gender, age, nationality). It would be valuable for future studies to focus on the quality of reporting to strengthen the generalisability and transparency of the findings.

Our mapping of social issues in the esports field shows that research on mental health and gaming addiction, gender, integrity issues, violence, racism, and social inequality represents the emerging trends in academic explorations. Esports and gaming might not be novel phenomena, but research on social issues in esports certainly is. As an academic field, the studies barely span two decades. Moreover, there has been considerable growth in this field over the last five years. Hence, there are many knowledge gaps to be filled in research on social issues in esports.

Notes

1 Also known as 'cyber doping'; see Chapters 7 and 8 in this book.
2 Esports Integrity Coalition (now named Esports Integrity Commission [ESIC]) is an association that works with esports stakeholders to protect the integrity of esports through disruption, prevention, investigation, and prosecution of all forms of cheating (i.e. similar to organisations such as the World Anti-Doping Agency [WADA] in traditional sports).
3 See www.esportsearnings.com.

References

Abarbanel, B., & Johnson, M. R. (2018). Esports consumer perspectives on match-fixing: Implications for gambling awareness and game integrity. *International Gambling Studies*, 19(2). https://doi.org/10.1080/14459795.2018.1558451

Bányai, F., Griffiths, M. D., Demetrovics, Z., & Király, O. (2019). The mediating effect of motivations between psychiatric distress and gaming disorder among esports gamers and recreational gamers. *Comprehensive Psychiatry*, 94. https://doi.org/10.1016/j.comppsych.2019.152117

Bányai, F., Zsila, Á., Kökönyei, G., Griffiths, M. D., Demetrovics, Z., & Király, O. (2021). The moderating role of coping mechanisms and being an e-Sport player between psychiatric symptoms and gaming disorder: Online survey. *JMIR Mental Health*, 8(3). https://www.doi.org/10.2196/21115

Bascón-Seda, A., & Macías, G. R. (2022). Análisis ético de los deportes electrónicos:¿ un paso atrás respecto al deporte tradicional? (Ethical analysis of esports: A step backwards compared to traditional sports?). *Retos*, 44, 433–443. https://doi.org/10.47197/retos.v44i0.90717

Bornmann, L. (2013). What is societal impact of research and how can it be assessed? A literature survey. *Journal of the American Society for Information Science and Technology*, 64(2), 217–233. https://doi.org/10.1002/asi.22803

Brickel, A. (2017). Addressing integrity and regulatory risk in esports: The responsibility of the whole esports community. *Gaming Law Review*, 21(8), 603–609. https://doi.org/10.1089/glr2.2017.21810

Brock, T. (2017). Roger Caillois and E-Sports: On the problems of treating play as work. *Games and Culture*, 12(4), 1–19. https://doi.org/10.1177/1555412016686878

Browne, M., Goodwin, B. C., & Rockloff, M. J. (2018). Validation of the short gambling harm screen (SGHS): A tool for assessment of harms from gambling. *Journal of Gambling Studies*, 34, 499–512. https://doi.org/10.1007/s10899-017-9698-y

Butovskaya, M. L., & Chargaziya, L. D. (2020). The involvement in competitive gaming and aggressive behavior in young men. *Voprosy Psikhologii*, 2, 91–103.

Chan, D. (2005). Playing with race: The ethics of racialized representations in e-games. *International Review of Information Ethics*, 4(12), 24–30.

Choi, C., Hums, M. A., & Bum, C.-H. (2018). Impact of the family environment on juvenile mental health: Esports online game addiction and delinquency. *International Journal of Environmental Research and Public Health*, 15(12). https://doi.org/10.3390/ijerph15122850

Chung, T., Sum, S., Chan, M., Lai, E., & Cheng, N. (2019). Will esports result in a higher prevalence of problematic gaming? A review of the global situation. *Journal of Behavioral Addictions*, 8(3), 384–394. https://doi.org/10.1556/2006.8.2019.46

Columb, D., Griffiths, M. D., & O'Gara, C. (2020). A descriptive survey of online gaming characteristics and gaming disorder in Ireland. *Irish Journal of Psychological Medicine*, 1–9. https://doi.org/10.1017/ipm.2020.5

Conroy, E., Kowal, M., Toth, A. J., & Campvell, M. J. (2021). Boosting: Rank and skill deception in esports. *Entertainment Computing*, 36. https://doi.org/10.1016/j.entcom.2020.100393

Cote, A. C. (2017). 'I can defend myself': Women's strategies for coping with harassment while gaming online. *Games and Culture*, 12(5), 136–155. https://doi.org/10.1177/1555412015587603

Cullen, A. L. (2018). 'I play to win!': Geguri as a (post) feminist icon in esports. *Feminist Media Studies*, 18(5), 948–952.

Darvin, L., Holden, J., Wells, J., & Baker, T. (2021). Breaking the glass monitor: Examining the underrepresentation of women in esports environments. *Sport Management Review*, 24(3), 475–499. https://doi.org/10.1080/14413523.2021.1891746

Esports Integrity Coalition. (2016). *Threats to the integrity of esports: A risk analysis*. https://www.documentcloud.org/documents/3004661-Esports-match-fixing-threat-assessment

Fiskaali, A., Lieberoth, A., & Spindler, H. (2020). *Exploring institutionalised esports in high school: A mixed methods study of well-being* [Conference presentation]. Proceedings of the 14th European Conference on Game Based Learning, ECGBL. https://doi.org/10.34190/GBL.20.045

Freitas, B. D. A., Contreras-Espinosa, R. S., & Correia, P. Á. P. (2021). A model of the threats that disreputable behavior present to esports sponsors. *Contemporary Management Research*, 17(1), 27–64. https://doi.org/10.7903/cmr.20779

Gainsbury, S. M., Abarbanel, B., & Blaszczynski, A. (2017). Intensity and gambling harms: Exploring breadth of gambling involvement among esports bettors. *Gaming Law Review*, 21(8), 610–615. https://doi.org/10.1089/glr2.2017.21813

Ghoshal, A. (2019). Ethics in esports. *Gaming Law Review*, 23(5), 338–343. https://doi.org/10.1089/glr2.2019.2357

Goh, C. L. (2021). The social licence to operate in esports: The glorification of violence, discrimination, and gaming addiction in esports. *SSRN*, 1–26. http://doi.org/10.2139/ssrn.3814567

Gray, K. L. (2012). Deviant bodies, stigmatized identities, and racist acts: Examining the experiences of African-American gamers in Xbox live. *New Review of Hypermedia and Multimedia*, 18(4), 261–276. https://doi.org/10.1080/13614568.2012.746740

Greer, N., Rockloff, M. J., Russell, A. M. T., & Lole, L. (2021). Are esports bettors a new generation of harmed gamblers? A comparison with sports bettors on gambling involvement, problems, and harm. *Journal of Behavioral Addictions*, 10(3), 435–446. https://doi.org/10.1556/2006.2021.00039

Gupta, D., Sharma, H., & Gupta, M. (2021). Doping as a barrier in universal acceptance of esports. *International Journal of Sports Marketing and Sponsorship*, 1–20. https://doi.org/10.1108/IJSMS-05-2021-0105

Higgins, C. (2020, September 30). How esports teams are fighting back against social injustice. *HyperX*. https://ag.hyperxgaming.com/article/10977/how-esports-teams-are-fighting-back-against-social-injustice

Holden, J. T., Kaburakis, A., & Rodenberg, R. (2017a). The future is now: Esports policy considerations and potential litigation. *Journal of Legal Aspects of Sport*, 27(1), 46–78. https://doi.org/10.1123/jlas.2016-0018

Holden, J. T., Rodenberg, R. M., & Kaburakis, A. (2017b). Esports corruption: Gambling, doping, and global governance. *Maryland Journal of International Law*, *32*(1), 236–273. http://doi.org/10.2139/ssrn.2831718

Holden, J. T., Kaburakis, A., & Tweedie, J. W. (2019). Virtue(al) games—Real drugs. *Sport, Ethics and Philosophy*, *13*(1), 19–32. https://doi.org/10.1080/17511321.2018.1459814

Jesson, J., Matheson, L., & Lacey, F. M. (2011). *Doing your literature review: Traditional and systematic techniques*. SAGE Publications Ltd.

Jenson, J., & de Castell, S. (2018). 'The entrepreneurial gamer': Regendering the order of play. *Games and Culture*, *13*(7), 728–746.

Kelly, S., Magor, T., & Wright, A. (2021). The pros and cons of online competitive gaming: An evidence-based approach to assessing young players' well-being. *Frontiers in Psychology*, *12*, 1–9. https://doi.org/10.3389/fpsyg.2021.651530

Kew, F. (1997). *Sport: Social problems and issues*. Routledge.

Kobek, P. (2019, September 10). The double threat of addiction in esports gambling. *TheGamer*. https://www.thegamer.com/esports-gambling-addiction-gaming/

Lelonek-Kuleta, B., & Bartczuk, R. P. (2021). Online gambling activity, pay-to-win payments, motivation to gamble and coping strategies as predictors of gambling disorder among e-sports bettors. *Journal of Gambling Studies*, *37*, 1079–1098. https://doi.org/10.1007/s10899-021-10015-4

Leonard, D. (2003). 'Live in your world, play in ours': Race, video games, and consuming the other. *Studies in Media & Information Literacy Education*, *3*(4), 1–9. https://doi.org/10.3138/sim.3.4.002

Macey, J., & Hamari, J. (2018). Investigating relationships between video gaming, spectating esports, and gambling. *Computers in Human Behavior*, *80*, 344–353. https://doi.org/10.1016/j.chb.2017.11.027

Macey, J., & Hamari, J. (2019). Esports, skins and loot boxes: Participants, practices and problematic behaviour associated with emergent forms of gambling. *New Media & Society*, *21*(1), 20–41. https://doi.org/10.1177/1461444818786216

Macey, J., Abarbanel, B., & Hamari, J. (2020). What predicts esports betting? A study on consumption of video games, esports, gambling and demographic factors. *New Media & Society*, *23*(6), 1481–1505. https://doi.org/10.1177/1461444820908510

Mao, E. (2021). The structural characteristics of esports gaming and their behavioral implications for high engagement: A competition perspective and a cross-cultural examination. *Addictive Behaviors*, *123*, 1–7. https://doi.org/10.1016/j.addbeh.2021.107056

McLeod, C. M., Xue, H., & Newman, J. I. (2021). Opportunity and inequality in the emerging esports labor market. *International Review for the Sociology of Sport*, 1–22. https://doi.org/10.1177/10126902211064093

Menti, D. C., & de Araujo, D. C. (2017). Violência de gênero contra mulheres no cenário dos esports. *Conexão - Comunicação e Cultura*, *16*(31), 73–88. https://doi.org/10.18226/21782687.v16.n31.03

Murray, S., Birt, J., & Blakemore, S. (2020). Esports diplomacy: Towards a sustainable 'gold rush'. *Sport in Society*, 1–19. https://doi.org/10.1080/17430437.2020.1826437

Nairn, A. (2021, April 22). Underage esports gambling is a huge problem that parents need to know about. *Metro UK*. https://metro.co.uk/2021/04/22/underage-esports-gambling-is-a-huge-problem-that-parents-need-to-know-14425481/

Ohno, S. (2021). The link between battle royale games and aggressive feelings, addiction, and sense of underachievement: Exploring esports-related genres. *International Journal of Mental Health and Addiction*, 1–9. https://doi.org/10.1007/s11469-021-00488-0

Paaßen, B., Morgenroth, T., & Stratemeyer, M. (2017). What is a true gamer? The male gamer stereotype and the marginalization of women in video game culture. *Sex Roles*, 76, 421–435. https://doi.org/10.1007/s11199-016-0678-y

Palanichamy, T., Sharma, M. K., Sahu, M., & Kanchana, D. M. (2020). Influence of Esports on stress: A systematic review. *Industrial Psychiatry Journal*, 29(2), 191–199. https://doi.org/10.4103/ipj.ipj_195_20

Papaloukas, M. (2018). *E-sports explosion: The birth of esports law or merely a new trend driving change in traditional sports law?* [Conference presentation]. Proceedings at the 24th IASL International Sports Law Congress. http://doi.org/10.2139/ssrn.3323593

Parshakov, P., Paklina, S., Coates, D., & Chadov, A. (2020). Does video games' popularity affect unemployment rate? Evidence from macro-level analysis. *Journal of Economic Studies*, 48(4), 817–835. https://doi.org/10.1108/JES-07-2019-0339

Pereira, A. M., Teques, P., Verhagen, E., Gouttebarge, V., Figueiredo, P., & Brito, J. (2021). Mental health symptoms in electronic football players. *BMJ Open Sport & Exercise Medicine*, 7(4), 1–9. https://doi.org/10.1136/bmjsem-2021-001149

Peter, S. C., Li, Q., Pfund, R. A., Whelan, J. P., & Meyers, A. W. (2019). Public stigma across addictive behaviors: Casino gambling, esports gambling, and internet gaming. *Journal of Gambling Studies*, 35(1), 247–259. https://doi.org/10.1007/s10899-018-9775-x

Riatti, P., & Thiel, A. (2021). The societal impact of electronic sport: A scoping review. *German Journal of Exercise and Sport Research*, 1–24. https://doi.org/10.1007/s12662-021-00784-w

Rogstad, E. T. (2021). Gender in esports research: A literature review. *European Journal for Sport and Society*, 1–19. https://doi.org/10.1080/16138171.2021.1930941

Rosenthal, R. (2020). A tough pill to swallow: Making the case for why esports leagues must adopt strict banned substance policies to prevent disability discrimination. *Virginia Sports & Entertainment Law Journal*, Forthcoming, 1–52. Available at SSRN: https://ssrn.com/abstract=3589710

Rossi, R., & Nairn, A. (2020, October 1). Esports could be quietly spawning a whole new generation of problem gamblers. *The Conversation*. https://theconversation.com/esports-could-be-quietly-spawning-a-whole-new-generation-of-problem-gamblers-147124

Ruvalcaba, O., Shulze, J., Kim, A., Berzenski, S. R., & Otten, M. P. (2018). Women's experiences in esports: Gendered differences in peer and spectator feedback during competitive video gameplay. *Journal of Sport and Social Issues*, 42(4), 295–311.

Schelfhout, S., Bowers, M. T., & Hao, Y. A. (2021). Balancing gender identity and gamer identity: Gender issues faced by Wang 'BaiZe' Xinyu at the 2017 hearthstone summer championship. *Games and Culture*, 16(1), 22–41. https://doi.org/10.1177/1555412019866348

Sefiha, O. (2017). Riding around stigma: Professional cycling and stigma management in the 'clean cycling' era. *Communication & Sport*, 5(5), 622–644. https://doi.org/10.1177/2167479516640751

Shulze, J., Marquez, M., & Ruvalcaba, O. (2021). The biopsychosocial factors that impact esports players' well-being: A systematic review. *Journal of Global Sport Management*, 1–25. https://doi.org/10.1080/24704067.2021.1991828

Siutila, M., & Havaste, E. (2019). A pure meritocracy blind to identity: Exploring the online responses to all-female esports teams in Reddit. *Transactions of the Digital Games Research Association, 4*(3), 43–74.

Sleap, M. (1998). *Social issues in sport*. Palgrave Macmillan.

Talberg, N. (2019). *The princess is not in any castle: Kjennetegn ved jenter og gutter på 9. trinn og vg1 som bruker mye tid på dataspill*. Rapport KORUS Øst.

Taylor, N., Jenson, J., & De Castell, S. (2009). Cheerleaders/booth babes/Halo hoes: Pro-gaming, gender and jobs for the boys. *Digital Creativity, 20*(4), 239–252. https://doi.org/10.1080/14626260903290323

Taylor, N., & Stout, B. (2020). Gender and the two-tiered system of collegiate esports. *Critical Studies in Media Communication*. https://doi.org/10.1080/15295036.2020.1813901

Tjønndal, A. (2020). 'What's next? Calling beer-drinking a sport?!': Virtual resistance to considering esports as sport. *Sport, Business and Management, 11*(1), 1–17. https://doi.org/10.1108/SBM-10-2019-0085

Triberti, S., Milani, L., Villani, D., Grumi, S., Peracchia, S., Curcio, G., & Riva, G. (2018). What matters is when you play: Investigating the relationship between online video games addiction and time spent playing over specific day phases. *Addictive Behaviors Reports, 8*, 185–188. https://doi.org/10.1016/j.abrep.2018.06.003

Vermeulen, L., Núñez Castellar, E., & Van Looy, J. (2014). Challenging the other: Exploring the role of opponent gender in digital game competition for female players. *Cyberpsychology, Behavior and Social Networking, 17*(5), 303–309.

Winkie, L. (2021, May 5). The original kings of esports. *The Atlantic*. https://www.theatlantic.com/technology/archive/2021/05/why-esports-so-segregated/618768/

Woods, R. B., & Butler, B. N. (2020). *Social issues in sport*. Human Kinetics.

Xue, H., Newman, J. I., & Du, J. (2019). Narratives, identity, and community in esports. *Leisure Studies, 38*(6), 845–861. https://doi.org/10.1080/02614367.2019.1640778

Yan, J. (2018). How does match-fixing inform computer game security? In V. Matyáš, P. Švenda, F. Stajano, B. Christianson, & J. Anderson (Eds.), *Security Protocols XXVI. 26th International Workshop, Cambridge, UK, March 19–21, 2018. Revised Selected Papers* (pp. 166–170). Springer Nature.

Yu, B., Brison, N. T., & Bennett, G. (2022). Why do women watch esports? A social role perspective on spectating motives and points of attachment. *Computers in Human Behavior, 127*, 1–11. https://doi.org/10.1016/j.chb.2021.107055

Zhao, Y., & Zhu, Y. (2021). Identity transformation, stigma power, and mental wellbeing of Chinese esports professional players. *International Journal of Cultural Studies, 24*(3), 485–503. https://doi.org/10.1177/1367877920975783

Part II

Gender

Chapter 3

The representation of women in *Hearthstone* esports

Espen Sjoberg and Raquel Wilner

Introduction

Since the release of the online collective card game *Hearthstone* in 2014, several controversies have surrounded women in the game, in particular concerning women being underrepresented at official *Hearthstone* tournaments. However, there have also been other controversies relating to the exclusion of women, or accusations of cheating. The first gender-related controversy surrounding *Hearthstone* occurred in July 2014, when the International e-Sports Federation (IeSF) held regional qualifiers for a large esports event to be held in Azerbaijan (Inquirer.net, 2014). In the Finnish qualifier, women were banned from entering the competition (Stuart, 2014), allegedly because the main event only had a men's division (Savage, 2014). This gender division caused outrage in the gaming community and was widely reported in the media (Ingenito, 2014; Kastrenakes, 2014; Pitcher, 2014). Just one day after the issue was raised by the media, IeSF reverted its stance and opened the qualifiers for women as well (IeSF, 2014). The news coverage of this issue did not follow up on the Finnish event itself, which was called Assembly 2014. According to the tournament website (Koskivirta, 2014), one woman, Siiri 'Metsakeijju' Paananen, qualified for the top 16 events in Helsinki. When interviewed by the media, Paananen was typically asked questions relating to her gender, such as how it felt to be the only woman in the competition and whether her participation was a victory for all women players (e.g. Berchewsky, 2014). From what Paananen (personal communication, 2022) remembers from the event, she first heard of the tournament due to the controversy and signed up out of spite because she did not like differential gender treatment.

Six months after the IeSF controversy, another one ensued when a player was accused of being a man pretending to be a woman. Hyerim 'MagicAmy' Lee was an accomplished Korean *Hearthstone* player, who was awarded third place in the 2014 ESL *Hearthstone* Legendary Series (competing against 512 players) and was subsequently recruited by the organisation Tempo/Storm at the end of the same year (Chou, 2014). Lee had to cancel her attendance at the ESL Finals and after that an online discussion began that questioned whether Lee was a real person, or

DOI: 10.4324/9781003258650-5

a man posing as a woman (Reddit, 2015). Gender-swapping through characters and avatars in online games is not uncommon (e.g. Hussain & Griffith, 2008), although the implication in this case was that Lee, a woman, could not have achieved her esports performances on her own (Hernandez, 2015). Following these accusations, Tempo/Storm (2015) launched their own investigation into the matter and concluded that the accusations against Lee were unfounded. She was a real person and not a man posing as a woman, there was no evidence of any illegal activity or foul play, and her esports achievements were her own. Ironically, the controversy started when a former teammate of Hyerim Lee, Eric 'Specialist' Lee, accused her of match fixing, an activity that Eric Lee himself was guilty of (Sykes, 2014). Following Tempo/Storm's (2015) investigation, Lee was cleared from accusations and the team gave her full support to develop her esports career. However, Lee instead decided to step down from professional *Hearthstone* and has not been part of the community since then.

These two instances are examples of controversies surrounding women in the professional scene of *Hearthstone* during the game's early esports stages. However, between 2014 and 2021, women have been severely underrepresented in the *Hearthstone* competitive events, which this chapter sets out to examine further. Even though a quarter of *Hearthstone*'s viewers are women (Interpret, 2019), the number of females who have competed at the highest levels of *Hearthstone* esports is so low that each player can be addressed individually. Despite the underrepresentation of women, the competitive scene signalled a change when the 2019 world champion was a woman, a change that has not yet been fully materialised (Yim, 2019).

In this chapter, we outline how women have been vastly underrepresented in competitive *Hearthstone* and have had limited opportunities to attend promotional or invitational events compared to their male peers. As the number of women who have competed at the highest level of competitive *Hearthstone* is so few, each competitor is outlined individually. Changes to this pattern of male-dominant attendance have largely been bottom-up, meaning that increased participation of women has primarily been the result of community criticism, individual efforts by the female competitors themselves, or lawsuits against the game developers, as opposed to the developers taking initiatives to increase equal opportunities for women *Hearthstone* players. The chapter also highlights how a game such as *Hearthstone*, which is individually oriented with a significant portion of female viewership, still largely fails to encourage and include women competitors in its esports scene.

Hearthstone: an online collective card game

Before addressing the representation of women in *Hearthstone* esports, a brief explanation of the game and its tournament structure is warranted. *Hearthstone* is a digital card game developed by Blizzard Entertainment (Sims, 2014). It was first accessible in mid-2013 and officially released on March 11, 2014 (Sims, 2013a).

Inspired by physical card games such as *Magic the Gathering*, *Hearthstone* requires both pre-game planning and in-game decision making. It follows a player-vs-player format of ranked or casual play, where each player brings a deck of 30 cards picked in advance. However, card choice may also depend on the current meta-state of the game: if certain deck archetypes are very popular a player may want to include cards to counter the deck types they are likely to come up against. Due to this, the metagame of *Hearthstone*, known as Standard, is a continuous balance between building the best possible deck and countering such a deck. There are also several additional game modes, such as Arena (random selection of cards) and Battlegrounds (getting cards through game progression). In this chapter, the primary focus is on the Standard format, since most high-end *Hearthstone* esports events use this format.

The esports aspect of the game follows a tournament structure typically called *Hearthstone* Championship Tour (HCT). This consists of several rounds of qualifiers, which we here call tiers, leading up to the world championship. For a tournament event, the general match structure has remained relatively unchanged across most of *Hearthstone*'s history: a match between two players typically involves a best-of-five format where whoever gets three victories first is the winner. A player brings premade decks to the tournament, which are then available for all the players to see prior to a match so that they can decide how best to approach their opponents.

The HCT competitive system has been gradually changed since 2013, but the progression towards the world championship can generally be put into tiers. Prior to 2019, the HCT followed a system of open qualifiers (Tier 4), leading to regional (Tier 3) and seasonal qualifiers (Tier 2), before culminating in the world championship (Tier 1). The progression was region-specific, as competitive *Hearthstone* is categorised into four regions, each running its independent progression: Europe, Americas, Asia-Pacific, and China. In 2019 this system changed with the introduction of the Grandmaster League, which meant that each region (except China, which has its own Gold Series system) had a league of 16 players that competed in two seasons across the year. The idea was that the winner of each season would advance to the world championship, while the lowest placements would be relegated out of the league. Thus, the system changed to open qualifiers (Tier 4) leading to a seasonal Master's tournament (Tier 3), which could lead to an invitation to the Grandmaster League (Tier 2) and finally the World/Global Championship (Tier 1). In this chapter, we only look at Tiers 1 and 2, as they represent the highest level of *Hearthstone* esports and are typically also associated with the highest monetary rewards and prestige. It is also at these levels that events are livestreamed and receive the most media attention. Thus, in this chapter, top-tier competitive *Hearthstone* refers to the world championship and the qualifying round leading up to it, which from now on we collectively call 'HCT2'.

Women in *Hearthstone* esports

Between 2014 and 2021 a total of 39 events were categorised as HCT2. Based on numbers alone, it quickly becomes apparent how underrepresented women have been and still are. In total, only four competitors identifying as women have competed in *Hearthstone*'s HCT2 levels. In other events, such as Inn-vitationals, Master Tournaments, or Global Games, more women have taken part, but at the highest level of *Hearthstone* esports between 2014 and 2021 women represented only 2% of all participants.[1] The circumstances surrounding the four women competing at this level are unique and represent firsts in one way or another. Due to this, each competitor is elaborated on separately in the chapter.

The first woman in HCT2: Xinyu Wang

Xinyu 'BaiZe' Wang was the first woman to compete at the HCT2 level when she participated in the 2017 Summer Championship and, as a result, has received the most media and scholarly attention. In this championship, the four best players from each of the four regions met and the top four players advanced to the world championship. Originally, Wang was not meant to attend as she came fifth in her regional qualifier, but as one of the Chinese players was unable to attend the event she was sent instead (Dafa Esports, 2017). During the event, she was unfortunate enough to meet the reigning world champion, Pavel Beltukov, in the first match and lost 2–3. Her second match, in which she faced Korean player Chang-Huyn 'cocosasa' Kim, became a topic of controversy.

In their first match, Kim made a play that made it likely for him to win the game. He proceeded to wave and then smile at Wang, to which one of the casters immediately reacted by saying, 'Did he just wave bye? He just waved goodbye to BaiZe in this game' (PlayHearthstone, 2017, 5:57:12). This was perceived as disrespectful behaviour towards an opponent, especially the first woman to attend a *Hearthstone* tournament at this level (Calixto, 2017). Kim (2017) later explained that he was actually waving 'hello' to the card he played, which was customary among Korean players, but admitted that his actions could have been misinterpreted and apologised for his behaviour. Wang later stated that she did not notice this gesture at the time, but that she generally did not appreciate Kim's eccentric behaviour during the match (Schelfhout et al., 2021). A study by Mavromoustakos-Blom et al. (2020) has looked at players' facial expressions during *Hearthstone* matches and found that during offline events (such as the one Wang attended), a player's mood is influenced by the opponent. It was argued that if one player expressed happiness, it could lead to anger or frustration in the opponent. In the Kim v. Wang match, Kim (2017) admitted that he was being highly expressive in the hope that it would cause Wang to make a mistake, a psychological tactic that Mavromoustakos-Blom et al. (2020) argue can work to decrease the mood of the opponent.

Wang's participation in this HCT is important not only because she represented the first woman to attend at this level, but also because her appearance illustrates an unfortunate focus on her gender. Schelfhout et al. (2021) argued that her appearance at the event acted as a reinforcer to exclude women from esports because her gender was constantly emphasised over her skill. Interviews with the competitors that played during the HCT event largely commented on Wang being a woman, and Wang herself was often asked questions about other players or her outside interests, while men competitors were asked about their skills at the game. It is possible that this unwanted attention to her gender affected her performance: studies have found that women underperform in male-dominated sports if they are reminded of stereotypes associated with the sport (e.g. Hermann & Vollmeyer, 2016). A study by Vermeulen et al. (2014) also found that facing male opponents in a video game leads to increased stress and a lower self-perception of one's own skill. These factors may have contributed towards Wang's game focus during the event, although it must be noted that Wang herself felt that she played as well as she could and had no regrets about her performance (Schelfhout et al., 2021).

After this event Wang was not seen in another HCT event again, although she did make appearances in several other tournaments, most notably coming in third place in the Titanar *Hearthstone* Elite Invitational in 2018 (Liquipedia, 2018a). However, one of her non-HCT tournament appearances is relevant to this chapter, namely when she competed in the 2017 Gold Club World Championship team event through her team Royal Never Give Up. Her team came third and netted $50,000 (Liquipedia, 2017). Of relevance here are the interviews with the players in the event describing their teammates. Wang's teammates were both men (Gao 'Leaoh' Yang and 'Kylins', real name not known). During the event, pre-recorded interviews of the competitors were played between games and here Wang's gender was clearly emphasised, exactly how it also happened in the 2017 Summer Championship.

When Kylins was asked to describe Gao Yang, he said that he was 'really good', 'the best on our team', and that 'he will defeat the opponents all by himself' (GCWC, 2017, 59:53). In comparison, when Kylins described Xinyu Wang, he hardly made any reference to her skills, e.g.

> BaiZe is the goddess of our team. She is pretty and good at playing *Hearthstone*. Admired by many boys [...] we'll try our best so BaiZe will not have to play in the competition. You will be disappointed because you may not see her on this [event].
>
> (MitsuhideHS, 2017, 6:39)

Yang also described her as a 'creative female player', once again underlining her gender. This interview appeared during the match between Xinyu Wang and Wang 'TiddlerCelestial' Xieyu, and caster Cora Georgiou immediately commented that 'it sounds like these guys ... they are crushing on BaiZe a little bit' (MitshuhideHS, 2017, 7:36). In other words, Wang, being the only woman competitor at the event, was described by her teammates as *a woman* and not as *a player*.

Wang did not continue her *Hearthstone* career after 2018 but stated in 2019 that she was optimistic about *Hearthstone* becoming more equitable and including women (Schelfhout et al., 2021).

The first woman world champion: Xiaomeng Li

When Xiaomeng 'Liooon' Li entered the Hearthstone World Championship 2019 she was virtually unheard of. This also marked her first HCT appearance (although she did come second in the 2018 Women's World Electronic Sports Games). As China uses its own qualifying system, which is not usually broadcast to the English-speaking *Hearthstone* environment, she was effectively an unknown yet had to compete against 1,086 other players in order to take part in the championship (Chen, 2021). Her participation was also the first time a woman had competed in a World Championship final (Tier 1). Li dominated the competition and became the *Hearthstone* World Champion undefeated, making her the first woman to win the title (Miller, 2019). This was also the first time a player from China had won the tournament. In her speech after winning the championship, she said that she was discouraged from competing in *Hearthstone* because she was a woman but hoped that her victory would act as a symbol for all women wanting to compete. This is what she said in her victory speech:

> A few years ago, I remember when I was competing in a huge tournament. I was waiting in line for backup signups and there is this guy telling me that if you are a girl, you should not wait in line here; it is not for you. And now today, I am here with all the support from the fans. So, I want to say to all the girls out there who have a dream for esports for competition, for glory: If you want to do it and you believe in yourself, you should just forget about your gender and go for it.
>
> (PlayHearthstone, 2019, 59:05)

Following her victory, she continued to be a dominating presence in professional *Hearthstone* in 2020, including getting three top-eight placements in major tournaments (Tier 3 level; Liquipedia, 2020). Unfortunately, as she was Chinese she could not be part of the Grandmaster League, which China does not take part in. This is because Blizzard's Chinese esports scene, including *Hearthstone*, follows its own competitive format known as the Gold Series. This is organised by Blizzard's Chinese distributor NetEase, and the esports scene is heavily domestic-oriented, running its own internal progression system until players reach Tiers 1 or 2 and enter the global stage (Kolev, 2017). This meant that Li did not appear on livestreams from other tournaments very often. In mid-2021 it was reported that she had retired from professional *Hearthstone* (Chen, 2021).

The first woman Grandmaster: Pathra Cadness

When the Grandmaster league format was introduced in 2019, the very first competitors were all invited, with subsequent seasons following a qualifier format. Of the 48 participants, only one was a woman: Pathra Cadness from New Zealand (Schelfhout et al., 2021). Cadness played for two seasons but ended up in 15th place and was relegated out of the league at the end of the year. However, her HCT appearances did not end there. In 2018, Blizzard arranged what was to be the last of the *Hearthstone* Global Games, where New Zealand participated in the finals.[2] In a team of four players, with Cadness as the only woman, the team secured third place in the championship.[3] Since then Cadness has continued to be a professional streamer, although she no longer competes in *Hearthstone*. She stated in 2021 that she felt like a 'guinea pig in a social experiment', in that she was one of the few women to take part in competitive *Hearthstone* and received unwanted negative attention in the chats during her Grandmaster performances (Winkie, 2021). This was likely due to the male gamer stereotype, which associates video gaming (and skill in the game) with men (Paaßen et al., 2017). As a result, women who compete at higher levels are typically overshadowed by their male peers and become marginalised (Rogstad, 2021). They are labelled as the exception or the outsider, rather than the norm, and stand out because they are women rather than gamers. When only one woman competes, she receives additional unwanted attention due to her gender, and it is well documented that women gamers with an online presence receive substantially more negative comments and attention than their male peers (e.g. Nakandala et al., 2017). This appears to be exactly what happened to Cadness.

The first transgender woman in HCT2: Luna Eason

Xiaomeng Li won the Hearthstone World Championship in 2019 against Brian 'bloodyface' Eason in the final. Shortly after this, Eason made an official announcement about being transgender and started to wear a facemask when competing. In 2020, Eason announced a gender change and was instead known as Luna Eason, going by the pronouns she/her (Eason, 2020). Her handle changed from 'bloodyface' to 'lunaloveee' (inspired by Harry Potter). Although this happened after the finals, it nevertheless meant that Eason was the first transwoman to compete in an HCT event. This also made 2019 a milestone event in *Hearthstone* in many ways, as it was both the first time that a woman and a transwoman had attended a world championship and were awarded first and second place respectively. Eason continued to play professional *Hearthstone* and qualified for the World Championship a second time in 2020 (coming in eighth place) and only narrowly failed to qualify in 2021 (Liquipedia, 2021).

It is interesting to note that Eason's gender has received significantly less attention in the media than the other women mentioned in this chapter. Xinyu Wang, Xiaomeng Li, and Panthra Cadness have all been discussed in the media in terms of how their gender relates to their *Hearthstone* performances. Eason was an established *Hearthstone* competitor prior to the gender change (Weiss, 2019) and has the longest and most accomplished *Hearthstone* career out of the four women outlined in HCT, having participated in the Grandmaster League for six seasons and attended the world championship twice (Liquipedia, 2021). Despite this, there are practically no media articles to be found about Eason's transition, gender, or performance in *Hearthstone* esports. The only one we could find was how she was initially excluded from the Cross-Roads Inn-vitational event in 2021 (outlined in more detail in the following) but was invited after two men withdrew their invitations so that she could attend (Chen, 2021b). Apart from this, Eason has received little public attention regarding her gender. This may be because debates about the inclusion of transwomen in women's sports tend to focus on transwomen having an unfair biological advantage (Cleland et al., 2021; Knox et al., 2019). However, *Hearthstone* is an esports in which all genders compete together and where skill in the game is not determined by physical attributes. It also bears similarities to technical sports such as archery, where Hamilton et al. (2021) argued that the physical advantage of transwomen over women is negligible and that transwomen should therefore be allowed to compete in the women's division as a principle of fairness.

The first woman at an official *Hearthstone* event: Rumay Wang

In addition to the four women outlined above, a fifth woman's contribution to the esports scene deserves recognition. Rumay 'Hafu' Wang is an American player and competed in the very first Blizzcon tournament in 2013, called the Innkeeper's Invitational (Sims, 2013b). The competitors were all invited players and did not qualify through performance. For this reason, we have not categorised it as an HCT2 event in this chapter, even though it was the very first of its kind. Nevertheless, this tournament saw eight renowned *Hearthstone* players competing for the title, where Wang was the only woman. She lost both of her matches and ended in sixth–eighth place. Since then, Wang has not attended many Standard *Hearthstone* competitions but has instead moved towards variety streaming. She is considered to be one of the world's best *Hearthstone* players in the Arena format (where a player builds a deck based on randomly offered cards), coming fourth in the 2014 Lord of the Arena tournament (Liquipedia, 2018b). In 2015, Tempo/Storm named her the third best Arena player in the world (Captain-planet, 2015) and in 2017 she was ranked second in the world in the official Blizzard rankings (Hill, 2017). Even though Wang may not have competed in an HCT2 event in *Hearthstone* Standard esports, she was the first woman to compete in an official event and has established herself as a celebrity player ever since.

Thus, as of 2022, only four women have competed in an HCT2 event, in comparison to hundreds of men. Women are clearly underrepresented and this has also been apparent in invitational events, where popular *Hearthstone* personalities were invited to compete in promotional tournaments. This gender disparity continued until the game developers were sued for sexual harassment, as outlined in the following.

The lawsuit and representation of women in *Hearthstone* invitational events

In 2021 the Hearthstone esports scene was criticised for the underrepresentation of women in its events (Winkie, 2021). This was in response to the

'Inn-vitational' (a deliberate misspelling with reference to the Inn in the game) events that Blizzard often organised. These events were non-HCT events in which top *Hearthstone* streamers or players were invited to compete using newly released cards. Even though more women have appeared in these invitational events than in HCT2 competitions, they still remain underrepresented. In total, there have been 13 such events, starting with the first 2013 Innkeeper's Invitational that Rumay Wang attended, as outlined earlier. Looking at all the participants between 2013 and 2021, women account for 15% of the participants in these events. The number of participants varied greatly from event to event, although a typical event consisted of 16 players, of which one or two were women. The 2016 One Night in Karazhan Disco Tournament event did not have a single woman participant. There also seems to be a pattern of tokenism. Prior to 2021, Alexandra 'Alliestrasza' Macpherson attended six out of the 11 invitational events and in all but one she was either the only woman or one of two.

In April 2021, an article in *PC Gamer* (Winkie, 2021) outlined the criticism against Blizzard concerning women at an Inn-vitational. This related to the Cross-Roads Inn-vitational event, where 20 invited participants competed for a $100,000 prize pool. Only two out of the 20 invited participants were women. Some of the invited men offered to give up their place in favour of getting more women involved, which Blizzard ultimately responded to, and in the end, four women participated (PlayHearthstone, 2021).

Three months after this criticism, the news broke that California's Department of Fair Employment and Housing was suing Activision Blizzard for sexual discrimination (Betancourt, 2021). The lawsuit outlined a variety of sexism issues present in the company, including sexual harassment and lower salaries for women employees (Superior Court of California, 2021). The company consisted of only 20% women, had only men in top leadership positions and gave newly appointed women lower salaries than their male counterparts and fewer promotion opportunities. Another issue that was widely reported in the media was the company's 'frat boy' culture (Betancourt, 2021; Lioa, 2021; Schreier, 2021), which is where women employees are victims of sexual harassment, inappropriate behaviour, and unwanted sexual comments without consequences for the offenders. This, regrettably, is reflective of the struggles that women face in the esports environment generally, as women executive employees and esports competitors face toxic masculinity and hostile environments in their profession (Darvin et al., 2021). It is also a continuous problem in online gaming, where women players face significantly more harassment than men, both when playing online (McLean & Griffiths, 2019) or when streaming (Nakandala et al., 2017).

Since the lawsuit started, several employees have left and walkouts have been arranged (Fahey, 2021). Some of the Blizzard leaders have acknowledged that they failed to ensure a good working environment for their women employees (Zwiezen, 2021). It is possible that the lawsuit will influence how the company organises esports events in the future. In terms of *Hearthstone*, one noticeable change has already happened with regard to the inclusion of women.

Prior to the lawsuit, the highest number of women attending an Inn-vitational event was four (at the 2019 Uldum Inn-vitational and the 2021 Cross-Roads Inn-vitational), but typically only one or two attendants were women. Seen in the light of the lawsuits, which highlighted sexism and toxic masculinity in a male-dominated workplace responsible for organising esports tournaments, it is perhaps hardly surprising that women were not given the same opportunities as men to attend these invitational events. After all, no qualifiers were necessary to attend them and the competitors were typically well-known *Hearthstone* personalities from streaming, content creation, and/or HCT. While many women were active in the *Hearthstone* streaming community, the game developers instead largely favoured inviting men to these events, with women acting as tokens. However, shortly after the lawsuits were announced, another Inn-vitational was held: the *Hearthstone* Global Inn-vitational tournament in November 2021 saw 36 invited players (nine from each region), of which ten were women (Delgado, 2021). China was the only region in the event to bring a male-only roster. The women competed across a variety of game formats and not only the Standard, competitive HCT format. During the writing of this chapter, this is the only Inn-vitational event to have happened post-lawsuit, so it is too early to suggest whether a higher inclusion of women players will become the norm, or if this was an exception. Nevertheless, at the *Hearthstone* Global Inn-vitational, women represented 28% of all the participants, the highest ratio of women to attend any official *Hearthstone* in history (outside of women-only tournaments).

Conclusion

The *Hearthstone* esports scene has seen its fair share of controversy since the game's release in 2014, with women being vastly underrepresented at major events, including those organised by invitation. Only in late 2021 did the pattern appear to show signs of changing, coincidentally shortly after a lawsuit was brought against the company for sexual misconduct. However, the fact that the many gender controversies in *Hearthstone* created a community outrage would suggest that a large percentage of players are supportive of better gender inclusivity. Regrettably, the fact that some women were invited to the Cross-Roads Inn-vitational only because men relinquished their spot means that gender equality at the event comes at the expense of male competitors, as opposed to the organisers making it gender equal in the first place. Had the organisers invited an equal ratio of men and women to promotional events, then gender equality would have been achieved without a sense of loss for one gender and gain for another. Such acts by the community also shift the responsibility of equal gender inclusion to the individual, whereas it is the game developers themselves who should ideally be the driving force behind such equality. Instead, Blizzard's actions to be gender-inclusive in competitive *Hearthstone* seem to largely grow in response to criticism or legal action, rather than their own initiative, thus suggesting that a permanent change in equal opportunities in competitive *Hearthstone* (and other Blizzard games) still has a long way to go.

It is clear that many women are involved in *Hearthstone* esports, either as competitors, streamers, or casters. However, it is also apparent from the historical data that women were usually left out of high-level competitive events. When women did compete, the focus was often on their gender rather than their skill. Four of the women competitors outlined earlier typically received questions from interviewers about their gender or felt that they were tokens in a male-dominated scene. Even after a woman won the *Hearthstone* world championship, the competitive scene hardly saw any change: the only woman to compete at an HCT2 event after 2019 was Luna Eason. The Hearthstone Global Inn-vitational marked the first event in which women were markedly better represented, accounting for 28% of the invited players. Whether this marks a trend for change or is simply an anomaly is too early to tell.

Notes

1 This includes retrospectively classifying Luna Eason as a woman prior to her gender change. If we count her as a man before she announced the gender change, then women represented only 0.9% of all participants.
2 A minor version of this event (with fewer and smaller teams) was held in 2019 as well, but was discontinued afterwards.
3 It should be noted that although Cadness was the only woman to attend the finals of this event, several women represented their countries in the group stages of this esports category between 2017 and 2018, such as Mirijam 'Wifecoach' Koy for Austria, Cara Vergel 'CaraCute' De Dios for the Philippines, and Estefanía 'Epsylon' Almague for Mexico.

References

Berchewsky, T. (2014). Assemblyilla tehtiin historiaa: Naiset vihdoinkin pelikisoihin. *Ilta-Sanomat*, July 31st. Available at: https://www.is.fi/taloussanomat/oma-raha/art-2000001844993.html.

Betancourt, S. (2021). Video game company activision blizzard sued over 'frat boy culture' allegations. *The Guardian*, July 22nd. Available at: https://www.theguardian.com/us-news/2021/jul/22/activision-blizzard-sued-frat-boy-culture-allegations.

Calixto, J. (2017). Hearthstone player waves his hand, sets off controversy. *Kotaku*, October 19th. Available at: https://kotaku.com/hearthstone-player-waves-his-hand-sets-off-controversy-1819676695.

Captain-planet. (2015). Hearthstone top 5: Arena masters. *Tempostorm.com*. Available at: https://tempostorm.com/articles/hearthstone-top-5-arena-masters.

Chen, A. (2021a). #7 most influential player – Xiaomeng 'VKLiooon' Li, the Trailblazer. *Esports.gg*, December 17th. Available at: https://esports.gg/guides/hearthstone/liooon-most-influential/.

Chen, A. (2021b). Hearthstone responds to call for diversity and inclusion. *Upcomer*, April 20th. Available at: https://upcomer.com/hearthstone-responds-to-call-for-diversity-and-inclusion.

Chou, D. (2014). Tempo/Storm adds Hyerim 'MagicAmy' Lee to Roster. *Tempostorm.com*, December 31st. Available at: https://tempostorm.com/articles/tempostorm-adds-hyerim-magicamy-lee-to-roster.

Cleland, J., Cashmore, E., & Dixon, K. (2021). Why do sports fans support or oppose the inclusion of trans women in women's sports? An empirical study of fairness and gender identity. *Sport in Society*, 1–16.

Dafa Esports. (2017). 2017 hearthstone summer championship: Event preview. *Dafa Esports*, October 11th. Available at: https://en.dafaesports.com/2017-Hearthstone-summer-championship-event-preview/.

Darvin, L., Holden, J., Wells, J., & Baker, T. (2021). Breaking the glass monitor: Examining the underrepresentation of women in esports environments. *Sport Management Review*, 24(3), 475–499.

Delgado, M. (2021). Hearthstone global Inn-vitational ft. Thijs, Dog, Jia, and other personalities, starts tonight. *Esports.gg*, November 10th. Available at: https://esports.gg/news/hearthstone/hearthstone-global-inn-vitational-ft-thijs-dog-jia-and-other-personalities-starts-tonight/.

Eason, L. (2020). Coming out transgender. Go by Luna now, use she/her pronouns. *Twitter*. Available at: https://twitter.com/lunaloveee8/status/1335709607361179650.

Fahey, M. (2021). Activision blizzard employees plan walkout wednesday to protest working conditions [update]. *Kotaku*, July 27th. Available at: https://kotaku.com/activision-blizzard-employees-plan-walkout-wednesday-to-1847362030.

GCWC. (2017). GCWC_Group Stage_Day 5_RNG vs EVO [Video File]. Available at: https://www.twitch.tv/videos/205746865.

Hamilton, B. R., Guppy, F. M., Barrett, J., Seal, L., & Pitsiladis, Y. (2021). Integrating transwomen athletes into elite competition: The case of elite archery and shooting. *European Journal of Sport Science*, 21(11), 1500–1509.

Hermann, J., & Vollmeyer, R. (2016). 'Girls should cook, rather than kick!' – Female soccer players under stereotype threat. *Psychology of Sport and Exercise*, 26, 94–101. http://doi.org/10.1016/j.psychsport.2016.06.010.

Hernandez, P. (2015). Why people believed a top hearthstone player was tricking everyone. *Kotaku*, February 20th. Available at: https://kotaku.com/why-people-believed-a-top-hearthstone-player-was-tricki-1687042036.

Hill, J. (2017). Top 100 arena players – February 2017. *PlayHearthstone.com*, October 3rd. Available at: https://playhearthstone.com/en-us/news/20601712.

Hussain, Z., & Griffiths, M. D. (2008). Gender swapping and socializing in cyberspace: An exploratory study. *CyberPsychology & Behavior*, 11(1), 47–53. http://doi.org/10.1089/cpb.2007.0020.

IeSF. (2014). IeSF board has made decision to make their event 'open for all'. *Iesf.com*, July 3rd. Available at: https://ie-sf.com/bbs/board.php?bo_table=iesf_notice&wr_id=105.

Ingenito, V. (2014). No women allowed at upcoming hearthstone tournament. *IGN*, July 2nd. Available at: https://www.ign.com/articles/2014/07/02/no-women-allowed-at-upcoming-hearthstone-tournament.

Inquirer.net. (2014). IESF 2014 world championship blog. *Inquirer.net*, November 13th. Available at: https://esports.inquirer.net/1657/iesf-2014-world-championships-blog.

Interpret. (2019). Females and esports viewership – 2019 update. *Interpret Research Brief*, February 21st. https://interpret.la/wp-content/uploads/2019/02/PR_BITE_FEB_19_ESPORTS.pdf.

Kastrenakes, J. (2014). This game tournament won't let female players compete. *The Verge*, July 2nd. Available at: https://www.theverge.com/2014/7/2/5864491/iesf-hearthstone-tournament-bans-female-players.

Kim, C.-H. (2017). [잡담] 코코사사입니다 인성질하고 원팩드려 죄송합니다 *Inven*, October 15th. Available at: https://m.inven.co.kr/board/hs/3509/1837321.

Knox, T., Anderson, L. C., & Heather, A. (2019). Transwomen in elite sport: Scientific and ethical considerations. *Journal of Medical Ethics*, 45(6), 395–403.

Kolev, R. (2017). How Chinese hearthstone is going through its biggest makeover yet. *Esports Heaven*, March 29th. Available at: https://www.esportsheaven.com/features/how-chinese-hearthstone-is-going-through-its-biggest-makeover-yet/.

Koskivirta, M. (2014). Qualifiers for the IeSF hearthstone championship at assembly. *Assembly Summer 2014* tournament page. Available at: https://tournaments.peliliiga.fi/summer14/tournaments/view/asms14-hsquali.

Liao, S. (2021). At Blizzard, groping, free-flowing booze and fear of retaliation tainted 'magical' workplace. *The Washington Post*, August 6th. Available at: https://www.washingtonpost.com/video-games/2021/08/06/blizzard-culture-sexual-harassment-alcohol/.

Liquipedia. (2017). 2017 gold club world championship. *Liquipedia*. Available at: https://liquipedia.net/hearthstone/Gold_Club_World_Cup/2017.

Liquipedia. (2018a). Titanar hearthstone elite invitational 2018. *Liquipedia*. Available at: https://liquipedia.net/hearthstone/Titanar_Hearthstone_Elite_Invitational/2018.

Liquipedia. (2018b). Hafu. *Liquipedia*. Available at: https://liquipedia.net/hearthstone/Hafu.

Liquipedia. (2020). Liooon. *Liquipedia*. Available at: https://liquipedia.net/hearthstone/Liooon.

Liquipedia. (2021). Lunaloveee. *Liquipedia*. Available at: https://liquipedia.net/hearthstone/Lunaloveee.

McLean, L., & Griffiths, M. D. (2019). Female gamers' experience of online harassment and social support in online gaming: A qualitative study. *International Journal of Mental Health and Addiction*, 17(4), 970–994.

Mavromoustakos-Blom, P., Kosa, M., Bakkes, S., & Spronck, P. (2020). Correlating facial expressions and subjective player experiences in competitive hearthstone. The 16th International Conference on the Foundation of Digital Games (FDG), 1–5. https://doi.org/10.1145/3472538.3472577.

Miller, H. (2019). 'Just forget your gender': Xiaomeng 'VKLiooon' Li becomes first female Hearthstone Grandmasters Global Finals champion. *The Washington Post*, November 2. Available at: https://www.washingtonpost.com/video-games/esports/2019/11/02/just-forget-your-gender-xiaomeng-vkliooon-li-becomes-hearthstones-first-female-grandmaster-champion/

MitsuhideHS. (2017). [Hearthstone] team celestial VS RNG – Gold club world championship 2017 [Video File]. Available at: https://www.youtube.com/watch?v=26kUYb5yFAo.

Nakandala, S., Ciampaglia, G., Su, N., & Ahn, Y. Y. (2017, May). Gendered conversation in a social game-streaming platform. *Proceedings of the International AAAI Conference on Web and Social Media*, 11(1), 162–171.

Paaßen, B., Morgenroth, T., & Stratemeyer, M. (2017). What is a true gamer? The male gamer stereotype and the marginalization of women in video game culture. *Sex Roles*, 76(7), 421–435.

PlayHearthstone. (2017). HCT summer championship – Day 2 [Video File]. Available at: https://www.twitch.tv/videos/182175083

PlayHearthstone. (2019). Hearthstone global finals – Finals – VKLiooon vs bloodyface [Video File]. Available at: https://www.youtube.com/watch?v=tmPx1O1-t9k

PlayHearthstone. (2021). Twitter tweet on adding two new players. *Twitter*, April 20th. Available at: https://twitter.com/PlayHearthstone/status/1384307923136913412.

Pitcher, J. (2014). Previously male-only hearthstone competition now open to all genders. *Polygon*, July 3rd. Available at: https://www.polygon.com/2014/7/3/5867015/international-esports-federation-reverses-gender-segregation-policy.

Reddit. (2015). MagicAmy Megathread. Available at: https://www.reddit.com/r/hearthstone/comments/2wcfzv/magicamy_megathread/.

Rogstad, E. T. (2021). Gender in esports research: A literature review. *European Journal for Sport and Society*, 1–19.

Savage, P. (2014). IeSF removes male-only restriction from its e-sports tournaments. *PC Gamer*, July 3rd. Available at: https://www.pcgamer.com/iesf-removes-male-only-restriction-from-its-e-sports-tournaments/.

Schelfhout, S., Bowers, M.T. & Hao, Y.A. (2021). Balancing gender identity and gamer identity: Gender issues faced by Wanf 'BaiZe' Xinyu at the 2017 hearthstone summer championship. *Games and Culture*, 16(1), 22–41.

Schreier, J. (2021). Claims of 'frat boy' culture tarnish Blizzard's successful image. *Aljazeera*, August 6th. Available at: https://www.aljazeera.com/economy/2021/8/6/claims-of-frat-boy-culture-tarnish-blizzards-successful-image.

Sims, C. (2013a). Hearthstone at BlizzCon – Fireside chat panel highlights. *PlayHearthstone*, August 11th. Available at: https://playhearthstone.com/en-gb/news/11524460/hearthstone-at-blizzcon-fireside-chat-panel-highlights-08-11-2013.

Sims, C. (2013b). Hearthstone Innkeeper's invitational: Player spotlight. *PlayHearthstone*, October 22nd. Available at: https://playhearthstone.com/en-us/news/11315877.

Sims, C. (2014). Welcome to the hearthstone launch! *PlayHearthstone*, March 11th. Available at: https://playhearthstone.com/en-us/news/13154923.

Stuart, K. (2014). Hearthstone gaming tournament bans women players – Ignites 'sexism' row. *The Guardian*, July 2nd. Available at: https://www.theguardian.com/technology/2014/jul/02/hearthstone-heroes-warcraft-tournament-ban-female-finland.

Superior Court of California. (2021). Department of fair employment and housing vs. Activision blizzard, case no. 21STCV26571.

Sykes, T. (2014). Blizzard issues permanent bans to hearthstone win traders. *PC Gamer*, October 31st. Available at: https://www.pcgamer.com/blizzard-issues-permanent-bans-to-hearthstone-win-traders/.

Tempo/Storm. (2015). Tempo/Storm parts ways with Hyerim 'MagicAmy' Lee. *Tempostorm.com*, February 20th. Available at: https://tempostorm.com/articles/tempostorm-parts-ways-with-hyerim-magicamy-lee.

Vermeulen, L., Castellar, E. N., & van Looy, J. (2014). Challenging the other: Exploring the role of opponent gender in digital game competition for female players. *Cyberpsychology, Behavior, and Social Networking*, 17(5), 1–7. http://doi.org/10.1089/cyber.2013.0331.

Weiss, N. (2019). Exclusive interview with bloodyface. *BlizzPro*, March 13th. Available at: https://blizzpro.com/2019/03/13/exclusive-interview-with-bloodyface/.

Winkie, L. (2021). Blizzard pledges to do better after wave of criticism from female hearthstone pros. *PC Gamer*, April 23rd. Available at: https://www.pcgamer.com

/blizzard-pledges-to-do-better-after-wave-of-criticism-from-female-hearthstone-pros/.

Yim, M. (2019). Hearthstone champ Lioon hopes Blizzcon victory will encourage other women in esports. *ESPN*, November 3rd. Available at: https://www.espn.com/esports/story/_/id/27994177/hearthstone-champ-liooon-hopes-blizzcon-victory-encourage-other-women-esports.

Zwiezen, Z. (2021). Everything that has happened since the activision blizzard lawsuit was filed. *Kotaku*, December 26th. Available at: https://kotaku.com/everything-that-has-happened-since-the-activision-blizz-1847401161.

Chapter 4

Leadership and gender inclusion in esports organisations

Lucy Piggott, Anne Tjønndal, and Jorid Hovden

Introduction

Sport leadership and governance are widely recognised as gender-imbalanced and gender-inequitable at all levels across the world (Elling et al., 2019; Evans & Pfister, 2021). With the emergence of esports, new organisations inside and outside the sports sector are rapidly being established at international, national, and local levels. Unlike most other sporting contexts, esports performance does not depend on physical ability. This has led practitioners to argue that esports has the potential to provide gender-inclusive sporting spaces (Ratan et al., 2015). Yet, a substantial body of research suggests that the marginalisation and discrimination of women is a major issue in esports (Rogstad, 2021). For example, in their review of the societal impact of esports, Riatti and Thiel (2021, p. 5) found that 'several studies thematize condescending behaviour towards women like sexist behaviour and exclusion, namely harassment or male hedonism'. It has been suggested that such issues of discriminatory behaviour are becoming an overarching problem in esports due to the possibility of playing anonymously (Hayday & Collison, 2020). Gender inequity in esports is also thought to be enhanced by the application of gender-normative roles of playable characters in many games (Lynch et al., 2016).

The findings from esports research mirror those from other sports. Most studies tend to focus on athletes and gender inclusion, i.e. the discrimination and harassment of women esports players, while there is limited knowledge about gender equity in leadership and management positions. Although the athlete perspective is undoubtedly valuable, Acker (2006a, p. 441) positioned the organisation as an important research site, because 'much of the social and economic inequality in ... industrial countries is created in organisations, in the daily activities of working and organising the work'. From this point of departure, the aim of this chapter is to explore the complex and interrelated ways in which esports organisations contribute to the production of gender inequity in esports leadership. Specifically, the research question guiding the chapter is: how do organisational structures, processes, and practices influence the gendering of power in leadership and governance positions in Norwegian esports organisations? To address this

DOI: 10.4324/9781003258650-6

research question, we have conducted qualitative interviews with elected and employed male and female leaders in Norwegian esports organisations. We draw on Acker's (1990; 2006a; 2006b) theoretical concept of inequality regimes in organisations to aid our analysis. In the following section, we briefly describe the limited research that exists on women in non-playing roles in esports in various national contexts.

Esports and women in leadership

Research on gender equity in esports leadership is limited. There are few empirical investigations on this topic, thus marking a notable gap in the existing body of literature that has mostly focused on women players (Cote, 2017; Hussain et al., 2021; Choi et al., 2020). Two exceptions are the works of Darvin et al. (2021) and Taylor and Stout (2020).

Darvin et al. (2021) interviewed ten women working in the esports industry as professional esports players, executives, and content creators. Eight participants were from the USA, one from Canada, and one from England. Their study explored the career experiences of women players and leaders in esports and the general underrepresentation of women in the esports industry. Based on their analysis, the researchers highlighted three main findings: that the esports industry was hostile towards women and plagued by blatant sexism, that women employed in the esports industry faced numerous barriers and obstacles, and finally, that women experienced toxic masculinity and adopted different survival skills (e.g. grit and resilience) to promote gender equity in the esports industry. The findings of Darvin et al. (2021) illustrate that women who make it into leadership positions in esports organisations have broken through a 'seemingly impenetrable barrier sustained through normalized male-dominance' (p. 484). Their analysis concludes that the obstacles women must overcome to become leaders in esports include gendered stigmas associated with gaming, a lack of support from family members for pursuing a career in esports management and challenges associated with building mixed-sex communities in esports.

Similar to the above study, Taylor and Stout (2020) interviewed 21 collegiate esports leaders from the USA and Canada and found that there was a greater gender diversity in student-run esports clubs, while well-funded varsity programmes remained male-dominated. Specifically, Taylor and Stout (2020) reported few indications of attempts to proactively promote gender diversity (i.e. the inclusion of non-male-identified individuals) in participation and management, both in student-run clubs and in varsity programmes. Yet, the informal nature of student-run clubs appeared to have a more gender-inclusive atmosphere than among varsity programmes, even when no explicit efforts at inclusivity were in place among club leadership. Taylor and Stout (2020) demonstrate that this is likely due to the efforts of female esports players to recruit their female friends into the student-run clubs. Recruitment in varsity programmes on the other hand is much more formalised, and therefore more dependent on active efforts to ensure gender diversity.

Despite the limited research on gender equity in esports organisations and leadership, the findings from two recent literature review studies suggest that gender and esports is an established field of research (Riatti & Thiel, 2021; Rogstad, 2021). For example, in their literature review, Riatti and Thiel (2021) identified 13 studies tackling social equality and inclusion in esports, while Rogstad (2021) analysed 21 studies on gender and esports. As already noted, most studies focus on the experiences of women esports players. Two topics that have received a fair amount of scholarly attention are the gender discrimination and sexual harassment of women players (e.g. Taylor et al., 2009; Voorhees, 2015; Paaßen et al., 2017; Ruvalcaba et al., 2018; Schelfhout et al., 2021). A recent example is that of Darvin et al. (2020), which examined the presence of discrimination and hostility in playing environments for men and women players. By means of a quantitative survey recruiting participants from the social media platform Reddit, they found that 'women esports participants experience higher rates of treatment discrimination during their time engaging in esports as players and are less likely to contribute to hostility in this environment' (Darvin et al., 2020, p. 45). Other studies have focused on male esports players and how they might contribute to a toxic sporting environment for women. For instance, Voorhes and Orlando (2018) observed an all-male *Counter-Strike: Global Offensive* (CS: GO) team and found that the different ways in which the male players performed gender in the esports scene revealed masculinity configurations that served to reinforce notions of toxic masculinity. Overall, studies of both female and male esports players support Rogstad's (2021, p. 15) conclusion that the esports industry is 'organised by and for men, resulting in a highly masculine environment'. Within this chapter, we build on this work to explore the extent to which this highly masculine environment extends to leadership in Norwegian esports organisations.

The organisation of esports in Norway

To contextualise our findings and analysis, it is necessary to provide a brief overview of the organisation of esports in Norway. Whilst gaming has been a popular activity amongst young Norwegians for years (Children and Media Survey, 2018), organised esports at the grassroots, semi-professional, and professional levels is a relatively new phenomenon (Tjønndal & Skauge, 2021). Some esports organisations and teams have developed as part of the Norwegian Olympic and Paralympic Committee and Confederation of Sports (NIF) as independent non-profit organisations. This organisational development mainly applies to esports organisations that operate within the Sports Video Games (SVGs) game genre, including game titles such as *FIFA*, *NBA2K22*, or *Rocket League* (Tjønndal, 2021). In some cases, voluntary sports clubs who are a part of NIF have begun to include esports activities for youth (Tjønndal & Skauge, 2021). Besides these organisations, there are independent national esports actors such as Norges e-sportforbund (NESF, n.d.) and Hyperion (Hyperion, n.d.) who, just like NIF, are voluntary non-profit organisations with a democratically elected leadership. However, the majority of Norwegian esports organisations are small private (for-profit) business organisations (Tjønndal, 2021). These organisations often organise professional teams that compete both nationally and internationally in game genres such as multiplayer online battle arenas (MOBA), first-person shooters, fighting, and real-time strategy. Some examples of such organisations are 00 NATION DNB (00 NATION DNB, n.d.) or Oilers esports (Oilers esports, n.d.). In many cases, these business organisations have originated as entrepreneurial ventures between a small group of friends, often all-male groups that have gaming as a leisure activity and want to turn that passion into a profession (Rogstad et al., 2021). While these small businesses often excel at social media promotion, it can be difficult to decipher how many people are employed and whether or not players and management receive a monthly salary that is enough to live on.

To complicate the esports landscape further, several national organisations aim to take a governing role in either one specific game, a specific game genre, or esports broadly. These organisations include both non-profit organisations and for-profit businesses. Furthermore, there is an ongoing debate about the potential inclusion of an esports federation into NIF. Today, some esports organisations welcome this initiative and others oppose it. The esports organisations that welcome the inclusion into NIF are mainly non-profit organisations that represent the sports video games (SVGs) genre (Rogstad et al., 2021). Among these are some sports clubs that offer esports activities for children and youth.

In contrast to the Norwegian esports industry, most sport organisations in Norway are organised under the umbrella organisation NIF, and so differ substantially from business organisations by being independent voluntary, non-profit, and democratic organisations. NIF positions gender equality as a basic organisational value and all sports organisations under NIF are required to adhere to NIF's laws. This includes a gender quota regulation which requires that one-third of the representatives in all elected organisational boards and committees must be women or men (Fasting & Sisjord, 2019). Furthermore, non-compliance with the gender quota regulation is met with strong sanctions. For example, if the gender quota on the board of a sports federation is not fulfilled, the election can be disapproved. For small private business organisations, there are no such regulations, even though working for gender balance in all societal sectors is stated as a central political aim in Norwegian society. Thus, small private esports organisations do not have the same regulation or incentive to work for gender inclusion in their leadership and governance as those under the NIF umbrella. As will be discussed within this chapter, this makes esports' potential future inclusion under NIF particularly relevant in relation to gender inclusion policy and practice.

Theoretical framework: gender regimes in organisations

In this chapter, we draw on Joan Acker's (2006a) inequality regimes framework to guide our analysis of how the structures, processes, and practices of Norwegian esports organisations influence the gendering of power in leadership and governance positions. The framework is based on Acker's claim that all organisations have inequality regimes, which she loosely defines as 'interrelated practices, processes, action, and meanings that result in and maintain class, gender, and racial inequalities within particular organisations' (Acker, 2006a, p. 443). Acker's (2006a) definition of inequality in organisations encompasses systematic inequalities between individuals in relation to their power and control over goals, resources, and outcomes, workplace decisions, opportunities for promotion or new roles, security in employment and benefits, pay and bonuses, respect and enjoyment of work, and the work environment. Sports organisations have previously been positioned as inequality regimes because they often reflect a culture that privileges men and masculinity, as well as other dimensions of inequality such as whiteness, heteronormativity, and ableism (Adriaanse & Schofield, 2013; Simpkins et al., 2022).

Acker (2006a) outlines six core components of inequality regimes. First, *the basis of inequality* refers to how power relations related to particular social characteristics have historical roots and thus continue to be embedded in organisations. Second, *the shape and degree of inequality* conceptualise how the structures of organisations affect inequitable hierarchies of power. Third, *organising processes that produce inequality* focus on how different organisational processes produce inequality. Fourth, *the visibility of inequalities* addresses the degree to which individuals in organisations are aware of the existence and impact of inequalities. Fifth, *the legitimacy of inequalities* concentrates on the extent to which inequality is legitimised and taken seriously by organisations, as well as the differences in legitimacy given to different forms of inequality. Finally, *control and compliance* explore how control is exerted in organisations and the extent to which dominant and oppressed groups comply with it.

In this chapter, we concentrate on four of Acker's core components of inequality regimes to help us to identify and analyse the ways in which certain structures, processes, and practices in esports organisations contribute to the production of gender inequality. First, we focus on *the shape and degree of inequality* by exploring the extent to which the hierarchies of esports organisations are characterised by vertical and horizontal forms of gender segregation. Second, we examine one particular *organising process that produces inequality* in Norwegian esports organisations by scrutinising the recruitment processes for leadership and governance positions within the organisations featured in our study. Third, we explore variances in the *control* that Norwegian esports organisations have over gender inclusion, with a particular focus on the significance of esports' potential inclusion under NIF in relation to gender inclusion policy. Finally, we analyse *the visibility and legitimacy of inequalities* in esports organisations to understand the extent to which individuals are aware of the existence and impact of inequalities as well as the degree to which such inequalities are taken seriously and given legitimacy.

Methods: digital interviews with esports leaders

The empirical basis of this study derives from qualitative interviews with male and female leaders in Norwegian esports organisations. Due to the strict COVID-19 rules and travel restrictions, all the interviews were conducted digitally. To create a face-to-face interview situation, we conducted our interviews synchronously (researcher and interviewee online simultaneously) using a video call service (Zoom). According to Salmons (2021), this approach represents a digital interview situation that is closest to a physical face-to-face conversation with participants.

We developed a semi-structured interview guide centred around four topics related to gender equity in leadership: (a) the interviewees' background and experiences with esports, (b) the recruitment and selection processes for their current leadership position, (c) the daily tasks and responsibilities in their leadership position, and (d) aspirations and ambitions for themselves and their organisations. The interviews, which lasted between one and two hours, were conducted in Norwegian and were transcribed in full before being translated into English.

The participants were 11 leaders (seven men and four women) from nine different esports organisations. The sample of participants was strategically selected to represent the complexities of the Norwegian esports landscape. The selection criteria were that the sample should include representatives from (1) esports organisations at different levels (national/regional/local, professional/grassroots), (2) different game genres (sports video games [SVGs], multiplayer online battle arenas [MOBAs], strategy games, shooters), and (3) include both male and female leaders. The participants' characteristics are summarised below in Table 4.1. All the participants have been given pseudonyms to protect their identities.

We have analysed the data material using a qualitative thematic content analysis approach (Thagaard, 2018) and structured our analysis of the interview data according to core components of Acker's theory of inequality regimes (2006a). The results of this process are presented in the next section of the chapter.

Findings and discussion

In this section, we critically analyse the ways in which organisational structures, processes, and practices influence the gendering of power in leadership and governance positions in Norwegian esports organisations. Primarily drawing on four of Acker's core components of inequality regimes, we split the findings across four sub-sections: (1) the shape and degree of gender inequality, (2) an organising process that produces gender inequality, (3) control over systems of gender inequality, and (4) the visibility and legitimacy of gender inequalities.

Table 4.1 Description of the participants

Pseudonym	Gender	Age	Ethnicity	Leadership role	Organisation	For-profit/non-profit
Arve	Man	27	White/Norwegian	Responsible for eFootball	National sport organisation	Non-profit
Ingrid	Woman	27	Minority	Board member	National esports organisation	Non-profit
Thea	Woman	29	White/Norwegian	CEO	Professional esports team	For-profit
Eva	Woman	34	White/Norwegian	Former coach and team manager	Experiences from a variety of esports organisations	Non-profit and for-profit
Pål	Man	39	White/Norwegian	Director	esports event management	For-profit
Rasmus	Man	43	White/Norwegian	Co-founder and co-owner	esports event management	For-profit
Jorunn	Woman	48	White/Norwegian	General manager	Professional esports team	For-profit
Martin	Man	56	White/Norwegian	Secretary-general	National esports organisation	Non-profit
Bjørn	Man	30	White/Norwegian	Coaching manager	Professional esports team	For-profit
Andreas	Man	39	White/Norwegian	CEO and founder	Professional esports team	For-profit
Trym	Man	31	White/Norwegian	Commercial director	Professional esports team	For-profit

The shape and degree of gender inequality

When looking at the shape and degree of gender inequality in Norwegian esports organisations, we found that these organisations aligned with the findings of existing research (Darvin et al., 2021; Taylor & Stout, 2020) in that they appear to be representationally male dominated. Whilst we did not conduct a statistical analysis of gender representation across Norwegian esports organisations, our qualitative findings indicate that there is an absence of women across all levels and positions:

> There are few women in esports, few women in leadership, few women on the investor side of things.
>
> (Eva)

> [Norwegian esports is] extremely male dominated; I have only met two or three women per one thousand men.
>
> (Jorunn)

> At the moment I can actually only think of one esports club leader who is a woman.
>
> (Pål)

From these findings, the extent to which vertical gender segregation (the segregation of men and women in relation to seniority of position) is prevalent is unclear as the interviewees mostly spoke of a broader underrepresentation of women across the sector.

Qualitative findings such as those presented in this chapter provide an important first step in identifying a problematic underrepresentation of women in Norwegian esports leadership and management positions. They also crucially contribute novel insights into how organisational structures, processes, and practices influence the gendering of power in the industry. To better understand the shape and degree of gender inequality in (Norwegian) esports organisations, we suggest that it would be fruitful for future research in this area to also include a statistical analysis of gender representation across esports organisations. As Elling (2015) argued, 'hard figures' can help to provide important evidence on the extent of the issue of representational male dominance. This is important because it reflects the extent to which the esports sector accords equal voice and fair representation in decision-making (Fraser, 2013). The lack of quantitative data available on gender representation in Norwegian esports indicates the under-researched nature of this topic.

Where women are present in Norwegian esports organisations, interviewees reported examples of gender segregation of roles. Specifically, some interviewees spoke of how women are absent from performance-related roles within their organisation, yet visible in camera-facing or creative roles:

Researcher: Do you have female managers and coaches?
Bjørn: Not managers and coaches, no. But we have them in other leadership roles. So, for example, the Leader of Creativity is a woman.

> Now we've acquired [female employee], she can do a lot. Also, all our sponsors are interested in seeing her face on camera.
>
> (Pål)

This aligns with findings in the sport governance literature that have found that women are underrepresented in roles that hold high volumes of symbolic capital, such as high-performance and financial roles (Piggott & Matthews, 2021; Tjønndal & Hovden, 2016).

There was also one notable example of an interviewee being pigeonholed into a community role, which she perceived as being a result of gender stereotyping in relation to her assumed behaviours, qualities, and interests as a woman:

Researcher: I saw that on your website, it says that you have set up a community committee?
Ingrid: Yes, it's me and the other female board member … they included me without asking me. … They probably assumed that we as women would like to be put there, because they think community is a 'female issue' that only women care about.

Such a gendered division of labour is problematic when 'women's roles' or 'women's issues' are not valued or respected, or where the decision-making power in the organisation is ghettoised and/or reinforces gender role stereotypes that categorise men and women into certain roles and tasks (Piggott & Matthews, 2021; Hovden & Tjønndal, 2021). Organisational processes contribute to such gendered representational trends (Acker, 2006a), and in the next section, we will discuss the impact of the recruitment process on gender inequality in Norwegian esports organisations.

Recruitment: an organising process that produces gender inequality

Within our study, the recruitment process was identified as an organisational process that produced gender inequality in Norwegian esports leadership and management. Hovden (2000, p. 17) has argued that 'leader selection is a very important micro-process in the web of organisational gender relations and *a site for identifying constructions of gendered substructures*' (italics in the original). Nine out of the 11 interviewees in our study discussed their experiences of being recruited into their current positions without going through formal employment processes. For some of these individuals, this was due to their role being self-made:

> But I've not been chosen, no. That is, I have found the way myself.
>
> (Rasmus)

> I joined as general manager from Day One, because it was my vision and my dream to create that club.
>
> (Thea)

For others it was a process of informal recruitment via existing contacts:

> I was only informed at a meeting in a café by the Chairman of the Board of the new company, and simply asked if I would like to be the Director.
>
> (Pål)

> I was asked by an acquaintance if I would like to help a bit with this association. Simply and straightforward, I was asked and that's enough.
>
> (Martin)

> I was contacted directly by the leader. He thought that my track record in esports had been excellent for many years, and he wanted me to be part of the club.
>
> (Bjørn)

> There were no other candidates for that position. … . It was recruitment through networks, and there were no job advertisements for the position
>
> (Jorunn)

Of the two interviewees who did go through a formal recruitment process, one was employed in a national sports federation under the NIF umbrella and was therefore influenced by NIF's policy on good democratic employment practices (NIF, 2019; NIF, 2020).

It was also clear that a background and existing network in gaming or esports were influential factors in interviewees being recruited for positions through informal processes. For example, several of the male interviewees were part of the gaming community long before taking up their current positions:

> I've played a lot of major online games. So I'm familiar with a lot of the culture surrounding online gaming. (Pål)

> I had a fantastic internet community that I was already part of. … So, I found, as very, very many others, that the web and gaming and all the social stuff around it was very good for me. (Rasmus)

> I played because I thought it was fun, and gradually I got better and better, and then people noticed my qualifications. And one thing followed another, sort of. (Bjorn)

Only one of the female interviewees talked about a serious background in gaming, which had led her to become one of the few professional female players in Norway:

> I started playing *Counter Strike*'s earlier version almost twenty years ago. So I've been playing computer games for quite some time. (Eva)

Recruitment and networking appear to be organisational processes that are influenced by the history, culture, and values of the esports sector. Esports is a creative industry and researchers have found that other male-dominated creative industries have a similarly high prevalence of informal networked recruitment processes. For example, informal recruitment processes are very commonplace in the film industry, with a constant need for networking to enjoy a successful career (Wreyford, 2015). Wreyford (2015) found that key contributing reasons for this included risk aversion by hiring known individuals with a track record in the industry, a narrative of meritocracy where such individuals were categorised as 'what the market wants', and a culture where familiarity with prospective workers fostered feelings of trust, confidence, and predictability (Wreyford, 2015). Similarities can be seen in the structure and culture of esports, with its evolution into a commercial industry and its tribalistic culture that is characterised by 'exclusionary boundaries and tribal mentalities developing between esports games and participant groups' (Hayday & Collison, 2020, p. 204).

The existence of informal recruitment processes within an esports industry characterised by both commercialisation and tribalism becomes problematic from a gender inclusion perspective. When the esports industry continues to be representationally dominated by men and culturally dominated by masculinity, informally hiring men for meritocratic reasons who are perceived to know 'what the market wants' can be used to justify not taking actions to redress gender inequalities. As will be discussed later in the chapter, many of the interviews were characterised by equality discourses that positioned esports as an industry that offers equal opportunity to prospective employees of all genders. Yet, gender organisational researchers have found that 'the clubbier the culture, the less likely women are to make the top' (Franks, 1999, p. 52). This is due to homosocial reproduction processes that result in an active preference for the recruitment of men, even amongst men who are not aware of the discrimination against women (Kanter, 1977). Kanter (1977) found that people draw on social similarity as a basis for trust, meaning that women and minority groups tend *not* to be trusted by the white, middle-class men who continue to dominate decision-making positions within industries such as esports. Therefore, if esports leaders and administrators continue to be informally recruited through male-dominated gaming and esports networks, the organisation of esports will likely continue to be run by men, for men.

Control over systems of gender inequality

The extent to which esports organisations have control over maintaining systems of gender inequality (i.e. failing to address both representational and recognitional gender injustice) to instead prioritise the organisation's goals depends on the type and sectoral location of the organisation (Acker, 2006a). As shown in Table 4.1, our organisational sample consisted of both for-profit and non-profit organisations, which reflects the diverse organisational nature of the Norwegian esports sector. This is notably different to the Norwegian sport sector which is dominated by non-profit organisations that are members of NIF. Just one of the organisations in our study is a member of NIF, but it became clear from the interviews that the inclusion of an esports federation under the NIF umbrella is a prominent current debate in the Norwegian esports sector. This is significant from a gender inclusion perspective because all NIF members are required to adhere to NIF laws, including a gender quota regulation that requires that one-third of the representatives in all elected organisational boards and committees must be women or men. Subsequently, not only would an esports federation under NIF have to comply with this quota regulation, but also any esports teams or clubs that subsequently would become members of NIF. Some of the interviewees saw the benefits of esports sitting under NIF:

> If we get some proper regulations and are taken seriously and are given greater opportunities to be able to keep up, promote our sport, then I am positive to it. It must be done properly. (Bjorn)

> The legislation of NIF, which everyone generally uses, is good. Meaning, how to organise club teams and associations. That's very good. They're a bit like Norwegian laws. (Martin)

However, it was clear that there were several significant challenges to including esports in NIF. This included NIF's position on which esports games were 'acceptable' or 'unacceptable', thus suggesting that esports in its current form would not be welcome under the NIF umbrella:

> In order to be accepted [by NIF], ... esports must also exist in reality. So, football, FIFA, Formula 1, Car games are fine. But many, many games fall outside because there is, they are just fictional things. You cannot accept Anti-terrorism against Terrorists, you cannot take in Rocket League or League of Legends or Fantasy. Right. Everything falls outside, so what's the point? (Rasmus)

Another challenge was that the interviewees characterised NIF as conservative and rigid, which was felt to be incompatible with the young and developing esports sector:

> They sit with old rules or statutes from the 80s that should sort of, 'yes, you should fit in here', or 'no, you don't fit here', right? And then we become the weird people, because we do not fit their old-fashioned sports system. (Rasmus)

> This is too early for both parties, because sports are conservative in nature. A little old-fashioned. I think NIF had a major problem admitting this association into its organisation. They were not ready for it. (Martin)

This raises the question of the extent to which the values and incentives of esports organisations and NIF align (Rogstad et al., 2021), and how much movement should be made by each party to create a better alignment of values. This includes values and incentives relating to gender inclusion.

Finally, the lack of an existing overarching esports federation was seen as a further obstacle to joining NIF. Despite the existing independent Norwegian esports association claiming to 'represent e-sports in Norway and internationally' (NESF, n.d.) and being the organisation to hold initial talks with NIF, esports remains fragmented in its organisation and governance:

> The association is very messy, no one believes that we will become members of NIF. (Ingrid)

> We're a thoroughly organised country. Sports are organised. So, everything is organised, but esports is not. (Martin)

These ongoing debates and negotiating processes on the inclusion of esports under NIF will likely have significant implications on future gender inclusion across the sector. This is because NIF membership influences the extent to which esports organisations hold full control over the maintenance of gender inequality systems that currently demonstrate a lack of voluntary incentive to achieve gender equity. Affirmative action measures, such as NIF-enforced gender equality quotas and good practice recommendations for sports federations, have been important in contributing to increased proportions of women in organisational leadership positions (Fasting & Sisjord, 2019; Hovden et al., 2019). Across Norwegian national sport federations, the average female representation on boards increased from 15% in 1985 to 44% in 2020, thereby demonstrating a positive impact of the NIF gender quota law (Fasting & Sisjord, 2019). However, as our findings demonstrate, the inclusion of esports under NIF is a contested issue that is influenced by the fragmented nature of the sector, the domination of for-profit businesses across the organisational landscape and the competing interests of Norwegian esports organisations. In the next sub-section, we discuss some of these competing vested interests in relation to the visibility and legitimacy of gender inequality.

The visibility and legitimacy of gender inequality

Despite our interview data indicating that women are underrepresented in leadership and management positions of Norwegian esports organisations, it was notable that gender issues were largely silenced until specific gender-related questions were asked by the researchers. This aligns with Acker's (2006a, p. 452) claim that 'gender and gender inequality tend to disappear in organisations or are seen as something that is beside the point of the organisation'. When gender was discussed, several of the interviewees (male and female) maintained that there were no problems relating to gender inequality in esports:

> When it comes to the administration, there are no obstacles preventing that new person with us from being a woman. (Arve)

> There's not a hint of gender discrimination or anything else. (Martin)

> We in the administration are very open to bringing in women. It's not the case that we actively recruit men because they're more experienced. (Bjørn)

> There are no barriers in esports, they want to include more women. (Jorunn)

Such comments align with gender equality narratives that focus on formal equality/lack of visible discrimination but fail to consider gendered cultural issues and informal practices that are known to continue to create gender inequity across the esports sector (Rogstad, 2021).

For some male esports leaders, the interviews indicated low ambitions in terms of what constituted an adequate female representation in management positions. For example, Bjørn claimed that as his organisation had 'several female employees', it was 'good at recruiting women', despite having no women in leadership positions in their organisation. Rasmus, on the other hand, stated that there 'are ample' women in the administration of Norwegian esports organisations as there are 'few clubs that don't have a woman in the management team in one way or another'. These quotes indicate a lack of awareness and legitimacy of the issue of inequality by some male leaders when it comes to the degree of male dominance in Norwegian esports organisations that is acceptable, and aligns with Acker's (2006a, p. 452) claim that 'men tend not to see their gender privilege'.

In terms of the legitimacy of having a greater female representation across the hierarchies of esports organisations, only one male interviewee (Pål) talked about the 'business case' for having more women leaders in esports, including that 'having a woman increases profits', that women employees 'break up the environment', and that 'it's nice to have as diverse an input as possible'. Additionally, some of the interviewees made it clear that their organisations were not proactive in implementing strategies to increase the number of women in esports leadership positions, thereby demonstrating a lack of legitimacy of the gender equality measures in Norwegian esports:

> Yes, we don't actually actively do anything, for example with regard to the leadership roles and our staff. (Bjørn)

> We've done far too little. But that's because we think this is terribly, terribly difficult. This is perhaps one of the most difficult aspects. (Rasmus)
>
> We could, of course, have done much more, but we haven't made it a major priority, because we've not experienced this as a problem yet. (Jorunn)

One explanation for a lack of action in resisting male-dominated esports leadership was a lack of organisational resources and capacity. For example, Arve said that actions to increase gender inclusivity in esports are:

> Automatically lower priority ... because, at the moment, there are not enough hours during the workday, to do this while you have all the other activities that must also continue. I don't have enough hours in a day to somehow sit and find solutions to just that problem [of gender inclusion] when there are a hundred other urgent challenges. (Arve)

Arve's comments seem to demonstrate that gender equality is not given legitimacy in his organisation or that women are not perceived as organisational resources for increased effectivity and income generation (Hovden, 2001; Sørhaug, 2004).

The legitimacy given to diversity and inclusion in esports organisations was also discussed as being influenced by competing vested interests. For example, Ingrid talked about how the financial instability of her organisation has led to leaders deciding to enter into 'very shady agreements', such as a 'million kroner deal' with an institution that was known to be actively against gay marriage and a sponsorship deal with a foreign betting company. According to Ingrid, these deals were 'completely opposed to Norwegian cultural values' and to her own values as a member of the LGBT community, which made it 'very, very painful to be a representative of that organisation'. This example highlights that 'simultaneous inequality-producing processes' exist in some Norwegian esports organisations, with gender being only one dimension of the inequality regimes at play (Acker, 2006a, p. 442). It also highlights that limited companies' accountability to shareholders can lead to 'non-responsibility for human and environmental survival and well-being unless these goals enhance profit' (Acker, 2006b, p. 9). Esports organisations as private businesses are not democratic enterprises, and the representation of women across the hierarchies of these organisations is dependent on the perspectives, willingness, and motivations of esports leaders in line with the vested interests of their organisations. That is, in organisations where profit-making is a primary interest, the inclusion of women is reliant on a belief amongst esports leaders that an increased representation of women can have a profitable outcome for the organisation. As Acker (2006a) warned, gender equality as a democratic value is not central to the values of private (market/commercial) organisations as part of a capitalist economy. The lack of legitimacy and visibility of gender inequality, combined with a lack of regulation of the male-dominated esports sector, raises concerns about the likelihood of esports becoming a gender-inclusive sector in the foreseeable future.

Conclusion

Acker (2006a) claimed that all organisations have inequality regimes that result in and maintain inequalities. The aim of this chapter has been to explore the complex and interrelated ways in which esports organisations contribute to the production of gender inequality in esports leadership. Our findings align with previous research showing that women are underrepresented across all levels and positions in esports organisations (Darvin et al., 2021; Taylor & Stout, 2020). However, whereas the limited research on this topic has predominantly focused on gender representation, individual experiences, and organisational cultures in esports organisations, our findings have generated new insights into the impact of formal organisational structures, processes, and practices on gender inequality in esports leadership.

Several of Acker's (2006a) inequality regimes are visible in the findings presented in this chapter. For example, the degree of inequality became visible through reports of a minimal representation of women across all roles and levels in the sector. There was also evidence of gender segregation of roles, with women tending to be absent in roles that hold the highest volumes of symbolic capital. We suggest that a statistical analysis of gender representation across the esports sector would be beneficial to get a true sense of the shape and degree of gender inequality in the sector at both the national and international levels. Additionally, we found that recruitment is an example of an organisational process rooted in the structure and culture of the esports industry that produces inequality in Norwegian esports organisations. This is through problematic informal recruitment processes in which male-dominated networks are highly influential. Furthermore, we discussed the influences of organisational type and sectoral location on variances in the control (and incentives) of esports organisations over maintaining unequal gendered systems. A significant and ongoing development in this regard is the debate surrounding the inclusion of esports under NIF. Such inclusion would result in member organisations being regulated by NIF (gender) laws and so losing some control over the maintenance of gender unequal systems. That said, some esports organisations would continue to sit outside of NIF and so continue to maintain full control over their (lack of) action to redress gender imbalance. Finally, we found that the visibility of gender inequalities is clearly lacking in some instances, with examples of both male and female interviewees failing to see the extent to which the Norwegian esports administration is male dominated. Inequality as an issue also lacks legitimacy in some instances, with examples of unambitious goals for female representation in esports administration, as well as inequality being seen as a less legitimate concern compared to, for example, income generation or everyday operations. This presentation of an array of inequality regimes in Norwegian esports organisations demonstrates the complex and varied ways in which gender power relations are played out in the sector.

According to Acker (2006a, p. 455), 'inequality regimes can be challenged and changed', although such change 'is difficult and change efforts often fail'. She argues that a key reason for this is because 'owner and managerial class interests and the power those interests can mobilize usually outweigh the class, gender, and race interests of those who suffer inequality' (Acker, 2006a, p. 455). Norwegian esports is part of a global esports market that is growing at a blistering pace (Cranmer et al., 2021). Therefore, an important factor in Norwegian esports becoming a more inclusive sector will be that equality, diversity, and inclusion are valued and seen as enablers, rather than hindrances to the economic interests of those who own and lead esports organisations.

References

Acker, J. (1990). Hierarchies, jobs, bodies: A theory of gendered organizations. *Gender & Society*, 4(2), 139–158.
Acker, J. (2006a). Inequality regimes: Gender, class, and race in organizations. *Gender and Society*, 20(4), 441–464.
Acker, J. (2006b). *Class questions: Feminist answers*. Rowman & Littlefield.
Adriaanse, J., & Schofield, T. (2013). Analysing gender dynamics in sport governance: A new regimes-based approach. *Sport Management Review*, 16(4), 498–513. http://www.sciencedirect.com/science/article/pii/S1441352313000089
Children and the Media Survey. (2018). *Barn og dataspill* [Children and Computer Games]. Norwegian Media Authority. https://www.medietilsynet.no/globalassets/publikasjoner/barn-og-medier-undersokelser/dataspilltallgrunnlag-februar-2018.pdf
Choi, Y., Slaker, J. S., & Ahmad, N. (2020). Deep strike: Playing gender in the world of overwatch and the case of Geguri. *Feminist Media Studies*, 20(8), 1128–1143. https://doi.org/10.1080/14680777.2019.1643388
Cote, A. C. (2017). 'I can defend myself': Women's strategies for coping with harassment while gaming online. *Games and Culture*, 12(2), 136–155. https://doi.org/10.1177/1555412015587603
Cranmer, E., Danny Han, D., van Ginsbergen, M., & Jung, T. (2021). Esports matrix: Structuring the esports research agenda. *Computers in Human Behavior*, 117. https://doi.org/10.1016/j.chb.2020.106671
Darvin, L., Holden, J., Wells, J., & Baker, T. (2021). Breaking the glass monitor: Examining the underrepresentation of women in esports environments. *Sport Management Review*, 24(3), 475–499. https://doi.org/10.1080/14413523.2021.1891746
Darvin, L., Vooris, R., & Mahoney, T. (2020). The playing experiences of esports participants: An analysis of treatment discrimination and hostility in esports environments, *Journal of Athlete Development and Experience*, 2(1), Article 3. https://doi.org/10.25035/jade.02.01.03
Elling, A. (2015). Assessing the sociology of sport: On reintegrating quantitative methods and gender research. *International Review for the Sociology of Sport*, 50(4–5), 430–436.
Elling, A., Hovden, J., & Knoppers, A. (2019). *Gender diversity in European sport governance*. Routledge.

Evans, A., & Pfister, G. (2021). Women in sports leadership: A systematic narrative review. *International Review for the Sociology of Sport*, 56(3), 317–342. https://doi.org/10.1177/1012690220911842

Fasting, K., & Sisjord, M. (2019). Norway: Gender, governance and the impact of quota regulations. In A. Elling, J. Hovden, & A. Knoppers (Eds.), *Gender diversity in European sport governance* (pp. 131–140). Routledge.

Franks, S. (1999). *Having none of it: Women, men and the future of work*. Granta.

Fraser, N. (2013). *Fortunes of feminism: From state-managed capitalism to neo-liberal crisis*. Verso.

Hayday, E. J., & Collison, H. (2020). Exploring the contested notion of social inclusion and gender Inclusivity within esports spaces. *Social Inclusion*, 8(3), 197–208. https://doi.org/10.17645/si.v8i3.2755

Hovden, J. (2000). 'Heavyweight' men and younger women? The gendering of selection processes in Norwegian sport organizations. *NORA: Nordic Journal of Women's Studies*, 8(1), 17–32.

Hovden, J. (2001). *Makt, motstand og ambivalens. Betydningar av kjønn i idretten*. Upublisert dr.avhandling. Universitetet i Tromsø.

Hovden, J., & Tjønndal, A. (2021). 'If there were more women coaches around, I think things would be different': Women boxing coaches' struggles to challenge and change a male dominated sport. In L. Norman (Ed.), *Improving gender equity in sports coaching* (pp. 251–269). Routledge.

Hovden, J., Elling, A., & Knoppers, A. (2019). Meta-analysis: Policies and strategies. In A. Elling, J. Hovden, & A. Knoppers (Eds.), *Gender diversity in European sport governance* (pp. 192–204). Routledge.

Hussain, U., Yu, B., Cunningham, G. B., & Bennett, G. (2021). 'I can be who I am when I play tekken 7': E-sports women participants from the Islamic Republic of Pakistan. *Games and Culture*, 16(8), 978–1000. https://doi.org/10.1177/15554120211005360

Hyperion. (n.d.). *Nye foreninger våren 2021!* https://n4f.no/artikkel/nye-foreninger-varen-2021/

Kanter, R. (1977). Some effects of proportions in group life: Skewed sex ration and responses to token women. *American Journal of Sociology*, 82(5), 965–990.

Lynch, T., Tompkins, J. E., Van Driel, I. I., & Fritz, N. (2016). Sexy, strong, and secondary: A content analysis of female characters in video games across 31 years. *Journal of Communication*, 66(4), 564–584. https://doi.org/10.1111/jcom.12237

NIF. (2019). *Årsrapport 2019*. https://www.idrettsforbundet.no/contentassets/3fa4c97bbabf4446b3867eb04fc8e102/23_20_nif-arsrapport-2019.pdf

NIF. (2020). *Nøkkeltall - Rapport 2019*. https://www.idrettsforbundet.no/contentassets/9f94ba79767846d9a67d1a56f4054dc2/20201001-nokkeltallsrapport-2019.pdf

NESF. (n.d.). *Om e-sportforbundet*. https://e-sportforbundet.no/om.html

Oilers esports. (n.d.). *Elite Team Counter Strike*. https://www.oilersesports.gg/

Paaßen, B., Morgenroth, T., & Stratemeyer, M. (2017). What is a true gamer? The male gamer stereotype and the marginalization of women in video game culture. *Sex Roles*, 76(7–8), 421–435.

Piggott, L., & Matthews, J. (2021). Gender, leadership, and governance in English national governing bodies of sport: Formal structures, rules, and processes. *Journal of Sport Management*, 35(4), 338–351. https://doi.org/10.1123/jsm.2020-0173

Ratan, R. A., Taylor, N., Hogan, J., Kennedy, T., & Williams, D. (2015). Stand by your man: An examination of gender disparity in league of legends. *Games and Culture*, 10(5), 438–462. https://doi.org/10.1177/1555412014567228

Riatti, P., & Thiel, A. (2021). The societal impact of electronic sport: A scoping review. *German Journal of Exercise and Sport Research.* https://doi.org/10.1007/s12662-021-00784-w

Ruvalcaba, O., Shulze, J., Kim, A., Berzenski, S. R., & Otten, M. P. (2018). Women's experiences in esports: Gendered differences in peer and spectator feedback during competitive video gameplay. *Journal of Sport and Social Issues, 42*(4), 295–311.

Rogstad, E. (2021). Gender in esports research: A literature review. *European Journal for Sport and Society.* https://doi.org/10.1080/16138171.2021.1930941

Rogstad, E., Blaalid, B., & Tjønndal, A. (2021). Hvem inkluderes? Et kjønnsperspektiv på IOCs strategi for esports i OL. In A. Tjønndal (Ed.). *Idrett, kjønn og ledelse* (pp. 211–229). Fagbokforlaget.

Salmons, J. (2021). *Doing qualitative research online.* SAGE Publishing.

Schelfhout, S., Bowers, M. T., & Hao, Y. A. (2021). Balancing gender identity and gamer identity: Gender issues faced by Wang 'BaiZe' Xinyu at the 2017 hearthstone summer championship. *Games and Culture, 16*(1), 22–41.

Simpkins, E., Velija, P., & Piggott, L. (2022). The sport intersectional model of power (SIMP) as a tool for understanding intersectionality in sport governance and leadership. In P. Velija & L. Piggott (Eds.), *Gender equity in UK sport leadership and governance* (pp. 37–50). Emerald Publishing Limited.

Sørhaug, T. (2004). *Managementalitet og autoritetenes forvandling -Ledelse i en kunnskapsøkonomi.* Fagbokforlaget.

Taylor, N., Jenson, J., & De Castell, S. (2009). Cheerleaders/booth babes/Halo hoes: Pro-gaming, gender, and jobs for the boys. *Digital Creativity, 20*(4), 239–252.

Taylor, N., & Stout, B. (2020). Gender and the two-tiered system of collegiate esports. *Critical Studies in Media Communication.* https://doi.org/10.1080/15295036.2020.1813901

Thagaard, T. (2018). *Systematikk og innlevelse.* Fagbokforlaget.

Tjønndal, A. (2021). 'What's next? Calling beer-drinking a sport?!': Virtual resistance to considering esports as sport. *Sport, Business and Management, 11*(1), 72–88. https://doi.org/10.1108/SBM-10-2019-0085

Tjønndal, A., & Hovden, J. (2016). Kjønn som sparringspartner-Ledelsesformer og betydninger av kjønn blant norske boksetrenere. *Tidsskrift for kjønnsforskning, 40*(3-4), 38–54.

Tjønndal, A., & Skauge, M. (2021). Youth sport 2.0? The development of esports in Norway from 2016 to 2019. *Qualitative Research in Sport, Exercise and Health, 13*(1), 166–183. https://doi.org/10.1080/2159676X.2020.1836509

Wreyford, N. (2015). Birds of a feather: Informal recruitment practices and gendered outcomes for screenwriting work in the UK film industry. *The Sociological Review, 63*(S1), 84–96.

Voorhees, G. (2015). Neoliberal masculinity: The government of play and masculinity in e-sports. In R. A. Brookey & T. P. Oates (Eds.), *Playing to win: Sports, video games, and the culture of play* (pp. 63–91). Indiana University Press.

Voorhees, G., & Orlando, A. (2018). Performing neoliberal masculinity: Reconfiguring hegemonic masculinity in professional gaming. In N. Taylor & G. Voorhees (Eds.), *Masculinities in play* (pp. 211–227). Palgrave Macmillan.

00 NATION DNB [@zerozeronation]. (n.d.). *Posts [Instagram profile]. Instagram.* Retrieved April 27, 2022, from https://www.instagram.com/zerozeronation/

Chapter 5

The importance of female characters in esports

A quantitative analysis of players' perceptions of gendered character representations in sports video games

Egil Trasti Rogstad and Mads Skauge

Introduction

The growing popularity of esports and its similarities with traditional sport have recently attracted the attention of many leading sports organisations, professional and local sports clubs, and sports media outlets, all of which are becoming increasingly and systematically involved with esports games that simulate sports. This game genre is often referred to as sports video games (SVGs) and includes popular franchises such as *FIFA* and *NBA 2K*. Although the increasing popularity of SVGs has been met with curiosity and excitement by many esports and sports stakeholders, a major issue regarding the convergence of esports and traditional sport relates to the overwhelming absence of women represented as both players and characters in esports based on SVGs (Bailey et al., 2021; Darvin et al., 2021). In fact, research indicates that girls and women only make up about 2% of all SVGs players (Yee, 2017). Moreover, female character options have long been significantly underrepresented in SVGs and other game genres (Lynch et al., 2016; Williams et al., 2009). Until the 2010s only a few of the most popular SVGs franchises included female characters (Brown, 2015; Jenson & de Castell, 2011). As a result, SVGs appear to constitute one of the least diverse genres of esports in terms of female representation (Yee, 2017).

The representation and proliferation of female characters play an important role in the overall marginalisation and negative stereotyping of women in esports and gaming (Paaßen et al., 2017). This issue encompasses a variety of esports game genres, including SVGs. Previous research has documented how female characters are often aligned with harmful stereotypes that portray female characters in overly sexualised ways and/or in subordinate roles (Bertozzi, 2008; Dill & Thill, 2007; Downs & Smith, 2010; Lynch et al., 2016; Williams et al., 2009). For instance, before the release of the popular American football game series *Madden* in 2015, the only women in the stadiums were lightly dressed cheerleaders (Brown, 2015). Such limited and stereotypical representations of women are problematic because they serve to reinforce the idea of esports as a male domain and discourage girls and women from playing (Consalvo, 2013; Lynch et al.,

DOI: 10.4324/9781003258650-7

2016; Olsson, 2013). Furthermore, they also serve to perpetuate biased perceptions of women players' skills and capabilities (McArthur, 2021).

As the convergence of esports and traditional sport continues to increase, equal and balanced gender representation is crucial for achieving a gender-balanced and equal sport (Kruthika, 2020). A welcomed increase in female characters in most SVGs in recent years may be an important step towards increasing the inclusiveness and representation of women in gaming (Darvin et al., 2021). However, as this increase does not necessarily lead to more inclusive and equal esports environments, a better understanding of players' perceptions about the increased number of female characters is needed (Darvin et al., 2021).

In this chapter, we examine players' perceptions of female characters in SVGs and their importance to the players themselves. The research question is: *how do players perceive gendered character representations in the SVGs genre?*

To begin with, we present a brief overview of previous research on gender, identity, and esports. Next, we outline the context of our study and methods before presenting and discussing our findings on players' perceptions of female characters in SVGs.

Research on gender, identity, and esports

Issues concerning gender and esports are closely connected to broader cultural and research discussions about gender, gameplay, and technology (Jenson & de Castell, 2018; Rogstad, 2021). Abbiss (2008) reviewed three decades of research on gender and technology and revealed that computing is constructed as a masculine activity. In particular, girls were found to be portrayed as impaired due to limited interest in internet technology and 'hard' computing (Abbiss, 2008). Massanari (2017) describes video games as part of a larger, toxic techno-culture centred around 'an othering of those perceived as outside the culture … and a valorization of masculinity masquerading as a particular form of "rationality"' (p. 5). This othering of players who are not perceived as part of the majority norm of young, white, heterosexual men has led to a male gamer stereotype that positions women as players with limited dedication and gaming skills (Paaßen et al., 2017). Conversely, men are thought to be 'hard-core' gamers who actively identify as gamers, play more competitive and advanced games on gaming consoles, and occasionally compete for prize money in esports competitions (Taylor, 2012). Paaßen et al. (2017) argue that the male gamer stereotype contributes to the marginalisation of women in video game culture, including negative psychological consequences, such as feelings of unwelcomeness, reduced self-identification, and direct and destructive psychological impacts of gender-based harassment. Furthermore, they argue that the longevity of this stereotype is related to the fact that men are almost exclusively represented in most professional roles and are prominent characters in the gaming culture. Similarly, women are significantly underrepresented as players, employees, fans, and playable characters in the esports industry (Bailey et al., 2021; Darvin et al., 2021). Shen et al. (2016) argue that the male gamer stereotype generates a self-perpetuating cycle, wherein women players perceive themselves as outsiders and are discouraged from playing esports, thereby leading to the reinforcement of such stereotypes.

Game content and gendered media representations

The male gamer stereotype influences game producers' presumed core audiences, which results in the development of game content and marketing strategies directed at the stereotypical interests of young, male audiences (Paaßen et al., 2017). This includes the underrepresentation of female game characters and proliferation of sexualised female character representations, such as emphasised breasts, buttocks, and provocative clothing (Jansz & Martis, 2007; Lynch et al., 2016; Shen et al., 2016). The consequences of such female representations have been debated in scholarly literature. While some researchers argue that such content has no effect on female players (Daviault & Schot, 2013;Reinhard, 2009), others suggest that sexualised depictions of female characters may discourage female players from participating in esports and gaming (Hartmann & Klimmt, 2006; Reinecke et al., 2007; Vermeulen et al., 2011)

To develop a deeper understanding of gendered media representations and how these tend to foster the reproduction of existing gender norms, Shaw (2015) suggests drawing on Butler's (2006, 2009) theoretical concepts of performativity and precarity as an explanatory framework. According to Shaw (2015), media representations are inextricably linked with processes in which gender is produced in certain social settings to fulfil various objectives and are dependent on a cultural acceptance of intelligibility. Performativity refers to Butler's (2006) understanding of identity as a continuous performance rendered natural by individuals. These identity performances are greatly influenced by the media, which frequently promotes certain representations of gender identities as desirable (Dixon, 2019). Precarity is closely related to performativity and is used to describe the process by which these performances are made comprehensible to others through larger networks of meaning (Butler, 2009). To destabilise categories individuals can perform in several different ways, although, 'to be a subject at all requires first complying with certain norms that govern recognition – that make a person recognizable. And so, non-compliance calls into question the viability of one's life, the ontological conditions of one's persistence' (Butler, 2009, p. xii). Shaw (2015) argues that this articulation is useful in the context of consumer culture, as precarity allows for a politics of representation that favours the margins instead of reconceiving the core. Butler's notions of performativity and precarity may help to reveal how media representations make certain identities possible, plausible, and liveable (Shaw, 2015). Thus, Butler's ideas help to demonstrate the political relevance of visibility beyond a basic reconstruction of profitable audiences without specifically focusing on 'true' or 'good' representations (Shaw, 2015).

Data and methods

Participant recruitment

The participants in the study were selected by a convenience sampling of members of multiple online SVG platforms, such as Reddit and Discord. The respondents were primarily recruited by posting on subreddits (sub-sections of the online discussion forum reddit.com), which was chosen due to the high representation of most SVGs and high levels of member interaction. Each of the sampled subreddits had between 6,500 and 1,100,000 subscribers. The SVGs included games simulating real sports (*FIFA, Madden, MLB The Show, NBA 2K, NBA Live, NHL, The Golf Club, Zwift*), racing games (*Assetto Corsa, iRacing, rFactor, F1*), and 'hybrid' games with a mixture of sport and fantasy elements (*Rocket League, Mario Tennis, Mario Kart*). Questionnaires were distributed via online survey and data management software. The respondents were asked about their perceptions of gendered character representations in SVGs, playing habits, and demographic information. Due to the initial low number of female respondents, the survey was additionally distributed on female-specific gaming forums and Discord channels. A total number of 444 SVG players participated in the study. The data collection and analysis were performed in compliance with national research ethics norms, and the study was approved by the Norwegian Centre for Research Data.

Variables and descriptive statistics

To explore players' perceptions of gendered character representations in SVGs, the participants were asked to rate four statements: (1) '*I believe most sports video games portray women poorly*', (2) '*Being able to play characters of the same gender as myself is important to me*', (3) '*I feel that there are too few female characters in sports video games*', and (4) '*I believe that more girls and women would engage in sports video games if there were more female characters in the games*'.

These four statements were developed based on similar studies related to perceptions of gendered character representations in video games (Duggan, 2015; Hall, 2015). The responses were rated on a seven-point Likert scale (1 = '*Strongly disagree*', 7 = '*Strongly agree*'). As the study aimed to compare differences in responses at both ends of the Likert scale, rather than various levels of agreement and disagreement, the responses were dichotomised with a cut-off value between 4 ('*Neither disagree nor agree*') and 5 ('*Somewhat agree*'). As media consumption may be influenced by demographics other than gender (Brown et al., 2018), participants were asked to provide demographic information, such as age, education, and ethnicity, which was then used as explanatory variables in the data analysis. Gaming frequency was included as a control variable to determine any potential variances between people playing SVGs at least once a week (core players) and people playing less than once a week (casual players). Descriptive (univariate) statistics on the respondents' locations were included, although this variable was not used in the regression models. No changes (re-coding) were made to the explanatory variables compared to their initial (original) operationalisations in the questionnaire.

Analytical design and strategy

The ordinal (a numeric variable ordered categorically) dependent variables (the explained variation in Y) were utilised by applying logistic regression. With regard to effect, the *sizes* (impact) odds and probabilities were used (Acock, 2014). As the output of multiple logistic regression – apart from positive or negative direction – is difficult to interpret directly based on coefficients, ORs and AVEs were predicted by calculating the predicted changes in odds and probabilities depending on social background. Stata 15 (Acock, 2014) was used to analyse the data.

Results

Tables 5.1a and 5.1b show the distribution of the dependent and explanatory variables in the analysis (descriptive statistics). Approximately half (53%, N = 166) of the respondents agreed that '*most sports video games portray women poorly*'. In addition, 61% (N = 258) of the respondents disagreed that '*being able to play characters of the same gender*' as themselves was important to them. In addition, 65% and 66% agreed that there were '*too few female characters in sports video games*' and that '*more girls and women would engage in sports video games if there were more female characters in the games*'.

As Table 5.1b shows, the sample consisted of 350 men (79%) and 94 women (21%). The participants were primarily between the ages of 16 and 35 (75%), located in North America, Central America (55%), or Europe (32%). Most of the respondents could be defined as core players (83%, N = 378) and 77 (17%) as casual players. Most of the participants were white (78%), with Asian (6%) and Hispanic (5%) as the second and third highest ethnicities.

The results indicate that female respondents had stronger preferences for gender representations generally and female representations, especially in SVGs, than men when controlled for social background and gaming frequency (Tables 5.2a–d). These findings are homogeneous and point in the same direction. All four dependent variables had significant gender effects at the < 0.01 level. This did not apply to any of the other explanatory variables, except for education and age in one case each. Furthermore, the gender effects are stronger (based on ORs and AVEs) and more statistically robust (lower sig.-values) than those for education and age. That is, the outputs for gender are more substantial than those for education and age, implying that gender is the most crucial variable when analysing gendered SVG play reasons using this data.

Most of the variance is explained by '*Being able to play characters of the same gender as myself is important to me*' (Table 5.2b; McFadden = 0.241, LR-test = 122.66), while the least explained variable variance is '*I believe more girls and women would engage in sports video games if there were female characters in the games*' (Table 5.2d; McFadden = 0.064, LR-test = 33.13).

Table 5.1a Descriptive statistics of dependent variables

Statements	N	%
I believe most sports video games portray women poorly		
Disagree	149	47
Agree	166	53
Disagree male	129	60
Agree male	87	40
Disagree female	14	16
Agree female	75	84
Being able to play characters of the same gender as myself is important to me		
Disagree	258	61
Agree	162	39
Disagree male	238	75
Agree male	79	25
Disagree female	13	14
Agree female	79	86
I feel that there are too few female characters in sports video games		
Disagree	148	35
Agree	275	65
Disagree male	137	43
Agree male	183	57
Disagree female	8	9
Agree female	85	91
I believe more girls and women would engage in sports video games if there were more female characters in the games		
Disagree	149	34
Agree	283	66
Disagree male	132	40
Agree male	197	60
Disagree female	11	12
Agree female	82	88

The greatest discrepancy in the gender outcomes is demonstrated for '*Being able to play characters of the same gender as myself is important to me*' (Table 5.2b). Applying the *margins* command in Stata reveals that holding the control variables constant, according to the formula (OR-1) *100 equals the mean percentage change in odds by one unit change in the explanatory variable (X). The odds of agreeing rather than disagreeing with this statement are 1,976% higher among women than men (95% CI [2.2253–3.812]), corresponding to a 63% higher probability (AVE statistics) for women ($p = 0.865$) compared to men ($p = 0.236$). This implies that white female core players with mean scores on age and education are 87% more likely to agree that playing characters of the same gender as

Table 5.1b Descriptive statistics of explanatory variables and respondents' locations

Variable	N	%
Gender		
Male	350	79
Female	94	21
Age		
15 or younger	22	5
16–20	75	17
21–25	132	29
26–30	85	19
31–35	47	10
36–40	40	9
41–45	27	6
46–50	14	3
51–55	6	1
61 or older	3	1
Education		
Less than high school diploma	33	8
High school degree or equivalent	121	28
Bachelor's degree	159	37
Master's degree	101	24
Doctorate	12	3
Ethnicity		
White	349	78
Hispanic or Latino	24	5
Black or African American	12	3
Native American or American Indian	8	2
Asian or Pacific Islander	26	6
Other	26	6
Gaming frequency		
Casual player (less than once a week)	77	17
Core player (at least once a week)	378	83

themselves is important to them, compared to a similar male respondent having a 24% probability of obtaining level 1 on the dependent variable.

The gender gap in the variables is the smallest for '*I believe more girls and women would engage in sports video games if there were female characters in the games*' (Table 5.2d, OR = 6.263). The odds of agreeing rather than disagreeing with this statement are 5,206% [6.263–1] *100) higher among female than male respondents (95% CI [1.047–2.621]), corresponding to a 31% higher probability among women (p = 0.905) compared to men (p = 0.604).

The odds of agreeing compared with disagreeing with the statement '*I believe most sports video games portray women poorly*' are 43% (OR = 1.434) higher for each additional education level attained (Table 5.2a). As shown in Table 5.2b, the odds of agreeing rather than disagreeing with the statement '*Being able to play*

Table 5.2a Logistic regressions for 'I believe most sports video games portray women poorly' (1 = Agree) (N = 289)

Variable	Coef.	SE	OR	AVE/p	z	Sig.	[95% C. Int.]
Gender (1 = Female)	1.869	0.389	6.484	0 = 0.425 1 = 0.827	4.80	< 0.001**	1.105 2.633
Age (1–10)	–0.118	0.081			–1.46	0.145	–0.277 0.040
Education (1–5)	0.361	0.167	1.434	1 = 0.272 5 = 0.614	2.16	0.031*	0.033 0.688
Ethnicity (ref. = White)							
Hispanic/Latino	0.168	0.572			0.29	0.768	–0.952 1.289
Black/African American	0.003	1.087			0.00	0.997	–2.128 2.135
Native American/ American Indian	0.575	1.180			0.49	0.626	–1.738 2.888
Asian/Pacific Islander	0.279	0.467			0.60	0.549	–0.635 1.195
Other	0.644	0.520			1.24	0.216	–0.375 1.664
Gaming frequency (1 = Weekly)	–0.000	0.357			–0.00	0.999	–0.701 0.700
Constant	–0.878	0.600			–1.46	0.144	–2.056 0.299
-2LL	338.382						
LR chi²(9)	58.48					< 0.001	
McFadden	0.147						
H-L GOF chi²(8)	12.56					0.127	

Notes: * p < 0.05.
** p < 0.01.
Coef. is sig. if p-value < 0.05.

characters of the same gender as myself is important to me' are 18% (OR = 0.823) lower for each additional age category (ranging 1–10). This corresponds to a 26% lower probability among the oldest (age category 10, $p = 0.087$) than the youngest respondents (age category 1, $p = 0.354$).

Discussion

The representation of female characters in video games continues to be a source of concern for players, game developers, researchers, and the other parties involved. This study has investigated how players perceive gendered character representations in SVGs. In the following discussion about our findings, we specifically focus on two topics: (1) female character options and (2) gendered character representations and player motivation.

Female character options

Being represented in the media is important for marginalised groups in the media such as women, as they act as important frames of reference that validate

Table 5.2b Logistic regressions for 'Being able to play characters of the same gender as myself is important to me' (1 = Agree) (N = 376)

Variable	Coef.	SE	OR	AVE/p	z	Sig.	[95%. C. Int.]
Gender (1 = Female)	3.032	0.397	20.758	0 = 0.236 1 = 0.865	7.63	< 0.001**	2.253 3.812
Age (1–10)	–0.193	0.081	0.823	1 = 0.354 10 = 0.087	–2.37	0.018*	–0.354 –0.033
Education (1–5)	0.031	0.162			0.20	0.845	–0.286 0.350
Ethnicity (ref. = White)							
Hispanic/Latino	0.647	0.537			1.20	0.229	–0.406 1.701
Black/African American	0.098	0.724			0.14	0.892	–1.322 1.519
Native American/ American Indian	0.554	1.263			0.44	0.661	–1.922 3.031
Asian/Pacific Islander	0.401	0.474			0.85	0.397	–0.527 1.331
Other	0.187	0.510			0.37	0.713	–0.813 1.188
Gaming frequency (1 = Weekly)	–0.120	0.361			–0.33	0.740	–0.827 0.587
Constant	–0.377	0.574			–0.66	0.511	–1.503 0.749
-2LL	385.474						
LR chi²(9)	122.66					< 0.001	
McFadden	0.241						
H-L GOF chi²(8)	1.77					0.987	

Notes:
* p < 0.05.
** p < 0.01.
Coef. is sig. if p-value < 0.05.

certain identities, regardless of whether one identifies with those representations (Shaw, 2015). Although women have become increasingly represented as game characters in most SVGs in recent years, many players still feel that female character options are too limited (Newell, 2021). This is also reflected in the results of this study, which reveal that the majority of respondents, particularly women, feel that there are too few female characters in SVGs (see Table 5.2a). This is consistent with earlier studies of SVGs, which assert that female players wish to have the opportunity to play as female characters (De Jean et al., 1999; Olsson, 2013). The importance of game character options can be explained by how individuals identify with specific identities in certain social contexts. Using the concept of performativity, Butler (2006) argues that identity is a performance. In other words, gender performance is what constitutes our understanding of gender. However, according to Butler's (2009) discussions about precarity, in order to be recognised by others, such performances depend on larger structures of meaning. Shaw (2015) argues that this meaning process is closely linked to media representation. Butler's (2009) concept of precarity suggests that media representations make particular identities conceivable, credible, and liveable. As such, game character representations become sites that allow or deny players to assume certain identities depending on the available character options (Taylor, 2006).

Although embodied identities, such as gender, are often thought to be unimportant in video game culture due to the common assumption that all players are white, heterosexual males (Taylor, 2012), Shaw (2015) argues that these identities become important for players who do not hold gender, racial, and sexuality privilege. This argument is supported by this study, which demonstrates that being able to play characters of the same gender as themselves is more important to female than male participants (Table 5.2b). Furthermore, the perceived lack of representation of women in SVGs as game characters may contribute to the reinforcement of harmful differences between men's and women's sports that portray sport and esports as male domains (Consalvo, 2013; Darvin et al., 2021). Somewhat paradoxically, Williams et al. (2009) pointed out that female game characters may have the best chance of appearing in SVGs, as the games in this genre often aim to resemble rosters of real-life sports. If SVGs do not provide sufficient opportunities for girls and women to play female characters, they may feel excluded from the games and be discouraged from playing altogether (Consalvo & Harper, 2009; Reinecke et al., 2007; Vermeulen et al., 2011).

Gendered character representations and player motivation

Female character representations have long remained significantly underrepresented in video games and are depicted in ways that reflect traditional gender norms and stereotypes (Bertozzi, 2008; Dill & Thill, 2007). The sexualisation of characters is especially frequent in male-oriented esports titles (Lynch et al., 2016), which often include portrayals of provocatively dressed female characters emphasising physical attributes (Downs & Smith, 2010; Jansz & Martis, 2007). For instance, the only option to play as female characters in the early SVGs was as female beach volleyball characters in pixelated bikinis (Brown, 2015). Despite an overall increase in female character options and a decrease in sexualised characters in games (Lynch et al., 2016), the results of this study reveal that female respondents tend to feel that most SVGs portray women poorly (Table 5.2c). This overall negative perception of female character portrayals in SVGs may lead to negative playing experiences for girls and women and discourage them from playing (Hartmann & Klimmt, 2006). It could also negatively influence players' impressions of real-life athletes that the female characters in SVGs are often meant to resemble (Darvin et al., 2021). Furthermore, stereotypical representations of women in games contribute to reinforcing the overall sexist nature of gaming and esports environments, foster negative impressions of women players and increase sexual harassment of women players (Darvin et al., 2020; Darvin et

Table 5.2c Logistic regressions for 'I feel that there are too few female characters in sports video games' (1 = Agree) (N = 372)

Variable	Coef.	SE	OR	AVE/p	z	Sig.	[95% C. Int.]
Gender (1 = Female)	1.999	0.448	7.388	0 = 0.580 1 = 0.910	4.45	< 0.001**	1.120 2.879
Age (1–10)	0.104	0.071			1.47	0.142	–0.035 0.244
Education (1–5)	0.134	0.147			0.91	0.363	–0.155 0.423
Ethnicity (ref. = White)							
Hispanic/Latino	0.759	0.554			1.37	0.171	–0.328 1.846
Black/African American	0.513	0.714			0.72	0.472	–0.886 1.913
Native American/ American Indian	–	–			–	–	– –
Asian/Pacific Islander	0.514	0.475			1.08	0.279	–0.416 1.445
Other	–0.162	0.472			–0.34	0.731	–1.088 0.763
Gaming frequency (1 = Weekly)	0.151	0.347			0.43	0.664	–0.530 0.833
Constant	–0.628	0.549			–1.14	0.253	–1.704 0.448
-2LL	432.275						
LR chi²(8)	44.02					< 0.001	
McFadden	0.092						
H-L GOF chi²(8)	3.95					0.861	

Notes:
* p < 0.05.
** p < 0.01.
Coef. is sig. if p-value < 0.05.

al., 2021; Dill et al., 2008; Hartmann & Klimmt, 2006). As a result, this overall negative perception of female characters in SVGs could be one potential reason why so few girls and women play them.

Therefore, positive and non-sexualised representations of female characters may be a key aspect in attracting more girls and women to engage in esports and could contribute towards improving gender equity in esports environments (Lynch et al., 2016). This is supported by the study's findings, which show that most of the respondents believe that more girls and women would engage in SVGs if more female characters were included in them (see Table 5.2d). Although the potential of positive female representations to reduce social inequality and unequal power relations may vary depending on players' levels of identification with game characters (Shaw, 2015), video games are created in a culture in which sexualised representations of women are commonplace (Moultrop, 2004). Therefore, it is not only SVG environments that would benefit from including representations reflecting a wider range of modes of being in the world, but also culture as a whole (Shaw, 2015).

Table 5.2d Logistic regressions for 'I believe more girls and women would engage in sports video games if there were more female characters in the games' (1 = Agree) (N = 405)

Variable	Coef.	SE	OR	AVE/p	z	Sig.	[95% C. Int.]
Gender (1 = Female)	1.834	0.401	6.263	0 = 0.604 1 = 0.905	4.57	< 0.001**	1.047 2.621
Age (1–10)	–0.002	0.063			–0.05	0.964	–0.127 0.122
Education (1–5)	0.013	0.109			0.12	0.904	–0.200 0.226
Ethnicity (ref. = White)							
Hispanic/Latino	0.405	0.507			0.80	0.424	–0.589 1.401
Black/African American	–0.084	0.659			–0.13	0.898	–1.377 1.209
Native American/American Indian	0.013	1.160			0.01	0.991	–2.260 2.287
Asian/Pacific Islander	0.022	0.458			0.05	0.961	–0.876 0.921
Other	0.152	0.496			0.31	0.759	–0.820 1.124
Gaming frequency (1= Weekly)	0.188	0.322			0.58	0.559	–0.443 0.821
Constant	0.208	0.484			0.43	0.667	–0.740 1.157
-2LL	479.632						
LR chi^2(9)	33.13					< 0.001	
McFadden	0.064						
H-L GOF chi^2(8)	5.07					0.749	

Notes:
* $p < 0.05$.
** $p < 0.01$.
Coef. is sig. if p-value < 0.05.

Conclusion and limitations

This study examines how representations of women as playable game characters in sports video games are perceived by players. The results reveal a clear gendered pattern, indicating that women have clearer and stronger opinions about female characters in SVGs than men. Although the number of female characters and their portrayals has developed in a positive direction in recent years, the participants feel that female character options remain too limited and that being able to play female characters is important to them. Moreover, female respondents tend to believe that SVGs portray women poorly and that more girls and women would engage in SVGs if more female characters were included. As a result, our findings reinforce the view that female character options are important to female players as game characters become sites that either enable or disallow them to take on certain identities (Shaw, 2015; Taylor, 2006). While the results are based on limited data related to SVG-based esports, the findings are consistent with previous research on gendered character options in gaming (Consalvo & Harper, 2009; De Jean et al., 1999; Darvin et al., 2021; Hartmann & Klimmt, 2006; Olsson, 2013; Reinecke et al., 2007; Vermeulen et al., 2011). Scarce and marginalised representations of women in video games constitute an important part of a self-perpetuating cycle, in which girls and women are discouraged from participating in esports activities. Normalising female characters towards competent and non-objectified representations could reduce the gender disparities in esports environments (Lynch et al., 2016; Shen et al., 2016).

The present study has several limitations. When recruiting respondents online it is often more challenging to verify aspects related to the population, sample, and location (Tjønndal & Fylling, 2021). Furthermore, this study focuses solely on players' perceptions of gender characters in SVGs, i.e. people who are already *engaged in* these games. Thus, the study has not considered the potential of gender equality in SVG play to recruit and include more women who do not play SVGs in the first place. However, it does contribute to the unpacking of gendered preferences concerning gendered character representations among players who already play SVGs. Furthermore, the study focuses on players' perceptions of gendered character representations in SVGs as a whole but does not consider the potential differences that may exist between various subgenres of SVGs. This is due to our limited data, which limits our possibility to look into distinct subgenres of SVGs.

Moreover, the sample size (N = 444) on which our analyses are based is relatively small given the number of people engaged in esports globally. Therefore, the statistical power of the findings is weak, implying that they should be treated with caution (see Tjønndal, 2021). In addition, convenience sampling means that the results, including differences between male and female participants, are only generalisable to the sample analysed (Bornstein et al., 2013). Furthermore, convenience samples generally comprise a limited number of underrepresented sociodemographic sub-groups, such as ethnic minorities, resulting in inadequate power to identify variations in sociodemographic factors (Bornstein et al., 2013). Finally, another important limitation of this study is the use of non-validated items to quantitatively explore players' perceptions of gendered character representations, which may have influenced the interpretation of the items. Our recommendation is that future research should focus on developing scales and items to measure preferences for game content and continue exploring the complexities of interactions between identification and players' experiences with game characters.

References

Abbiss, J. (2008). Rethinking the 'problem' of gender and IT schooling: Discourses in literature. *Gender and Education*, 20(2), 153–165. https://doi.org/10.1080/09540250701805839

Acock, A. (2014). *A gentle introduction to Stata*. Stata Press.

Bailey, E. N., Miyata, K., & Yoshida, T. (2021). Gender composition of teams and studios in video game development. *Games and Culture, 16*(1), 42–64. https://doi.org/10.1177/1555412019868381

Bertozzi, E. (2008). 'You play like a girl!': Cross-gender competition and the uneven playing field. *Convergence, 14*(4), 473–487. https://doi.org/10.1177/1354856508094667

Bornstein, M. H., Jager, J., & Putnick, D. L. (2013). Sampling in developmental science: Situations, shortcomings, solutions, and standards. *Developmental Review: DR, 33*(4), 357–370. https://doi.org/10.1016/j.dr.2013.08.003

Brown, J. (2015, September 10). Where are all the women sports stars in video games? *Vocativ.* https://www.vocativ.com/213774/where-are-all-the-women-sports-stars-in-video-games/index.html

Brown, K. A., Billings, A. C., Murphy, B., & Puesan, L. (2018). Intersections of fandom in the age of interactive media: Esports fandom as a predictor of traditional sport fandom. *Communication and Sport, 6*(4), 418–435. https://doi.org/10.1177/2167479517727286

Butler, J. (2006). *Gender trouble: Feminism and the subversion of identity.* Routledge.

Butler, J. (2009). *Performativity, precarity, and sexual policies.* Routledge.

Consalvo, M. (2013). Women, sports and videogames. In M. Consalvo, K. Mitgutsch, & A. Stein (Eds.), *Sports videogames* (pp. 87–111). Routledge.

Consalvo, M., & Harper, T. (2009). The sexi(e)st of all: Avatars, gender and online games. In N. Panteli (Ed.), *Virtual social networks: Mediated, massive and multiplayer* (pp. 98–113). Palgrave Publishing.

Darvin, L., Holden, J., Wells, J., & Baker, T. (2021). Breaking the glass monitor: Examining the underrepresentation of women in esports environments. *Sport Management Review, 24*(3), 475–499. https://doi.org/10.1080/14413523.2021.1891746

Darvin, L., Vooris, R., & Mahoney, T. (2020). The playing experiences of esports participants: An analysis of treatment discrimination and hostility in esports environments. *Journal of Athlete Development and Experience, 2*(1), 36–50. https://doi.org/10.25035/jade.02.01.03

Daviault, C. & Schott, G. (2013). Looking beyond representation: Situating the significance of gender portrayal within game play. In C. Carter, L. Steiner, & L. McLaughlin (Eds.), *The Routledge Companion to Media & Gender* (pp. 341–359). Routledge.

De Jean, J., Upitis, R., Koch, C., & Young, J. (1999). The story of phoenix quest: How girls respond to a prototype language and mathematics computer game. *Gender and education, 11*(2), 207–223. https://doi.org/10.1080/09540259920708

Dill, K. E., & Thill, K. P. (2007). Video game characters and the socialization of gender roles: Young people's perceptions mirror sexist media depictions. *Sex Roles, 57*(11–12), 851–864. https://doi.org/10.1007/s11199-007-9278-1

Dill, K. E., Brown, B. P., & Collins, M. A. (2008). Effects of exposure to sex-stereotyped video game characters on tolerance of sexual harassment. *Journal of Experimental Social Psychology, 44*(5), 1402–1408. https://doi.org/10.1016/j.jesp.2008.06.002

Dixon, M. (2019). *Media theory for a level: The essential revision guide.* Routledge.

Downs, E., & Smith, S. L. (2010). Keeping abreast of hypersexuality: A video game character content analysis. *Sex Roles, 62*(11–12), 721–733. https://doi.org/10.1007/s11199-009-9637-1

Duggan, M. (2015). Gaming and gamers. *Pew Research Center.* http://www.pewinternet.org/2015/12/15/gaming-and-gamers/

Hall, C. (2015, March 5). The games industry is wrong about kids, gaming and gender. *Polygon.* https://www.polygon.com/2015/3/5/8153213/the-games-industry-is-wrong-about-kids-gaming-and-gender

Hartmann, T., & Klimmt, C. (2006). Gender and computer games: Exploring females' dislikes. *Journal of Computer-Mediated Communication, 11*(4), 910–931. https://doi.org/10.1111/j.1083-6101.2006.00301.x

Jansz, J., & Martis, R. G. (2007). The Lara phenomenon: Powerful female characters in video games. *Sex Roles, 56*(3–4), 141–148. https://doi.org/10.1007/s11199-006-9158-0

Jenson, J., & de Castell, S. (2011). Girls@Play: An ethnographic study of gender and digital gameplay. *Feminist Media Studies, 11*(2), 167–179. https://doi.org/10.1080/14680777.2010.521625

Jenson, J., & De Castell, S. (2018). 'The entrepreneurial gamer': Regendering the order of play. *Games and Culture, 13*(7), 728–746. https://doi.org/10.1177/1555412018755913

Kruthika, N. S. (2020). Esports and its reinforcement of gender divides. *Marquette Sports Law Review, 2*(30), 349–369. https://heinonline.org/HOL/LandingPage?handle=hein.journals/mqslr30&div=18&id=&page=

Lynch, T., Tompkins, J. E., Van Driel, I. I., & Fritz, N. (2016). Sexy, strong, and secondary: A content analysis of female characters in video games across 31 years. *Journal of Communication, 66*(4), 564–584. https://doi.org/10.1111/jcom.12237

Massanari, A. (2017). #Gamergate and the Fappening: How Reddit's algorithm, governance, and culture support toxic technocultures. *New Media and Society, 19*(3), 329–346. https://doi.org/10.1177/1461444815608807

McArthur, V. (2021). Damsel in this dress: An analysis of the character designs of women in post-secondary game design programs. *Feminist Media Studies, 21*(3), 381–397. https://doi.org/10.1080/14680777.2020.1715463

Moultrop, S. (2004). Response to Aarseth. In P. Harrigan & N. Wiardrip-Fruin (Eds.), *First person: New media as story, performance, and game* (pp. 47–48). MIT Press.

Newell, S. (2021, December 27). Every sports game finally featuring women's teams. *Screenrant.* https://screenrant.com/sports-video-game-women-players-team/

Olsson, C. (2013). Sports videogames and real-world exercise: Using sports videogames to promote real-world physical activity among adolescents. In N. Panteli (Ed.), *Virtual social networks: Mediated, massive and multiplayer* (pp. 98–113). Palgrave Publishing.

Paaßen, B., Morgenroth, T., & Stratemeyer, M. (2017). What is a true gamer? The male gamer stereotype and the marginalization of women in video game culture. *Sex Roles, 76*(7–8), 421–435. https://doi.org/10.1007/s11199-016-0678-y

Reinecke, L., Trepte, S., & Behr, K.-M. (2007). Why girls play: Results of a qualitative interview study with female video game players. Hamburger Forschungsberichte zur Sozialpsychologie (Hamburger Research Reports on Social Psychology No. 77). University of Hamburg.

Reinhard, C. D. (2009). Hypersexualism in video games as determinant or deterrent of game play: Do men want them and do women want to be them? *Roskilde Universitet.* https://forskning.ruc.dk/en/publications/hypersexualism-in-video-games-as-determinant-or-deterrent-of-game

Rogstad, E. T. (2021). Gender in esports research: A literature review. *European Journal for Sport and Society*, 1–19. https://doi.org/10.1080/16138171.2021.1930941

Shaw, A. (2015). *Gaming at the edge: Sexuality and gender at the margins of gamer culture.* University of Minnesota Press.

Shen, C., Ratan, R., Cai, Y. D., & Leavitt, A. (2016). Do men advance faster than women? Debunking the gender performance gap in two massively multiplayer online games. *Journal of Computer-Mediated Communication, 21*(4), 312–329. https://doi.org/10.1111/jcc4.12159

Taylor, T. L. (2006). *Play between worlds: Exploring online game culture*. MIT Press.

Taylor, T. L. (2012). *Raising the stakes: E-sports and the professionalization of computer gaming*. MIT Press.

Tjønndal, A. (2021). The impact of COVID-19 lockdowns on Norwegian athletes' training habits and their use of digital technology for training and competition purposes. *Sport in Society*, 1–15. https://doi.org/10.1080/17430437.2021.2016701

Tjønndal, A., & Fylling, I. (2021). *Digitale forskningsmetoder* [Digital Research Methods]. Cappelen Damm Akademisk.

Vermeulen, L., Van Looy, J., De Grove, F., & Courtois, C. (2011). You are what you play?: A quantitative study into game design preferences across gender and their interaction with gaming habits. In Proceedings of the 2011 DiGRA International Conference: Think Design Play. Digital Games Research Association (DiGRA). http://www.digra.org/digital-library/publications/you-are-what-you-play-a-quantitative-study-into-game-design-preferences-across-gender-and-their-interaction-with-gaming-habits/

Williams, D., Consalvo, M., Caplan, S., & Yee, N. (2009). Looking for gender: Gender roles and behaviors among online gamers. *Journal of Communication, 59*(4), 700–725. https://doi.org/10.1111/j.1460-2466.2009.01453.x

Yee, N. (2017, January 19). Beyond 50/50: Breaking down the percentage of female gamers by genre. *Quantic Foundry*. https://quanticfoundry.com/2017/01/19/female-gamers-by-genre/

Part III

Mental health and integrity issues

Chapter 6

Stress and coping in esports

Dylan Poulus and Remco Polman

In the last decade, esports competitions have become increasingly popular and lucrative. In 2021, esports audience numbers were estimated at 474 million and are predicted to reach half a billion in 2022 (Newzoo, 2021). The *Defense of the Ancients 2* (*DOTA 2*) International 10 prize pool totalled $40 million USD, with the competition winner, Team Spirit, taking $18 million USD in winnings (Valve Corporation, 2021). As esports competitions continue to grow, e-athletes will be required to perform under increasing amounts of pressure and stress. Researchers have realised the increasing psychological pressures placed on e-athletes and have begun to examine the factors associated with high performance in esports (Leis et al., 2021; Polman et al., 2018). One area of particular interest is how competitive and elite e-athletes experience and cope with stress.

The influence of stress and how athletes cope with it has received extensive academic interest in traditional sport (Polman, 2012). Research shows that an athlete's ability to cope with stress impacts their performance and well-being (Crocker et al., 2015; Nicholls & Polman, 2007). Over the last 20 years, stress and coping research in sport has been primarily guided by Lazarus's (1999) cognitive-motivational-relational theory (CMRT) of emotion (see Crocker et al., 2015, for a review). This theoretical model holds that stress and coping involve a dynamic and recursive relationship between the athlete and their environment (see Figure 6.1). Initially, an athlete will engage in two types of appraisal – primary and secondary – in response to a source of stress (stressor). Primary appraisal refers to the athlete evaluating the demands of a specific situation in relation to their personal goals, beliefs, or values and what is potentially at stake in relation to them (Lazarus, 1999). Through this process, athletes will assess how intense they perceive the stressor to be and how much control they feel they have to change the situation. Subsequently, the athlete will determine the stressor as a challenge (the evaluation of future benefit if the stressor is overcome) or a threat (the evaluation of future loss or harm if the stressor is not overcome). Athletes also engage in secondary appraisals of the stressor. In these appraisals, athletes engage in a complex evaluative process involving consideration of the internal resources they perceive they have in order to overcome the stressor and a focus on maximising favourable outcomes and minimising harm. Secondary appraisals

DOI: 10.4324/9781003258650-9

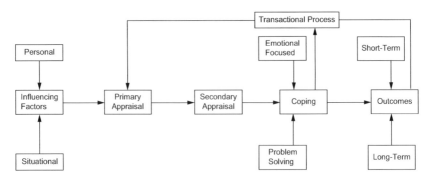

Figure 6.1 The cognitive-motivational-relational theory (CMRT) of emotion. (Lazarus, 1999.)

involve evaluating the resources that are available to the athletes, for example, the degree of control and the available coping strategies they perceive they have (Lazarus & Folkman, 1984; Polman, 2012). Athletes report feeling stressed when they perceive that the requirements of a situation (primary appraisal) tax or outweigh their perceptions of their internal resources (secondary appraisal) to cope with or succeed in that situation. When athletes experience stress, they employ a coping strategy or strategies. It is important to note that primary and secondary appraisals can be conducted in any order and constantly occur and reoccur throughout an athlete's experience of an event. These appraisals influence an athlete's coping strategy selection (thoughts and behaviour) in an attempt to change the stressor and/or regulate an emotional response (Crocker et al., 2015).

Coping can be defined as 'constantly changing cognitive and behavioural efforts to manage specific external and/or internal demands that are appraised as taxing or exceeding the resources of the person' (Lazarus & Folkman, 1984, p. 141). Initially, coping strategies aim to regulate athletes' emotions. Normally, coping is used to down-regulate negative emotions caused as a result of initially experiencing stress, as these can potentially interfere with more active ways of coping (Folkman & Moskowitz, 2004). Importantly, coping only reflects the implementation of a strategy or strategies aimed at reducing stress, not the effectiveness of that strategy. In addition, the act of coping does not ensure a positive outcome or a decrease in distress.

Coping strategies are often grouped at the macro level (see Crocker et al., 2015). Lazarus and Folkman (1984) initially grouped coping strategies into two higher-order categories: problem-focused coping (PFC) and emotion-focused coping (EFC). PFC strategies aim to change the stressor or stressful situation, whereas EFC strategies are efforts to regulate emotional distress or negative emotions that arise from experiencing the stressor (Nicholls & Polman, 2007). Roth and Cohen (1986) grouped coping strategies into approach coping and avoidance coping (AC). Approach coping strategies are direct actions aimed at confronting and eliminating the source of stress, while AC strategies involve cognitive and behavioural efforts to disengage from the stressor. Through the debate about coping classifications, other higher-order categorisations have been proposed by academics. For example, Gaudreau and Blondin (2004) suggested that PFC, EFC, AC, and approach coping as higher-order classifications did not adequately reflect the nature of coping and instead proposed task-oriented, disengagement-oriented, and distraction-oriented coping as more accurate alternatives. With task-oriented coping strategies, an athlete attempts to master a stressful situation; disengagement-oriented coping strategies involve the athlete no longer striving for their personal goals, while distraction-oriented coping involves the athlete focusing on cues that are not relevant to their sport (Gaudreau & Blondin, 2004). In their recent meta-analysis of performance and coping in sport, Nicholls et al. (2016) offered three new coping classifications: mastery, internal regulation, and goal withdrawal. Mastery coping strategies aim to control the situation and eliminate the stressor (similar to PFC and task-oriented coping). The athlete employs internal regulation coping strategies to manage their internal response to the stressor (similar to EFC), and goal withdrawal coping strategies are when an athlete no longer attempts to attain their goal (similar to AC).

Coping effectiveness refers to athletes' perceptions of how well a coping strategy or series of strategies alleviate stress (Nicholls, 2010). In the following we provide two examples of how events might be perceived as stressful and where coping strategies have been employed by an e-athlete.

> An e-athlete playing *Rainbow Six: Siege* (R6) is hours away from game one of a major invitational competition. The e-athlete is worried about how they will perform in game 1. This competition is the largest on the R6 calendar, and the game is important. Through primary appraisal, the e-athlete might appraise this stressor as intense (the game is only hours away and important) and controllable (the e-athlete has the ability to influence their own performance). This stressor is likely to be perceived as a challenge, because if the e-athlete can overcome their stress and play well then they might win game 1 (future benefit). Through secondary appraisal, the e-athlete will assess their abilities, including the coping strategies they could employ (i.e. what they could do to calm down or better prepare for game one). Finally, as the stressor is perceived as controllable, the e-athlete might implement a PFC strategy and choose to study their team's playbook. By studying the playbook, the e-athlete feels more confident that they will remember which angles they are meant to hold and where they need to place their equipment on each site.
>
> After completing game one, our e-athlete's team lost and one of their teammates had an intense verbal altercation, blaming them for the loss. The e-athlete is embarrassed and upset with the anti-social (toxic) way their teammate spoke to them. Through primary appraisal, the e-athlete might appraise this stressor as intense (they are upset and embarrassed) and with low levels of control (they have a limited capacity to control their teammate's actions).

This interpersonal conflict between teammates is likely to be perceived as a threat (if this interpersonal disagreement cannot be overcome, it could cause future harm). Through secondary appraisal, the e-athlete will assess their abilities, including the coping strategies they could employ (i.e. what they could do to regulate their negative emotions). Finally, as the e-athlete perceives they have limited control of the stressor, they might employ an EFC strategy and accept the reality of the situation. By accepting that there is currently little they can do to alter the stressor, they can down-regulate negative emotions and focus on the rest of the tournament.

A limitation of the CMRT of emotion is that it is difficult to test the model as a whole. As such, most traditional sport stress and coping research explores specific sections of the CMRT. Predominantly guided by the CMRT, esports researchers have begun to investigate the experiences of stress and coping in competitive and elite e-athletes (Leis & Lautenbach, 2020). This chapter sets out to outline the sources of stress, stress appraisals, coping, and coping effectiveness experienced by e-athletes.

Sources of stress experienced by e-athletes

In traditional sport, it was thought that athletes could encounter an infinite number of stressors (Anshel, 2001; Noblet & Gifford, 2002). However, longitudinal diary studies (Nicholls et al., 2005, 2006) have shown that the number of stressors experienced by athletes is very limited. The main stressors, which amount to 80% of those experienced, relate to performance, outcome, and mental error. In esports, several studies have examined the stressors experienced by e-athletes (see Table 6.1).

Himmelstein et al. (2017) did not specifically aim to investigate stress and coping in e-athletes, but in interviews exploring the mental skills of competitive LoL e-athletes they uncovered a series of obstacles encountered (stressors) by competitive e-athletes. The stressors identified in this particular study related to (a) performance (i.e. ineffective attentional control, making a mistake in-game, going on tilt), (b) an inability to regulate emotions, dwelling on past performances, and choking under pressure, (c) the e-athletes' team (lack of team resilience and ineffective communication), (d) the need for a balance between life and gaming (difficulty separating life and gaming, lack of commitment to gaming), and (e) a limited understanding of the game (LoL champions and current meta) and where to best gain new game-specific knowledge about stressors.

Through interviews, Smith et al. (2019) explored the stress and coping processes in seven professional *CounterStrike: Global Offensive* (CS:GO) e-athletes. Four higher-order themes were identified. The team issues encompassed outcomes of losing, intra-team criticisms, communication issues, communication/criticisms from IGL, lack of confidence in teammates, and a lack of shared team goals. Individual issues included life balance and lifestyle impacts, scrutiny, and criticism from the opposition and social media. Lastly, event issues were related to event audience, media interviews, and logistics.

In our own work (Poulus et al., 2021a), we collected stressor data via a self-report measure from 270 e-athletes ranked in the top 40% of one of the following five major esports: *R6*, *Overwatch*, *CS:GO*, *LoL*, and *DOTA 2*. The data was initially analysed deductively into stressor categories previously reported in sport (Nicholls & Polman, 2007; Nicholls et al., 2007). The data that did not fit traditional sport stressor categories was analysed inductively. E-athletes reported 11 sources of stress identified in traditional sport and four novel esports-specific stressors (technical issues, balancing life commitments, anti-social behaviour, and critical moment performance). Five first-order themes were identified in the data: performance, teammate, external individual, balancing life commitments, and technical issues. Teammate stressors were the most frequently reported (53.8%) and consisted of anti-social behaviour (21.6%), teammate general (15%), teammate communication (13.3%), and teammate mistake (4%). Performance-related stressors were reported by 26.9% of e-athletes and included general performance (13%), outcome (7%), critical moment performance (6.3%), and injury (0.7%). The first-order stressors teammate and performance accounted for 80.7% of the stressors reported, with external individuals, balancing life commitments, and technical issues accounting for the remaining 19.3%. Interestingly, achievement levels in esports influenced the stressors reported by e-athletes. E-athletes in the 99th–100th percentile reported more performance-related stressors, whereas e-athletes below the 99th percentile (98th–60th) were more likely to report teammate stressors. This may have been due to elite e-athletes playing in more organised teams and lower-level e-athletes relying more on in-game matchmaking to select their teammates.

Building on our initial exploration of the stressors experienced by e-athletes, with the use of diaries we (Poulus et al., 2021b) longitudinally examined the stress and coping process of elite LoL e-athletes. Over an 87-day competitive period, six elite e-athletes completed 397 diary entries. Using the same stressor categories as those reported in Poulus et al. (2021a), the elite LoL e-athletes reported performance (44%), teammate (35%), external individual (9%), balancing life commitments (7%), and technical issues (3%) as higher-order stressors. These results support previous findings in esports (Poulus et al., 2021a) and traditional sport (Nicholls et al., 2005, 2006) and suggest that elite e-athletes and athletes are more likely to report more performance-related stressors. Similarly, performance and teammate stressors accounted for ~80% of the higher-order stressors reported by our elite LoL e-athletes.

Leis et al. (2021) interviewed 12 professional LoL e-athletes to explore their stressors, stress responses, and coping strategies in relation to their best and worst competitions. The interview guide was primarily based on the CMRT (Lazarus, 1999). The stressors were categorised into five main groups: performance expectations, internal evaluation, team issues, audience and social media, and environmental constraints. Performance expectation stressors were experienced by

Table 6.1 Stressors experienced by e-athletes

Himmelstein et al. (2017)		Smith et al. (2019)		Poulus et al. (2021a)
Lower-order	Higher-order	Lower-order	Higher-order	Second-order
Ineffective attentional control	Barriers to optimal performance	Communication issues	Team issues	Teammate communication (13.3%)
Making a mistake in-game		Communication/ criticisms from IGL		Teammate mistake (4%)
Going on tilt and being harassed		Lack of confidence in teammates		Teammate general (15%)
Inability to regulate emotions		Outcomes of losing		Anti-social behaviour (21.6%)
Dwelling on past performances		Intra-team criticism		
Choking under pressure		Lack of shared goals		General performance (13%)
Confidence issues				Outcome (7%)
An inability to repeat flow experiences		Life balance	Individual issues	Critical moment performance (6.3%)
Inadequate physical and mental preparation		Lifestyle impacts		Injury (0.7%)
Lack of team resilience	Team obstacle	Opposition	Scrutiny and criticisms	Criticism (1.5%)
Ineffective communication		Social media		Crowd (1.1%)
				Coach (0.3%)
Difficulty separating life and gaming	Need for balance between life and gaming	Event audience	Event issues	Official (2.2%)
A lack of commitment to gaming		Media interviews		Opponent (4.4%)
		Logistics		
Limited understanding of the game	Limited understanding of the game			Balancing life commitments
				Technical issues

	Poulus et al. (2021b)		Leis et al. (2021)	
First-order	Lower-order	Higher-order	Competition-related stressor sub-categories	Competition-related stressor categories
Teammate (53.8%)	Teammate communication (6%)	Teammate (35%)	High self-expectations	Performance expectations
	Teammate mistake (10%)		Wanting to play without mistakes	
	Teammate general (7%)		Winning the finals	
	Anti-social behaviour (9%)		Winning for a teammate	
Performance (27.9%)	General performance (21%)	Performance (44%)	Players' perception of their performance	Internal evaluations
	Outcome (11%)		Opponents' abilities	
	Critical moment performance (5%)		Outcomes of competitions	
	Injury (3%)			
			Lack of confidence in teammates	Team issues
External individual (9.6%)	Criticism (3%)	External individual (9%)	Intra-team criticism	
	Crowd (1%)		Teammate evaluations of own performances	
	Coach (2%)			
	Official (0%)		Interviews	Audience and social media
	Opponent (3%)		Live audience	
			Social media	
Balancing life commitments (7.4%)	Balancing life commitments	Balancing life commitments (7%)		
Technical issues (3.7%)	Technical issues	Technical issues (3%)	Perceived organisational stressors	Environmental constraints
			Competitive setting	

all the interviewed e-athletes and included high self-expectations, wanting to play without mistakes, winning the finals, and winning for a teammate. Internal evaluation stressors consisted of e-athletes' perceptions of their performances, opponents' abilities, and competition outcomes. The elite LoL e-athletes reported a series of stressors related to team issues, which encompassed a lack of confidence in teammates, intra-team criticisms, and teammate evaluations of own performances. Audience and social media stressors were described as having various impacts on elite LoL e-athletes. For some, post-game media interviews and the presence of a live crowd affected their ability to relax and increased pressure. Interestingly, two e-athletes reported audience-related stress as something positive. Four e-athletes mentioned that they felt pressure from social media. Stressors related to environmental constraints included perceived pressure from the organisation and competitive setting.

Poulus et al. (2021) did not explicitly explore sources of stress in esports. In a more exploratory approach, they qualitatively investigated the perceived determinants of success in seven elite e-athletes. By exploring the e-athletes' experiences of playing well, a series of stressors and stressful situations were identified. The elite e-athletes primarily reported team communication breakdowns as their main source of stress. Team communication was also reported as one of the first things to break down when things started to go wrong and it was a 'huge limiter' to success.

Overall, the e-athletes appeared to experience a small number of recurring stressors. The competitive and elite e-athletes frequently reported teammate (i.e. communication issues and teammate evaluations of their play) and performance-related (i.e. game outcome and making mistakes) stressors, with some players reporting anti-social behaviour and balancing other life commitments as stressors. The elite e-athletes appeared to report more stressors related to performance, whereas competitive e-athletes reported more stressors related to their teammates. Such differences at the expertise level could have consequences for the coaching and psychological support of e-athletes. Following the experience of a stressful event, coping strategy selection and coping effectiveness could be influenced by how an individual appraised the stressor.

Stress appraisals

Stress appraisals for competitive and elite e-athletes have received limited academic attention. Behnke et al. (2020) experimentally investigated social challenge and threat responses in competitive CS:GO e-athletes. Social challenge and threat states were manipulated by informing participants that their performances were better (challenge) or worse (threat) than their opponents in previous performances. E-athletes who were more experienced appraised themselves as having higher internal resources relative to the demands of the contest and performed better than e-athletes who perceived that they had lower internal resources. Furthermore, e-athletes who appraised the contest as a challenge mobilised greater physiological resources (as measured by heart rate). These results suggest that confidence in one's own gaming ability may lead to more successful performances and buffer against threatening information during competitions. Threat and challenge appraisals have also been shown to impact performance in *FIFA 19* players. E-athletes who reported more positive challenge/threat evaluations achieved higher numbers of shots on target, lower foul numbers, higher goal difference, and higher accuracy of passes (Behnke et al., 2020).

In our own work (Poulus et al., 2021b), we found that for elite LoL e-athletes stressors relating to competitive matches were perceived as more intense than training stressors. In addition, stressors related to teammates and balancing life commitments were reported as being more intense than performance-related stressors. These findings were explained as e-athletes potentially having a lack of control over their teammates and other life commitments. This research also found that performance-related stressors in competition and training settings were more likely to be perceived as a challenge, whereas teammate-related stressors were more likely to be perceived as a threat. Perceiving a stressor as a threat has been linked to maladaptive avoidance coping (Smith et al., 2019) and could indicate that e-athletes need more support to cope with teammate-related stressors.

Whilst there is clearly a lack of stress appraisal research in esports, the current research suggests that self-confidence can influence appraisal and an e-athlete's allocation of physiological resources to a contest, and also that context (i.e. competition and training) and stressor type (i.e. performance and teammate) can influence stress intensity, challenge, and threat appraisals. These are important issues and provide a potential for interventions by sport psychologists that enhance the performances and well-being of e-athletes. By appraising an event as stressful and as a challenge or threat, an e-athlete is likely to employ a number of coping strategies.

Coping response and coping effectiveness

Coping and coping strategy selection has received extensive academic investigation in traditional sport (Nicholls et al., 2016). Mastery coping (PFC and task-oriented coping) is frequently reported by athletes and is generally accepted as being more adaptive than EFC and AC strategies (Nicholls et al., 2016; Polman, 2012). For example, athletes have frequently reported using strategies to increase concentration (PFC: Nicholls & Polman, 2007; Nicholls et al., 2005) or to overcome and avoid making psychical and mental errors. Internal regulation and EFC strategies are employed to cope with stressors that cause negative emotions (Ntoumanis & Biddle, 2000). Athletes have frequently reported utilising acceptance, visualisations, and taking advice to help to cope with negative emotions as a result of experiencing stress (Nicholls et al., 2006, 2007). Finally, athletes have used AC strategies like blocking (Nicholls et al., 2005, 2009) to stop thinking about the event. It should be noted that AC strategies can be effective in the short term, but avoiding coping with stressors over a longer term can be maladaptive (Carver et al., 1989). Hence, if the cause of the stress is a fundamental technical or tactical deficiency, then stress will recur over time. As such, a problem-focused coping strategy will have to be invoked to resolve the issue to avoid any future repetition of stress associated with the technical or tactical deficiency.

Smith et al. (2019) reported that elite CS:GO e-athletes employed an EFC, PFC, AC approach, and appraisal coping strategies. In their study, a series of EFC strategies were employed to cope with the immediate stress of a situation, such as having breaks from the game between rounds and adjusting their focus to regulate emotions better in competition situations. PFC strategies were reportedly used to manage short-term or immediate stressors. For example, positive talk from teammates and in-game leaders when a team was losing and for building up teammates' confidence after losing a game was reported by the elite CS:GO e-athletes. The e-athletes avoided doing interviews, engaging in debates on social media, shaking hands with certain opponents, and eventually leaving teams for which they didn't enjoy playing. AC strategies appear to have been employed in e-athletes play styles. When e-athletes were struggling in a match they reported playing more passively to avoid making mistakes. Elite CS:GO e-athletes used AC strategies in-game to avoid discussing difficult topics, as this could lead to arguments and detract from performance. Approach coping was reported by elite CS:GO e-athletes and referred to longer-term planned activities focused on confronting the source of stress and reducing it (Roth & Cohen, 1986). These strategies included training boot camps with a focus on living and training together. Lastly, appraisal-focused coping involved cognitive re-evaluations of a situation in an attempt to reduce its importance. One e-athlete reported reframing in-game statistics in CS:GO by viewing the game as a team sport, and stated that 'looking at stats doesn't really reflect on the context and how the game went. You can have someone who was, who was helping the team out in other ways' (p. 33). Overall, Smith and colleagues' (2019) findings showed that elite e-athletes could overuse AC strategies and lack effectively employed PFC and EFC strategies during gameplay. A lack of effective coping in traditional sport has been linked to reductions in athlete performance and overall well-being (McDonough et al., 2013), which could be a potential issue in esports.

Our own research (Poulus et al., 2020) investigated the influence of mental toughness on the stress and coping process in competitive and elite e-athletes (Top 40%). Overall, PFC strategies (planning, active coping, and positive reframing) were the most frequently employed coping strategies used by the e-athletes, followed by EFC (acceptance, humour, and self-blame) and AC (self-distraction). However, in situations in which the e-athletes appraised the stressor as more intense, they tended to use more EFC and AC coping strategies. Perceptions of control over the stressor, on the other hand, resulted in the e-athletes using more PFC strategies. Finally, appraising the stressor as a threat resulted in using more PFC and EFC strategies.

In our subsequent diary study with elite *LoL* e-athletes (Poulus et al., 2021b), PFC strategies were also the most frequently reported strategies for dealing with stress during both competition and training, followed by EFC and AC. The latter was mainly used when a teammate was the stressor in a training session or competition. Similar to the findings by Smith et al. (2019) with elite CS:GO e-athletes, elite *LoL* e-athletes appear to use AC too frequently, with the potential that coping is maladaptive. Not coping with teammate-related stressors during training or competitions can be maladaptive, as it is unlikely that the teammate stressor will improve without intervention and could lead to interpersonal and communication breakdowns.

In line with these results, Leis et al. (2021) reported that during competitions the main coping strategy used by elite *LoL* e-athletes was to focus on their performance (attention regulation, PFC). Five other coping themes were reported by Leis et al. (2021): self-regulation, social network, increasing effort, consumption strategies, and dissociation. Self-regulation strategies such as sleep, meditation, visualisation, cold showers, self-talk, and partying were used to regulate the pressures experienced in the competitive environment. Social network refers to the importance of the team environment when coping with stress. Being able to communicate with and trust coaches, teammates, partners, friends, and family was important for e-athletes' coping abilities. Elite *LoL* e-athletes reported strategies related to increasing efforts, such as watching other elite players, analysing games, and evaluating previous losses. Finally, consumption strategies (i.e. drinking coffee and energy drinks) and dissociation strategies (i.e. playing passively to avoid mistakes, avoiding thinking about mistakes and stopping intra-team communication) were used to minimise pressure and avoid stress.

The current esports stress and coping literature suggests that the coping strategies used by e-athletes and traditional sport athletes are similar. Generally speaking, competitive and elite e-athletes predominantly employ more PFC strategies (i.e. positive task, positive reframing, and attention regulation) and less EFC (i.e. acceptance and social support/network) and AC (i.e. self-distraction and passive playstyle). As previously indicated, the presence of coping strategies does not ensure the alleviation of stress, and it is therefore important to measure the effectiveness of coping.

Coping effectiveness has received limited attention in both traditional sport and esports. Overall, mastery coping (PFC and task-oriented coping) is reported by athletes to be most effective in alleviating stress and increasing performance. Internal regulation and EFC strategies appear to be less effective than PFC and are not associated with increased sporting performance, while AC appears to be negatively associated with performance (Nicholls et al., 2016). Poulus et al. (2021b) measured how effective elite *LoL* e-athletes perceived their coping strategy implementation to be. Their findings suggest that PFC and EFC were rated as more effective than AC in training and competition. This finding is unique to e-athletes and indicates that effective EFC strategy use could be important for success in esports. In further support of the potential importance of EFC in esports, for stressors related to performance and teammates, PFC and EFC were again rated as more effective than AC. AC being rated as least effective supports previous research in sport (Nicholls et al., 2016) and esports (Smith et al., 2019), thus suggesting that longer-term AC could be maladaptive.

Moderators and mediators to the stress and coping process: mental toughness

Traditional sport research has investigated various personality factors that moderate and mediate stress and coping processes (Polman et al., 2010). Specifically, mental toughness (MT) has been found to both directly and indirectly influence the stress and coping process (Levy et al., 2012). Figure 6.2 provides a conceptual framework of how personality factors and situations could influence stress and coping (adapted from: DeLongis & Holtzman, 2005).

Although there is an ongoing debate about the definition and classification of MT, it can be broadly defined as a collection of attitudes, emotions, cognitions, and behaviours that influence our ability to overcome challenges in the pursuit of our goals (Coulter et al., 2010). Athletes with higher MT report lower levels of perceived stress and higher levels of emotional control (Kaiseler et al., 2009). Furthermore, higher MT athletes are more likely to perceive stressors as challenges rather than threats (Levy et al., 2012). Higher levels of MT are also associated with the use of more adaptive PFC and task-oriented coping, and less with disengagement and AC strategies (Kaiseler et al., 2009; Nicholls et al., 2008).

As indicated previously, our own research (Poulus et al., 2020) investigated whether mental toughness influenced the stress and coping process in competitive and elite e-athletes. Higher levels of MT (specifically, emotional and life control) were associated with lower levels of stress intensity and increased stressor control. PFC overall and the PFC strategies, active coping, positive reframing,

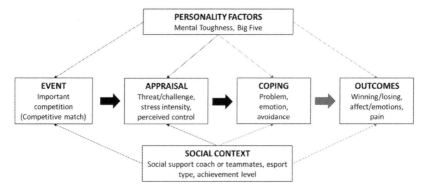

Figure 6.2 Diagram and conceptual framework of how situational aspects and personality could influence coping behaviour. (Adapted from DeLongis & Holtzman, 2005, p. 3.)

planning, and instrumental support were positively associated with MT. The use of AC strategies was negatively correlated with MT. Interestingly, higher levels of MT were also associated with increased in-game rank, thus suggesting that similar to traditional sport, MT could be associated with higher levels of esports performance (Cowden, 2016).

Practical implications

Experiencing stress appears to be an inherent part of competitive and elite esports performance. Current esports research is beginning to describe the stressors that are experienced, the coping strategies, and their effectiveness. Based on the limited esports literature and work previously conducted in traditional sport, we describe some of the practical implications for e-athletes, coaches, and other esports support staff (Watson et al., 2021; Leis et al., under review). E-athletes appear to experience teammate and performance stressors most frequently, in particular, teammate stressors related to communication issues, anti-social behaviour, and teammate evaluations of own play, and performance stressors related to the outcome of competitive matches, making mistakes, and meeting high self-expectations. Considering that e-athletes have reported experiencing a small number of recurring stressors, helping e-athletes to develop more effective coping strategies could be beneficial for performance and well-being. Specifically, developing PFC and EFC coping strategies that help elite e-athletes to better deal with performance stressors and competitive e-athletes to deal with teammate stressors could improve performance and well-being. An intervention developed for traditional athletes that could benefit e-athletes is coping effectiveness training (CET; Reeves et al., 2011). CET focuses on developing athletes' appraisals of stressors and use of PFC and EFC strategies and builds a general understanding of athletes' stress and coping processes. As current esports research suggests that PFC and EFC are important to esports performance, an esports-adapted CET that improves e-athletes' awareness of their coping and supports the development of PFC and EFC could be particularly beneficial to e-athletes.

For competitive (semi/sub-elite) e-athletes and practitioners supporting competitive e-athletes, psychological interventions that help e-athletes to cope more effectively with anti-social behaviour could also improve player performance and well-being. Competitive e-athletes have limited control over anti-social teammates and opponents' behaviour and therefore have a limited number of coping strategies to employ. A mindfulness-acceptance-commitment training (MAC) that is adapted to esports could help e-athletes to develop connections between their thoughts, feelings, and actions and better cope with their internal experiences (Gardner & Moore, 2004) – for example, an online programme that helps competitive e-athletes to become more aware of their internal experiences (mindfulness) and defuse negative thoughts and emotions (acceptance), instead of attempting to control and change the situation.

Higher-level e-athletes report using more PFC strategies. Coaches and esports support staff should therefore encourage e-athletes to actively cope with their stressors or the negative emotions caused by the stressful situation. One way of doing this could be by developing mental toughness in e-athletes (Nicholls et al., 2008). Traditional sport coaches have helped athletes to develop mental toughness by structuring training sessions/practices and entering appropriately demanding competitions (Crust & Clough, 2011). For example, esports coaches (and e-athletes) could create training situations in which e-athletes are challenged, pushed out of their comfort zones, and encouraged to creatively solve problems under pressure.

Future research directions: stress and coping in esports from a social issue perspective

From a social issue perspective, there are limitations to the current stress and coping research in esports. For example, no research has yet been conducted on potential gender or age differences in e-athletes' stress and coping mechanisms. This will become more important as women's participation in esports increases and more secondary school esports programmes are created. Research has already indicated that there are gender differences in the way that stressors are appraised (e.g. women appraise stress with higher intensity) and coping strategies are used (see, for example, Kaiseler et al., 2013), but there is a need for more empirical studies on these subjects. Similarly, adolescents do not have the coping repertoire of adults. Considering the younger age of some of the players, it will be important to establish these developmental differences, because this will have important implications for coaching and psychological interventions.

Future research could also explore how other factors (i.e. fitness level and social support) impact the stress and coping processes in esports (Behnke et al., 2021). Trotter et al. (2021) investigated social support, self-regulation, and psychological skill use in e-athletes. Their findings showed an increased perceived social support, self-regulation, and psychological skill use in e-athletes ranked in the top 10% of their chosen esports (as determined by in-game rank). Future investigations could explore the potential influence of social support and self-regulatory skills on stress and coping in esports. Research on fitness levels and physical activity levels in esports is also limited (Trotter et al., 2020). Future research could explore how exercise and physiological predictors (i.e. heart rate variability or cortisol levels) buffer against stress (i.e. lowering stress intensity appraisal) or increase coping effectiveness (i.e. more effective down-regulation of negative emotions).

This chapter has outlined the current stress and coping research in esports. Despite being a new area of research, the current literature has begun to explore the sources of stress, stress appraisals, coping, and coping effectiveness in elite and competitive e-athletes. A series of practical applications have been suggested for e-athletes, coaches, and support staff that could potentially improve player performance and well-being. Finally, future research directions related directly to e-athletes' stress and coping processes and how other factors might influence them have been outlined.

References

Anshel, M. H. (2001). Qualitative validation of a model for coping with acute stress in sport. *Journal of Sport Behavior; Mobile, 24*(3), 223–246.

Behnke, M., Gross, J. J., & Kaczmarek, L. D. (2020). The role of emotions in esports performance. *Emotion.* https://doi.org/10.1037/emo0000903

Behnke, M., Hase, A., Kaczmarek, L. D., & Freeman, P. (2021). Blunted cardiovascular reactivity may serve as an index of psychological task disengagement in the motivated performance situations. *Scientific Reports, 11*(1), 1–10.

Behnke, M., Kosakowski, M., & Kaczmarek, L. D. (2020). Social challenge and threat predict performance and cardiovascular responses during competitive video gaming. *Psychology of Sport and Exercise, 46*, 101584. https://doi.org/10.1016/j.psychsport.2019.101584

Carver, C. S., Scheier, M. F., & Weintraub, J. K. (1989). Assessing coping strategies: A theoretically based approach. *Journal of Personality and Social Psychology, 56*(2), 267–283. https://doi.org/10.1037/0022-3514.56.2.267

Coulter, T. J., Mallett, C. J., & Gucciardi, D. F. (2010). Understanding mental toughness in Australian soccer: Perceptions of players, parents, and coaches. *Journal of Sports Sciences, 28*(7), 699–716. https://doi.org/10.1080/02640411003734085

Cowden, R. G. (2016). Mental toughness, emotional intelligence, and coping effectiveness: An analysis of construct interrelatedness among high-performing adolescent male athletes. *Perceptual and Motor Skills, 123*(3), 737–753. https://doi.org/10.1177/0031512516666027

Crocker, P., Tamminen, K., & Gaudreau, P. (2015). Coping in sport. In S. Mellalieu & S. Hanton (Eds.), *Contemporary advances in sport psychology: A review* (pp. 28–67). Routledge.

Crust, L., & Clough, P. J. (2011). Developing mental toughness: From research to practice. *Journal of Sport Psychology in Action, 2*(1), 21–32. https://doi.org/10.1080/21520704.2011.563436

DeLongis, A., & Holtzman, S. (2005). Coping in context: The role of stress, social support, and personality in coping. *Journal of Personality, 73*(6), 1633–1656.

Folkman, S., & Moskowitz, J. T. (2004). Coping: Pitfalls and promise. *Annual Review of Psychology, 55*(1), 745–774. https://doi.org/10.1146/annurev.psych.55.090902.141456

Gardner, F. L., & Moore, Z. E. (2004). A mindfulness-acceptance-commitment-based approach to athletic performance enhancement: Theoretical considerations. *Behavior Therapy, 35*(4), 707–723. https://doi.org/10.1016/S0005-7894(04)80016-9

Gaudreau, P., & Blondin, J.-P. (2004). Different athletes cope differently during a sport competition: A cluster analysis of coping. *Personality and Individual Differences, 36*(8), 1865–1877. https://doi.org/10.1016/j.paid.2003.08.017

Himmelstein, D., Liu, Y., & Shapiro, J. (2017). An exploration of mental skills among competitive league of legend players. *International Journal of Gaming and Computer-Mediated Simulations (IJGCMS), 9*(2), 1–21. https://doi.org/10.4018/IJGCMS.2017040101

Kaiseler, M., Polman, R., & Nicholls, A. (2009). Mental toughness, stress, stress appraisal, coping and coping effectiveness in sport. *Personality and Individual Differences, 47*(7), 728–733. https://doi.org/10.1016/j.paid.2009.06.012

Kaiseler, M., Polman, R. C. J., & Nicholls, A. R. (2013). Gender differences in stress, appraisal, and coping during golf putting. *International Journal of Sport and Exercise Psychology, 11*(3), 258–272. https://doi.org/10.1080/1612197X.2013.749004

Lazarus, R. S. (1999). *Stress and emotion, a new synthesis*. Springer Publishing Company.

Lazarus, R. S., & Folkman, S. (1984). *Stress, appraisal, and coping*. Springer Publishing Company.

Leis, O., Franziska, L., Birch, P. D., & Elbe, A.-M. (2021). Stressors, perceived stress responses, and coping strategies in professional esports players: A qualitative study. *International Journal of eSports Research*. https://www.ijesports.org/article/76/html

Leis, O., & Lautenbach, F. (2020). Psychological and physiological stress in non-competitive and competitive esports settings: A systematic review. *Psychology of Sport and Exercise*, 101738. https://doi.org/10.1016/j.psychsport.2020.101738

Leis, O., Raue, C., Dreiskämper, D., & Lautenbach, F. (2021). To be or not to be (e)sports? That is not the question! Why and how sport and exercise psychology could research esports. *German Journal of Exercise and Sport Research, 51*(2), 241–247.

Levy, A., Nicholls, A., & Polman, R. (2012). Cognitive appraisals in sport: The direct and moderating role of mental toughness. *International Journal of Applied Psychology, 2*(4), 71–76. https://doi.org/10.5923/j.ijap.20120204.05

McDonough, M., Hadd, V., Crocker, P., Holt, N., Tamminen, K., & Schonert-Reichl, K. (2013). Stress and coping among adolescents across a competitive swim season. *Sport Psychologist, 27*, 143–155. https://doi.org/10.1123/tsp.27.2.143

Newzoo. (2021). *Global Esports & live streaming market report 2021*. https://resources.newzoo.com/hubfs/Reports/2021_Free_Global_Esports_and_Streaming_Market_Report_EN.pdf?utm_campaign=GEMR%202021&utm_medium=email&_hsmi=114762550&_hsenc=p2ANqtz-83uoY4g0SvOsSDlSMQdWPFiBmvL_NCJkxpyx6_wGTG_sceCJQqxa3HhMoOXIwYUaj2CntT1toC-4Ctd__0fxCm2zOj6A&utm_content=114762550&utm_source=hs_automation

Nicholls, A. (2010). Effective versus ineffective coping in sport. In A. Nicholls (Ed) *Coping in Sport: Theory, Methods, and Related Constructs* (pp. 263–276). Nova Science Pub Inc.

Nicholls, A., & Polman, R. (2007). Performance related stressors, coping, and coping effectiveness among international adolescent rugby union football players: A 31-day diary study. *Journal of Sport Behavior, 30*(2), 199–218.

Nicholls, A. R., Holt, N. L., Polman, R. C. J., & Bloomfield, J. (2006). Stressors, coping, and coping effectiveness among professional rugby union players. *The Sport Psychologist, 20*(3), 314–329. https://doi.org/10.1123/tsp.20.3.314

Nicholls, A. R., Holt, N. L., Polman, R. C. J., & James, D. W. G. (2005). Stress and coping among international adolescent golfers. *Journal of Applied Sport Psychology, 17*(4), 333–340. https://doi.org/10.1080/10413200500313644

Nicholls, A. R., Levy, A. R., Grice, A., & Polman, R. C. J. (2009). Stress appraisals, coping, and coping effectiveness among international cross-country runners during training and competition. *European Journal of Sport Science, 9*(5), 285–293. https://doi.org/10.1080/17461390902836049

Nicholls, A. R., & Polman, R. C. J. (2007). Coping in sport: A systematic review. *Journal of Sports Sciences, 25*(1), 11–31. https://doi.org/10.1080/02640410600630654

Nicholls, A. R., Polman, R., Levy, A. R., Taylor, J., & Cobley, S. (2007). Stressors, coping, and coping effectiveness: Gender, type of sport, and skill differences. *Journal of Sports Sciences*, 25(13), 1521–1530. https://doi.org/10.1080/02640410701230479

Nicholls, A. R., Polman, R. C. J., Levy, A. R., & Backhouse, S. H. (2008). Mental toughness, optimism, pessimism, and coping among athletes. *Personality and Individual Differences*, 44(5), 1182–1192. https://doi.org/10.1016/j.paid.2007.11.011

Nicholls, A. R., Taylor, N. J., Carroll, S., & Perry, J. L. (2016). The development of a new sport-specific classification of coping and a meta-analysis of the relationship between different coping strategies and moderators on sporting outcomes. *Frontiers in Psychology*, 7. https://doi.org/10.3389/fpsyg.2016.01674

Noblet, A. J., & Gifford, S. M. (2002). The sources of stress experienced by professional Australian footballers. *Journal of Applied Sport Psychology*, 14(1), 1–13. https://doi.org/10.1080/10413200209339007

Ntoumanis, N., & Biddle, S. J. H. (2000). Relationship of intensity and direction of competitive anxiety with coping strategies. *The Sport Psychologist*, 14(4), 360–371. https://doi.org/10.1123/tsp.14.4.360

Polman, R. (2012). Elite athletes' experiences of coping with stress. In J. Thatcher, M. Jones, & D. Lavallee (Eds.), *Coping and emotion in sport* (2nd ed., pp. 284–301). Routledge (Taylor & Francis Group). https://eprints.qut.edu.au/109880/

Polman, R., Trotter, M., Poulus, D., & Borkoles, E. (2018). eSport: Friend or Foe? In S. Göbel, A. Garcia-Agundez, T. Tregel, M. Ma, J. Baalsrud Hauge, M. Oliveira, T. Marsh, & P. Caserman (Eds.), *Serious games* (Vol. 11243, pp. 3–8). Springer International Publishing. https://doi.org/10.1007/978-3-030-02762-9_1

Polman, R. C. J., Clough, P. J., & Levy, A. R. (2010). Personality and coping in sport: The big five and mental toughness. In A. Nicholls (Ed.), *Coping in sport: Theory, methods, and related constructs* (p. 33). Nova Science Pub Inc.

Poulus, D., Coulter, T., Trotter, M., & Polman, R. (2021). Perceived stressors experienced by competitive esports athletes. *International Journal of Esports*. https://www.ijesports.org/article/73/html

Poulus, D., Coulter, T. J., Trotter, M. G., & Polman, R. (2020). Stress and coping in Esports and the influence of mental toughness. *Frontiers in Psychology*, 11. https://doi.org/10.3389/fpsyg.2020.00628

Poulus, D. R., Coulter, T. J., Trotter, M. G., & Polman, R. (2021a). Longitudinal analysis of stressors, stress, coping and coping effectiveness in elite esports athletes. *Psychology of Sport and Exercise*, 60(2). https://doi.org/10.1016/j.psychsport.2021.102093

Poulus, D. R., Coulter, T. J., Trotter, M. G., & Polman, R. (2021b). A qualitative analysis of the perceived determinants of success in elite esports athletes. *Journal of Sports Sciences*, 1–12. https://doi.org/10.1080/02640414.2021.2015916

Reeves, C. W., Nicholls, A. R., & McKenna, J. (2011). The effects of a coping intervention on coping self-efficacy, coping effectiveness, and subjective performance among adolescent soccer players. *International Journal of Sport and Exercise Psychology*, 9(2), 126–142. https://doi.org/10.1080/1612197X.2011.567104

Roth, S., & Cohen, L. J. (1986). Approach, avoidance, and coping with stress. *American Psychologist*, 41(7), 813–819.

Smith, M., Birch, P., & Bright, D. (2019). Identifying stressors and coping strategies of elite esports competitors. *International Journal of Gaming and Computer-Mediated Simulations (IJGCMS)*, 11(2), 22–39. https://doi.org/10.4018/IJGCMS.2019040102

Trotter, M. G., Coulter, T. J., Davis, P. A., Poulus, D. R., & Polman, R. (2020). The association between esports participation, health and physical activity behaviour. *International Journal of Environmental Research and Public Health*, *17*(19), 7329. https://doi.org/10.3390/ijerph17197329

Trotter, M. G., Coulter, T. J., Davis, P. A., Poulus, D. R., & Polman, R. (2021). Social support, self-regulation, and psychological skill use in e-athletes. *Frontiers in Psychology*, *12*, 722030. https://www.frontiersin.org/articles/10.3389/fpsyg.2021.722030/pdf

Valve Corporation. (2021). *Dota 2—The international 10 battle pass*. Dota2.Com. https://www.dota2.com/international/battlepass

Watson, M., Abbott, C., & Pedraza-Ramirez, I. (2021). A parallel approach to performance and sport psychology work in esports teams. *International Journal of Esports*, *2*(2), 1–6. https://www.ijesports.org/article/52/html

Chapter 7

Doping in esports

Joanna Wall Tweedie, Rebecca R. Rosenthal, and John T. Holden

Introduction

The popularity of esports has burgeoned in recent years and was further accelerated by the COVID-19 pandemic (López-Cabarcos et al., 2020). Scholars have predicted that by 2023 the esports market will exceed $200 billion in revenue and that around three billion people will be participating in some form of professional or recreational esports (Wijman, 2020). Due to the rapid rise in popularity of professional esports, many of the leagues and organisations that are part of the esports ecosystem have formed quickly, often without implementing formal regulations for competitors or adopting a traditional governance structure. Due to this, addressing integrity issues such as those in traditional professional sports is uniquely challenging in the esports space (Kelly et al., 2021). For example, as participation in esports necessitates long hours of sustained focus and requires players to remain alert and responsive without taking breaks mid-game, many participants seek a boost via pharmacological means. In fact, several well-known gamers have been forthcoming about the prevalence of stimulant and cognitive-enhancing drug use in the industry (e.g. Maiberg, 2015, Wingfield & Dougherty, 2015).

At present, the widespread use of performance-enhancing drugs is one of the greatest threats to the integrity of the professional esports industry. Certainly, if esports is to achieve legitimacy in the broader sports world, embracing antidoping policies will be essential. This chapter explores how doping currently functions in the world of esports and the ways in which future regulations could curtail the drug abuse that is currently authorised by the industry. This chapter begins by discussing doping in traditional sports and goes on to describe the emergence of doping concerns in the esports industry. Finally, the chapter identifies the challenges of regulating performance-enhancing substance use in esports and proposes policy recommendations to help move the industry forward.

Overview of doping in traditional sports

The history of doping and anti-doping

Cheating has been prevalent in sport at least since the earliest contests in Olympia, Greece. A person's desire to seek an advantage over their opponent

DOI: 10.4324/9781003258650-10

appears to be a natural by-product of human competition. Thus, the use of performance-enhancing substances has been demonstrated in all forms of competition, from sport to war. Yesalis and Bahrke (2002) note that at the early Olympic Games some forms of cheating, such as bribery, were prohibited and carried harsh punishments, but that the use of drugs or other substances to enhance athletic performance was not considered cheating. Further, as there were no apparent efforts to dissuade the use of performance-enhancing substances in the past (Yesalis & Bahrke, 2002), doping in sport became common practice (e.g. Engelberg et al., 2015; Dimeo, 2016).

Whereas in Greco-Roman times natural products, chemicals, and animal extracts were used to enhance athletic performance (Lippi et al., 2008), in recent years, and due to the advancements in science and biotechnology, ergogenic aids have included synthetic molecules, hormones, and gene manipulation (Lippi & Guidi, 2004). The multitude of strategies used for doping means that a variety of physiological systems may be targeted. The specific objectives for doping can and may include increased strength, improved endurance, weight management, delayed fatigue, pain desensitisation, and enhanced concentration (e.g. Lippi et al., 2008; Yesalis & Bahrke, 2002).

In the latter part of the nineteenth century, athletes involved in sports like swimming, running, cycling, and boxing used stimulants to boost their performances (Prokop, 1970). The development of amphetamines in 1929 led to increased use of powerful stimulants in sport, as well as in wider society (Rasmussen, 2008). Amphetamines were used systematically in the Second World War to help soldiers combat fatigue and improve endurance (Rosen, 2008). Following the Second World War, the use of stimulants like amphetamines to enhance sport performance burgeoned. Subsequently, in the mid-1960s, anabolic steroid use by athletes became prominent amongst strength-based Olympic athletes, and the utility of these drugs then extended to track athletes and other sports like American football (Yesalis & Bahrke, 2002). Doping technologies later advanced to include the misuse of peptide hormones, such as human growth hormone (hGH) and erythropoientin (EPO) (Lippi et al., 2008).

The turning point for anti-doping policies came in the early 1960s (Dimeo & Hunt, 2013; Todd & Todd, 2001). The death of Danish cyclist, Knud Enemark Jansen, at the 1960 Rome games was speculated to be the result of amphetamine use, and his death is seen as the catalyst for the International Olympic Committee's (IOC) adoption of anti-doping policies (Yesalis & Bahrke, 2002). Specifically, in 1967 the IOC implemented policies targeting performance-enhancing drugs (Todd & Todd, 2001). These anti-doping campaigns were shaped by the argument that drug use constituted cheating by being an unnatural and immoral advantage that also posed health risks for athletes (Dimeo & Hunt, 2013; Hunt et al., 2012). In the late twentieth century, the rise in anti-doping efforts ran parallel to the rise in doping – in the race between the drugs and the policies doping appeared as the victor. Recognising that an independent organisation with global authority would be needed if anti-doping efforts were to be at all effective, the World Anti-Doping Agency (WADA) was established in 1999 (Lippi et al., 2008; Dimeo & Hunt, 2013).

Sport has certainly grown exponentially in recent decades in both societal prominence and rewards. The high prestige and prizes associated with winning in sport generate a temptation for deviance to which some actors will succumb. Sociologists have explained this condition via anomie theory (Goode, 2017), which suggests that the magnitude of potential available rewards tempts actors to violate rules, irrespective of potential punishment. While anomie theory emphasises that the decision to violate the rules rests with an individual, scholars have highlighted that in elite sport, the decision to dope is unlikely to be made by an individual but rather requires a multitude of supporting actors, such as coaches, trainers, and teammates (Dimeo & Hunt, 2013; Overbye et al., 2013). Recent high-profile doping cases, such as that of Lance Armstrong, have illustrated a team approach to the use of performance-enhancing drugs.

The use of performance-enhancing drugs in sport has been explained by some scholars via game theory, which depicts that the advantages of using banned substances are powerful and that, conversely, the costs of not using drugs and performing poorly are devastating (Shermer, 2008). Other researchers have contended that the prevalence of doping and failed anti-doping efforts arise because athletes believe that the perceived likelihood of detection is extremely low (Engelberg et al., 2015; Overbye et al., 2013). Thus, WADA's emphasis on the deterrence value of its doping controls is criticised, with many arguing for a greater emphasis on doping prevention to begin with (Lippi et al., 2008; Lucidi et al., 2008).

The WADA Code and drug classes

As the global authority tasked with overseeing anti-doping in sport, WADA aims to harmonise anti-doping policies, rules, and regulations around the world (WADA, 2021). The WADA Code is the central document that details the anti-doping programme and publishes a list of prohibited substances and methods. The Prohibited List is updated annually and details substances and ingesting methods that are prohibited in and out of competition.

According to WADA, a substance or method is deemed to be in violation of the anti-doping rules if it fulfils two of the following three criteria: (1) a potential to enhance performance, (2) an actual or potential health risk, and (3) a violation of the 'spirit of sport' (WADA, 2021). WADA classifies the various substances on its Prohibited List by their drug class, with substances falling into the following categories: anabolic agents, peptides and growth factors, Beta-2 agonists, hormone and metabolic modulators, and diuretics and masking agents (WADA, 2021). Classes of drugs that are only prohibited in competition (instead of banned outright both in and out of competition) include stimulants, narcotics, cannabinoids, and glucocorticoids. The Prohibited List is designed to be all-encompassing and includes statements like: 'and other substance with similar chemical structure or biological effect, are also prohibited' (WADA, 2021, p. 6). These statements are designed to prevent any deliberate misuse of gaps on WADA's list. While WADA publishes a Prohibited List of substances, WADA's Code offers exemptions for athletes with a legitimate medical need for a particular drug on the Prohibited List.

Therapeutic use exemptions

Therapeutic use exemptions, abbreviated as TUEs, are permissions granted to competitors to utilise otherwise banned substances or methods whilst competing. The rise of TUEs began in the early 1990s, although almost immediately there were concerns that the system could allow some to claim illegitimate exemptions and thereby obtain a competitive advantage (Fitch, 2013). The rise in the use of amphetamines in sport followed the growing use of these drugs in society as a whole. Amphetamines were, and still are, widely available and prescribed, along with other stimulants, for a host of legitimate medical ailments, including mild depression and attention-deficit disorder (Rasmussen, 2008). Thus, the challenge faced by anti-doping authorities has long been to demarcate what constitutes the use of these substances as cheating versus a genuine medical need (Overbye & Wagner, 2013; Lentillon-Kaestner & Carstairs, 2010; Tscholl & Dvorak, 2012). For drugs that are widely prescribed for common ailments, the distinction between doping in the cheating sense and taking medications legitimately needed for a medical condition can be particularly challenging.

It is deemed essential that sport remains accessible to athletes irrespective of their medical conditions and, furthermore, that anti-doping rules do not negatively impact the health of athletes. TUEs are prominent at the highest level of sport but are also prone to misuse and exploitation (e.g. Fitch, 2020; Rodenberg & Holden, 2017; Overbye & Wagner, 2013). Adding a further challenge to the interpretation of TUEs is the fact that they can be granted retroactively in certain instances, such as medical emergencies (Pitsiladis et al., 2017). Therefore, the ongoing challenge for anti-doping authorities is to balance allowing access to drugs for medical treatment and unintentionally permitting doping. Consideration as to what such a regulatory balance would look like in esports is especially elusive. The next section includes a discussion about the history of doping and regulations in esports.

A history of doping in esports

The evolution of doping regulations in esports

Doping concerns first plagued the esports industry in 2015, when *Counter-Strike: Global Offensive* player Kory Friesen admitted that he and his teammates took Adderall while competing in a tournament for a prize of $250,000 (Maiberg, 2015). Friesen's admission sent esports leagues and tournament organisers into a frenzy, as they tried to (1) explore the extent to which there was a doping problem in professional esports and (2) alleviate rumours that could tarnish the burgeoning competitive esports industry. Immediately after Friesen's admission, the Electronic Sports League (ESL) – the league hosting the tournament during which Friesen and his *Counter-Strike* teammates took Adderall – enacted a doping policy (Gilbert, 2015). In formulating this policy, the ESL adopted WADA's list of prohibited substances, which includes steroids, stimulant medications like Adderall, and recreational drugs like cocaine and marijuana (Mueller, 2015). Under the ESL's doping policy, the ESL reserves the right to randomly drug-test players at any time 'from the start of the first day until the end of the last day of competition'. Players found in violation of the ESL's policy are subject to punishments ranging from reduced prize money to a two-year ban from all ESL events (Tach, 2015).

After the ESL enacted its doping policy in 2015, several other organisations, such as the Esports Integrity Coalition (ESIC), the World Esports Association (WESA), and the International Esports Federation (IESF), followed suit (Martinelli, 2019; Bogle, 2020). The policies enacted by the ESIC, WESA, and IESF all rely on WADA's list of prohibited substances, require players to submit to random doping tests, allow players to apply for TUEs, and highlight potential sanctions for doping violations (WESA, 2016; IESF, 2020; ESIC, 2021). Although the ESIC, WESA, and IESF have comprehensive doping policies in place, membership in these organisations is not mandatory (Bogle, 2020). Thus, the doping policies promulgated by these leagues only impact the esports leagues and tournament organisers that are members of the WESA, ESIC, or IESF. To date, the only prominent esports league that is a member of any of these organisations is the ESL (Rosenthal, 2021). As the ESL already has its own doping policy in place and is the only prominent esports league to have such a policy, its membership in organisations like the WESA and ESIC is unsurprising (Rosenthal, 2021). Overall, despite the formation of esports-regulating organisations like the WESA, ESIC, and IESF, doping in professional esports remains virtually unregulated. As recently as 2020, *The Washington Post* published an article in which a reporter interviewed the former *Call of Duty* World Champion, Adam Sloss (Hamstead, 2020). Sloss explained that Adderall abuse was something he experienced 'very frequently' at esports tournaments and that because 'Adderall abuse was too much to keep up with' he retired from professional gaming (Hamstead, 2020).

The key to success? Why professional esports players dope

Just as professional football and basketball players take steroids to become faster or stronger and thereby gain an advantage over their competitors, well-known and junior-level professional esports players also rely on drugs for an advantage. Whereas in a traditional sport like football, speed, strength, and agility are the name of the game, in esports success relies on reaction time and sustained focus (Rosenthal, 2021). For example, an average tournament held by the *League of Legends* Championship Series (LCS) can last for eight hours, with players often playing in back-to-back 30-minute matches (Hasan, 2020). This is distinguishable from a professional basketball game under the auspices of the National

Basketball Association (NBA), which usually only lasts somewhere between two and two and a half hours.

As cognition-enhancing drugs like Adderall, Vyvanse, and Ritalin can increase focus and speed up reaction times, they have become increasingly popular in professional competitive esports (Holden et al., 2019). In addition to gaming for hours on end without a break, professional esports players typically make close to 400 movements every minute on a mouse or keyboard (Schütz, 2016). The former semipro *Halo* player, Matthew 'MellowMajik' Murphy, explained that before taking Adderall he was 'exhausted, tired, and [would] lose motivation after only a couple hours' (Hamstead, 2020). However, with Adderall, he contended that he was able to play better than ever and could game for up to 12 hours straight (Hamstead, 2020). Other players share Murphy's sentiment. For example, professional esports athlete Tyler Mozingo said that when taking Adderall he had 'laser-like focus' which made him feel 'untouchable' (Loria, 2016).

In professional esports, sustained energy for making precise movements on a mouse or keyboard in long matches is significant because 'every fraction of a second counts, and the tiniest delay … can lead to disastrous loss' (Schütz, 2016). Specifically, top professional esports players can each take home a few million dollars if their team wins a major tournament (Lozano, 2021). As the average salary of professional esports players is much lower than the average salary of NBA players – for example, an esports player in a team in a top professional league makes approximately $50,000 per year, whereas a novice NBA player makes over $900,000 – professional esports players rely on tournament prize pools to supplement their income (Rosenthal, 2021; Adams, 2021). The income-driven nature of esports is primarily motivated by the fact that the average career of a professional esports athlete is shorter than that of an average professional traditional sports athlete (Yun, 2019). The significant amount of money on the line and the fewer years in which a professional esports athlete can earn this money underscores why esports players frequently resort to taking drugs like Adderall to gain a competitive advantage (Yun, 2019; Rosenthal, 2021).

In sum, doping in professional esports is ubiquitous, and unless top professional esports leagues like the *Call of Duty* League and the *League of Legends* Championship Series either create their own doping policies or adopt the policies proffered by organisations like the WESA, ESIC, or IESF, doping in esports is here to stay. In the short term, the widespread doping that transpires in the world of professional esports presents integrity issues and raises concerns about player health (Toomey, 2019; Berry, 2021). In the long term, the consequences of the pervasive doping that permeates the esports industry are far bleaker. Specifically, adolescents who hear that their favourite esports players are taking drugs like Adderall may be motivated to experiment with these drugs in the hope that they too can become top esports athletes (Hamstead, 2020).

The next section explores why the blanket adoption of doping regulations is critical to the future success of the esports industry, and how implementing these regulations presents a challenge for esports leagues.

Challenges to regulating doping in esports

Esports is not unique in its challenges. Indeed, sports have been fighting cheating and corruption since the earliest competitions (Weston, 2017). One of the challenges facing the regulation of the esports space has been the fragmented nature of professional competition, in that there is no overarching governing body akin to a national sport's governing body. Additionally, there are varying degrees of professionalisation across the space, with some leagues like the *Overwatch* League attempting to mirror the model of American professional sports (Holden & Baker III, 2019). In contrast, other leagues lack the development that is seen in professional sports. The absence of a 'central regulator' in esports has resulted in disparate rules and the ability of some competitors to avoid consequences even where there are efforts to stop violations of the rules (Czegledy, 2021).

How doping functions in esports

The use of performance-enhancing stimulants in esports is a long-documented problem (Holden et al., 2018; Holden et al., 2019; Rosenthal, 2021). Several factors have been blamed for stimulant use in esports, including: 'grueling lifestyles, nonexistent job security, and lack of advocates for professional esports players' (Czegledy, 2021). In addition, the fiercely competitive environment may incentivise competitors to bend the rules to stay competitive. As referenced in an earlier section, in 2015 esports doping took centre stage when professional gamer Kory Friesen, who played under the gamer tag 'SEMPHIS', announced that his whole team competed using the prescription stimulant Adderall (Kamen, 2015). Adderall, which is the trade name for the drug dextroamphetamine, is commonly prescribed for attention-deficit hyperactivity disorder (ADHD). The substance, which belongs to a class of drugs called stimulants, is used to 'help increase your ability to pay attention, stay focused on an activity, and control behavior problems' (WebMD, n.d.). Friesen's admission that his team had used stimulants set leagues and tournament organisers scrambling to implement some form of drug testing to lend legitimacy to the emerging sports sub-segment (Stivers, 2016).

Professional esports is hardly alone in the use of stimulants by competitors hoping to gain a competitive advantage. Stimulant-based doping has been observed in various settings, from online poker and chess to college campuses (Ip et al., 2021). Stimulants are also commonly used substances in other professional sports (Rodenberg & Holden, 2017). In one recent survey of gamers, more than 40% of those surveyed reported using performance-enhancing substances during gameplay. The most commonly used substance was caffeine-based energy drinks, followed by stimulants, with 6.1% of video gamers reporting that they used stimulant medications to gain a competitive advantage (Ip et al., 2021). Perhaps more concerning is that half of those who reported using a prescription stimulant noted that they did so *without* a valid prescription for the drugs (Ip et al., 2021). The prevalence of stimulant prescriptions has made it difficult to craft effective policies that permit legitimate use while ferreting out those who only seek to gain a competitive advantage. Numerous authors have documented the challenges of implementing a rigorous anti-doping system that permits the use of otherwise banned substances by some competitors (Holden et al., 2019; Lentillon-Kaestner & Carstairs, 2010; Overbye & Wagner, 2013; Tscholl & Dvorak 2012). The permitted use of stimulant medications makes it more challenging to assess legitimacy because stimulants are so readily prescribed to the general population (Holden et al., 2019).

As introduced earlier, TUEs are designed to afford athletes with a documented need for a medical intervention the ability to compete utilising an otherwise banned substance. TUEs are not intended to provide a competitive advantage but to only allow athletes to compete whilst receiving treatment for legitimate medical diagnoses (Rosenthal, 2021). While TUEs may risk exploitation, much of the esports world continues to operate without any drug testing at all. Even where there are policies in place, enforcement in many leagues seems to be a low priority. As former *Overwatch* League commissioner, Nate Nanzer, stated in 2018: 'Adderall is a legal prescription in the United States of America and ... there's no data that suggests that it makes you better at playing *Overwatch*' (Hamstead, 2020). While it may seem obvious that an increased focus would be a competitive advantage in a task that requires focused attention, even giving credence to those who do not believe that stimulants provide a competitive advantage, this is only one of the three prongs in WADA's banned substances programme. There are known risks associated with the use of amphetamine-based stimulants like Adderall, including hypertension, sudden cardiac death, stroke, kidney disease, and seizures (American Addiction Center, n.d.).

According to numerous industry insiders, the use of stimulants in the esports industry seems rampant (Hamstead, 2020). However, the response to the reports has been uninspiring. In much the same way that professional sports leagues like Major League Baseball were slow to respond to their own doping scandal, at least until the United States Congress took an interest in it (Mitchell, 2007), esports leagues have been slow to implement any meaningful changes. The reasons for the reluctance to implement effective policies could be twofold. First, we know that stimulant medications prescribed for the treatment of ADHD are incredibly prominent in society and sport (Rodenberg & Holden, 2017). Second, the risk of a major doping scandal could threaten the still-nascent esports space. The esports industry is still in its infancy and the reputational damage of a major player being banned for using a prohibited substance could cause irreparable harm (Holden et al., 2020).

Recommendations

Constructing and subsequently implementing an effective anti-doping programme has proved to be an endless pursuit for traditional sports organisations.

Indeed, one could ask how much progress has been made in the fight against doping, especially following the allegations of state-sponsored doping involving Russian athletes (Panja, 2021). Westmattelmann, Dreiskamper, Straub, et al. (2018) outline several methods that can be utilised to increase the detection of doping in sports. The adoption of these methods would be a positive step forward for the esports industry. First, the authors note that more frequent testing effectively discourages doping for some athletes, although they also note that it is not the only panacea. Second, the continued effort to ramp up detection methods is an aspect of anti-doping that has long been a struggle for agencies, as, by nature, anti-doping is reactive. Third, in traditional sports where the growth of synthetic drugs and biological alterations are changing conceptualisations of doping, Athlete Biological Passports are being used to monitor physiological changes in athletes' bodies over time. Finally, while testing procedures are one form of deterrence, along with educational programmes, the stick to those carrots comes from punishments. Anti-doping punishments have long been the primary means of discouraging doping, with sanctions ranging from fines to bans to criminal penalties in some countries (Westmattelmann et al., 2018). The United States followed the lead of many other countries by criminalising doping programme administrators at international events in 2020, although the legislation does not include athletes in its scope (Futterman, 2020). If the esports industry is to move forward, there needs to be an industry-wide commitment to enforcing anti-doping policies and recognising and enforcing the determinations and sanctions of sister organisations.

According to Michele Verroken, the former head of anti-doping at UK Sport, esports is having some success with implementing drug testing at tournaments. However, while identifying that Adderall use may be down, an increase in marijuana use came as a surprise. While marijuana has not historically been classified as a performance-enhancing drug in traditional sports circles, it has been suggested that the substance's calming effects could benefit esports competitors (Baldwin, 2019). While the ESIC has emerged from a crowded pack of regulatory groups seeking to be the guiding force behind the esports industry, the lack of unified oversight for the industry has effectively created a patchwork of policies. There has not yet been sufficient adoption or recognition of the ESIC's (or another governing body's) authority to indicate that there are meaningful efforts underway to rein in doping in professional esports (McCambridge, 2017). The policies proposed by the ESIC and similarly positioned organisations are a solid starting point to routing out doping-related integrity concerns. However, leagues must be committed to adopting and enforcing anti-doping policies in order to propel the industry forward.

Conclusion

Esports as an industry is still attempting to find its footing. In many ways, professional esports is trying to walk the line of staying authentic to the culture that brought it to this point, while at the same time trying to change so that investors are comfortable injecting billions of dollars into the industry. Thus far, one of the significant challenges for esports investors has been to envision how the industry will generate consistent revenue (Holden et al., 2020). As easy as it may be to draw a comparison between traditional sports and esports, that comparison fails to reflect some of the core differences that make governing the esports industry more challenging. Among the most prominent differences are the types of drugs used by athletes. In traditional sports, many of the performance-enhancing substances of choice lack widespread societal use. The growth of esports as a professionalised activity is dependent on the integrity of the matches. The money flowing into the industry for years will not continue to come if investors cannot trust the legitimacy of the competition. While much of the integrity-related focus in the industry has focused on high-profile match-fixing scandals, the eradication of doping should remain a paramount objective. However, there is a need to balance the integrity concerns associated with performance-enhancing substances and at the same time allow for therapeutic use exemptions so that competitors with a demonstrated medical need are not penalised with exclusion.

The implementation of biological passports and an ongoing evaluation of TUEs are steps that could be immediately adopted by esports leagues. Such changes could protect the integrity of professional esports in the short term *and* inform esports leagues about which methods are the most successful in eradicating doping in the long term. Indeed, for professional esports to continue generating billions in revenue, the time to act is now.

References

Adams, L. (2021, August 5). NBA minimum salaries for 2021/22. *Hoops Rumors*. Retrieved from https://www.hoopsrumors.com/2021/08/nba-minimum-salaries-for-2021-22.html.

Adderall oral: Uses, side effects, interactions, pictures, warnings & dosing. (n.d.). *WebMD*. Retrieved from https://www.webmd.com/drugs/2/drug-63163/adderall-oral/details.

American Addiction Center. (n.d.). Side effects of adderall: Depression, anxiety & raised heart rate. *American Addiction Centers*. Retrieved from https://americanaddictioncenters.org/adderall/side-effects.

Baldwin, A. (2019, April 17). Targeted doping tests having an impact in esports, says Verroken. *Reuters*. Retrieved from https://www.reuters.com/article/uk-sport-doping-idUKKCN1RT2EX.

Berry, M. (2021). Esports: The sharp edge of adderall in professional gaming. *American Addiction Centers*. Retrieved from https://americanaddictioncenters.org/blog/esports-adderall-abuse.

Bogle, J. (2020). Trying to think faster: Doping in esports. *Villanova University*. Retrieved from https://www1.villanova.edu/villanova/law/academics/sportslaw/commentary/mslj_blog/2020/TryingtoThinkFasterDopinginEsports.html.

Czegledy, P. K. (2021). Esports integrity policies. *Gaming Law Review*, 25(4), 161–170. https://doi.org/10.1089/glr2.2020.0017.

Dimeo, P. (2016). The myth of clean sport and its unintended consequences. *Performance Enhancement & Health, 4*(3–4), 103–110. https://doi.org/10.1016/j.peh.2016.04.001.

Dimeo, P., & Hunt, T. M. (2013). Anti-doping policy: Historical and contemporary ambiguities in the fight for drug-free sport. In I. Henry & L. M. Ko (Eds.), *Routledge handbook of sport policy* (pp. 267–276). New York: Routledge.

Engelberg, T., Moston, S., & Skinner, J. (2015). The final frontier of anti-doping: A study of athletes who have committed doping violations. *Sport Management Review, 18*(2), 268–279. https://doi.org/10.1016/j.smr.2014.06.005.

Esports Integrity Commission. (2021). *Anti-doping code*. Retrieved from https://esic.gg/codes/anti-doping-code/.

Fitch, K. (2020). Therapeutic use exemptions (TUEs) are essential in sport: But there is room for improvement. *British Journal of Sports Medicine, 54*(3), 191–192. http://doi.org/10.1136/bjsports-2018-100113.

Fitch, K. D. (2013). Therapeutic use exemptions (TUEs) at the olympic games 1992–2012. *British Journal of Sports Medicine, 47*(13), 815–818. http://doi.org/10.1136/bjsports-2013-092460.

Futterman, M. (2020, December 17). A new U.S. law would target doping's enablers. international watchdogs don't like it. *The New York Times*. Retrieved from https://www.nytimes.com/2020/11/18/sports/olympics/rodchenkov-doping-russia-olympics.html.

Gilbert, B. (2015). There's an Adderall doping scandal in the world of professional gaming. *Business Insider*. Retrieved from https://www.businessinsider.com/esl-drug-testing-for-adderall-2015-7.

Goode, E. (2017). Is concern about sports doping a moral panic? In V. Møller, I. Waddington, & Hoberman, J. (Eds.), *Routledge handbook of drugs and sport* (pp. 31–40). Routledge.

Hamstead, C. (2020, February 13). 'Nobody talks about it because everyone is on it': Adderall presents esports with an enigma. *Washington Post*. Retrieved from https://www.washingtonpost.com/video-games/esports/2020/02/13/esports-adderall-drugs/.

Hasan, U. (2020). How long does a league of legends tournament last? *Esports How*. Retrieved from https://esportshow.com/how-long-does-a-league-of-legends-tournament-last/.

Holden, J. T., & Baker III, T. A. (2019). The econtractor? Defining the esports employment relationship. *American Business Law Journal, 56*(2), 391–440. https://doi.org/10.1111/ablj.12141.

Holden, J. T., Edelman, M., & Baker III, T. A. (2020). A short treatise on esports and the law: How America regulates its next national pastime. *University of Illinois Law Review, 2020*(2), 509–582. https://illinoislawreview.org/print/vol-2020-no-2/a-short-treatise-on-esports-and-the-law/

Holden, J. T., Kaburakis, A., & Rodenberg, R. M. (2018). Esports: Children, stimulants and video-gaming-induced inactivity. *Journal of Paediatrics and Child Health, 54*(8), 830–831. https://doi.org/10.1111/jpc.13897.

Holden, J. T., Kaburakis, A., & Wall Tweedie, J. (2019). Virtue (al) games—Real drugs. *Sport, Ethics and Philosophy, 13*(1), 19–32. https://doi.org/10.1080/17511321.2018.1459814.

Hunt, T. M., Dimeo, P., & Jedlicka, S. R. (2012). The historical roots of today's problems: A critical appraisal of the international anti-doping movement. *Performance Enhancement & Health, 1*(2), 55–60. https://doi.org/10.1016/j.peh.2012.05.001.

International Esports Federation. (2020). *Anti-doping rules*. Retrieved from https://iesf.org/wp-content/uploads/2020/12/2021_IESF_Anti-Doping_Rules_Approved.pdf.

Ip, E. J., Urbano, E. P. T., Caballero, J., Lau, W. B., Clauson, K. A., Torn, R. A., ... Barnett, M. J. (2021). The video gamer 500: Performance-enhancing drug use and Internet Gaming Disorder among adult video gamers. *Computers in Human Behavior*, 106890, 1–7. https://doi.org/10.1016/j.chb.2021.106890.

Kamen, M. (2015, July 16). Pro-gamer admits to doping in esports. *WIRED UK*. Retrieved from https://www.wired.co.uk/article/esports-doping-admission.

Kelly, S. J., Derrington, S., & Star, S. (2021). Governance challenges in esports: A best practice framework for addressing integrity and wellbeing issues. *International Journal of Sport Policy and Politics*, 1–18. https://doi.org/10.1080/19406940.2021.1976812.

Lentillon-Kaestner, V., & Carstairs, C. (2010). Doping use among young elite cyclists: A qualitative psychosociological approach. *Scandinavian Journal of Medicine & Science in Sports*, 20(2), 336–345. https://doi.org/10.1111/j.1600-0838.2009.00885.x.

Lippi, G., & Guidi, G. C. (2004). Gene manipulation and improvement of athletic performances: New strategies in blood doping. *British Journal of Sports Medicine*, 38(5), 641–641. http://doi.org/10.1136/bjsm.2004.013623.

Lippi, G., Franchini, M., & Guidi, G. C. (2008). Doping in competition or doping in sport? *British Medical Bulletin*, 86(1), 95–107. https://doi.org/10.1093/bmb/ldn014.

López-Cabarcos, M. Á., Ribeiro-Soriano, D., & Piñeiro-Chousa, J. (2020). All that glitters is not gold: The rise of gaming in the COVID-19 pandemic. *Journal of Innovation & Knowledge*, 5(4), 289–296. https://doi.org/10.1016/j.jik.2020.10.004.

Loria, K. (2016). *Some competitive video gamers are abusing drugs to get an edge*. https://www.businessinsider.com/esports-doping-scandal-investigated-by-espns-otl-2016-1?r=US&IR=T

Lozano, K. (2021). Dota 2's The international 10 champions will win a whopping US $18 million. *Yahoo News*. Retrieved from https://news.yahoo.com/dota-2-the-international-10-champions-teams-win-money-070452102.html.

Lucidi, F., Zelli, A., Mallia, L., Grano, C., Russo, P. M., & Violani, C. (2008). The social-cognitive mechanisms regulating adolescents' use of doping substances. *Journal of sports sciences*, 26(5), 447–456. https://doi.org/10.1080/02640410701579370

Maiberg, E. (2015). Counter-strike esports pro: 'We were all on Adderall'. *Vice*. Retrieved from https://www.vice.com/en_us/article/gvy7b3/counter-strike-esports-pro-we-were-all-on-adderall.

Martinelli, J. (2019). The challenges of implementing a governing body for regulating esports. *University of Miami International and Comparative Law Review*, 26(2), 500–523.

McCambridge, E. (2017, July 21). Anti-doping efforts still in their infancy in esports. *Deutsche Welle*. Retrieved from https://www.dw.com/en/anti-doping-efforts-still-in-their-infancy-in-esports/a-39783790.

Mitchell, G. J. (2007). *Report to the commissioner of baseball of an independent investigation into the illegal use of steroids and other performance enhancing substances by players in major league baseball* (Vol. 13). New York: Office of the Commissioner of Baseball.

Mueller, S. (2015). Esports drug testing update: ESL announces list of banned substances including adderall, cocaine, post, steroids and more. *International Business Times*. Retrieved from https://www.ibtimes.com/esports-drug-testing-update-esl-announces-list-banned-substances-including-adderall-2050245.

Overbye, M., Knudsen, M. L., & Pfister, G. (2013). To dope or not to dope: Elite athletes' perceptions of doping deterrents and incentives. *Performance Enhancement & Health*, 2(3), 119–134. https://doi.org/10.1016/j.peh.2013.07.001.

Overbye, M., & Wagner, U. (2013). Between medical treatment and performance enhancement: An investigation of how elite athletes experience therapeutic use exemptions. *International Journal of Drug Policy*, 24(6), 579–588. https://doi.org/10.1016/j.drugpo.2013.03.007.

Panja, T. (2021, August 2). Russia banned from olympics and global sports for 4 years over doping. *The New York Times*. Retrieved from https://www.nytimes.com/2019/12/09/sports/russia-doping-ban.html.

Pitsiladis, Y., Wang, G., Lacoste, A., Schneider, C., Smith, A. D., Di Gianfrancesco, A., & Pigozzi, F. (2017). Make sport great again: The use and abuse of the therapeutic use exemptions process. *Current Sports Medicine Reports*, 16(3), 123–125. https://doi.org/10.1249/JSR.0000000000000364.

Prokop, L. (1970). The struggle against doping and its history. *Journal of Sports Medicine and Physical Fitness*, 10(1), 45–48.

Rasmussen, N. (2008). America's first amphetamine epidemic 1929–1971: A quantitative and qualitative retrospective with implications for the present. *American Journal of Public Health*, 98(6), 974–985. http://doi.org/10.2105/AJPH.2007.110593.

Rodenberg, R. M., & Holden, J. T. (2017). Cognition enhancing drugs ('nootropics'): Time to include coaches and team executives in doping tests? *British Journal of Sports Medicine*, 51, 1316. http://doi.org/10.1136/bjsports-2015-095474

Rosen, D. M. (2008). *Dope: A history of performance enhancement in sports from the nineteenth century to today*. Westport, CT: Praeger.

Rosenthal, R. (2021). A tough pill to swallow: Making the case for why esports leagues must adopt strict banned substance policies to prevent disability discrimination. *Virginia Sports & Entertainment Law Journal*, 20(1), 76–105.

Schütz, M. (2016). Science shows that esports professionals are real athletes. *Deutsche Welle*. Retrieved from https://www.dw.com/en/science-shows-that-esports-professionals-are-real-athletes/a-19084993.

Shermer, M. (2008). The doping dilemma. *Scientific American*, 298(4), 82–89. https://doi.org/10.1038/scientificamerican0408-82.

Stivers, C. (2016). The first competitive video gaming anti-doping policy and its deficiencies under European Union law. *San Diego International Law Journal*, 18, 263–293.

Tach, D. (2015). ESL adopts world anti-doping agency's prohibited substances list, like steroids and pot. *Polygon*. Retrieved from https://www.polygon.com/2015/8/12/9136721/esl-adopts-anti-doping-WADA-list-banned-substances.

Todd, J., & Todd, T. (2001). Significant events in the history of drug testing and the Olympic movement: 1960–1999. In W. Wilson & E. Derse (Eds.), *Doping in elite sport* (pp. 65–128). Champaign, IL: Human Kinetics.

Toomey, R. (2019). Upholding the integrity of esports to successfully and safely legitimize esports wagering. *Gaming Law Review*, 23(1), 12–18. https://doi.org/10.1089/glr2.2019.23112.

Tscholl, P. M., & Dvorak, J. (2012). Abuse of medication during international football competition in 2010-lesson not learned. *British Journal of Sports Medicine*, 46(16), 1140–1141. https://doi.org/10.1136/bjsports-2011-090806.

Westmattelmann, D., Dreiskämper, D., Straub, B., Schewe, G., & Plass, J. (2018). Perception of the current anti-doping regime–A quantitative study among German top-level cyclists and track and field athletes. *Frontiers in Psychology, 9*, 1890–1904. https://doi.org/10.3389/fpsyg.2018.01890.

Weston, M. (2017). The regulation of doping in US and international sports. In M. A. McCann (Eds.), *The Oxford handbook of American sports law*, (pp. 83–110). https://doi.org/10.1093/oxfordhb/9780190465957.001.0001.

Wijman, T. (2020). Three billion players by 2023: Engagement and revenues continue to thrive across the global games market. *Newzoo*. Retrieved from https://newzoo.com/insights/articles/games-market-engagement-revenues-trends-2020-2023-gaming-report/.

Wingfield, N., & Dougherty, C. (2015, July 23). Drug testing is coming to e-sports. *The New York Times*. Retrieved from https://www.nytimes.com/2015/07/24/technology/drug-testing-is-coming-to-e-gaming.html.

World Anti-Doping Authority. (2021). *Anti-doping code 2021*. Retrieved from https://www.wada-ama.org/sites/default/files/resources/files/2021list_en.pdf.

World Esports Association. (2016). *Code of conduct and compliance for teams and players*. Retrieved from http://www.wesa.gg/wp-content/uploads/2017/04/WESA-Code-of-Conduct-Teams-and-Players.pdf.

Yesalis, C. E., & Bahrke, M. S. (2002). History of doping in sport. *International Sports Studies, 24*(1), 42–76.

Yun, S. M. (2019). A comparative overview on esports against traditional sports focused in the legal realm of monetary exploitation, cheating, and gambling. *Cardozo Arts & Entertainment Law Journal, 37*(2), 513–550.

Chapter 8

'Virtually cycling'

The impact of technology, cheating, and performance enhancement in bicycle e-racing

Bryce Dyer

Introduction

Online-based cycling is a rapidly growing and popular form of esports. e-cycling (or 'virtual cycling') consists of the physical exertion of riding a bicycle in a virtual simulation of varying terrain, topography, or racing and also allows participants to remotely engage in competitive or social settings.

However, due to recent developments, such as greater awareness, the COVID-19 global pandemic, and better technology to facilitate it, e-cycling has developed its own culture. It has now evolved from simply being a simulation into a novel sporting discipline in its own right. It has done this by offering unique riding environments and gamification features that motivate and engage a range of users and facilitate national and world championships coordinated by cycling's own governing bodies. Sadly, like so many other forms of organised sport, this activity has seen the inevitable introduction of questionable ethics, dishonesty, and, in some cases, downright cheating by participants. As a result, this sport has created challenging and unique forms of performance enhancement and unfairness practices that have not been seen before in traditional competitive sports. This chapter explores the history of e-cycling, details the technology used to facilitate it and categorises the legal and illegal ergogenics that can occur as a result.

History of e-cycling

In 1951 the Nimrod game console was exhibited in Berlin for the first time and showcased a simple strategy game that human beings could play together (Abanazir, 2019). As time passed, gaming saw further technological developments in the 1990s in terms of online mass participation. By the turn of the twenty-first century, there were calls for some forms of computer or console-based gaming to be recognised as a sport in its own right (Wagner, 2006). Meanwhile, in parallel with those developments, indoor cycling had been the basis for scientific study since at least 1913 (Macdonald, 1913). Whilst rollers or ergometers had been in general use for assessing physical fitness since the early twentieth

DOI: 10.4324/9781003258650-11

century, the early foundations of indoor cycling outside scientific practice took place in 1975 with Wilfried Baatz's invention of one of the first wind resistance–based stationary trainers. This was known as the 'Racermate' (Anon,[1] 2018). The 'Computrainer' electronically controlled static bicycle system was later invented in 1986, which allowed computerised software to control the physical workload of a cyclist riding indoors. Ultimately, the computer gaming industry and indoor cycling seemingly merged and grew in popularity when, in the early twenty-first century, cycling apps such as Zwift, Rouvy, Sufferfest, RGT, and BKool provided effective visual stimuli to simulate or gamify the act of cycling outdoors inside. An example of this is shown in Figure 8.1.

Like general video gaming, indoor cycling technology has evolved, become more complex, and even diversified into the distinctly different markets of performance, gaming, or social networking. Nonetheless, regardless of the virtual experience selected by a user, it has proved to contribute significantly to health and well-being (Supriyanto & Liu, 2021). Its global popularity has been partly accelerated by the onset of the COVID-19 pandemic in 2020 (McIlroy et al., 2021).

However, the credibility of competitive racing on online platforms is a common concern. It has also been claimed that athletes cheat on such apps and platforms to obtain a performance advantage (Dyer, 2020). Despite such issues, several governing cycling bodies have already begun the process of incorporating e-cycling into their portfolios as a regulated competitive sport. Some examples of this were British Cycling hosting national championships in 2019 and the UCI holding their inaugural Esports World Championships in 2020 (Dyer, 2020). Although this sporting discipline is still in the early stages of development, various stakeholders have been quick to engage with it, promote it, and legitimise it.

Figure 8.1 e-cycling app example.

e-cycling equipment

Cycle-based e-racing is typically available on a range of commercial apps or digital platforms, with the basic equipment consisting of a computer, a static trainer with a bicycle fitted to it, and an internet connection. Essentially, the equipment measures the power output (in watts) from a rider and transmits it to the e-cycling app, which then controls the rider's avatar in the virtual space. The rider can then see their behaviour on a screen. However, like many other sports, there are variations of this process, each of which has its own benefits and drawbacks. In short, the power data is handled by a static trainer, which is sometimes referred to as a 'turbo' or an 'erg'. There are four main types of static trainers. The most expensive and specialised are known as 'smart bikes', which look like conventional exercise bikes. They are heavier, adjustable, and more stable than other types of static bicycles. The second type is known as 'smart' trainers. These allow for the wheel of a conventional bicycle to be removed and for the chain to run over a conventional set of rear gear sprockets attached to the trainer. This is also known as a 'direct drive' trainer. The e-cycling app then sends information to the smart trainer to provide resistance to the cyclist depending on the kind of virtual terrain they are cycling over in terms of gradients and surfaces. Thirdly, some static trainers are known as 'wheel on', which require the bicycle to be mounted into it. Here, the rear wheel contacts a roller that dictates the resistance and can be controlled by the computer. However, the most affordable option is known as 'dumb' trainers, which do not provide resistance to the cyclist as the simulated terrain changes. These are also 'wheel on' based and may require the user to have a separate power meter to transmit data to the e-racing app being used. If a power meter is not available, some apps can apply their own algorithms to estimate the power output of the rider based on the rear wheel speed.

Other optional supplementary equipment may also include a fan to aid rider cooling, a gradient simulation device to help simulate gradients, rocker boards to simulate the free movement of a bicycle when ridden, and steering pivots to allow riders to actively steer (rather than have the app do this for them automatically).

From doping to cyber doping

Technology is a fundamental part of many sports. In some cases it is standardised and its subsequent impact may be small. However, in other cases, it has a significant role to play in optimising an athlete's performance. As a result, it would be a foolish athlete who marginalises or disregards its influence when its impact or needs may well be mutually exclusive to their physical training. The ethical behaviour of both the athlete and their stakeholders is crucial to the well-being and future of the sport itself. However, as the ethics of a sport can be philosophical and relative or subjective in nature, a tightly defined set of rules is needed for athletes to follow and to legally maximise their performance. A diagrammatic illustration of this approach for an athlete is shown in Figure 8.2.

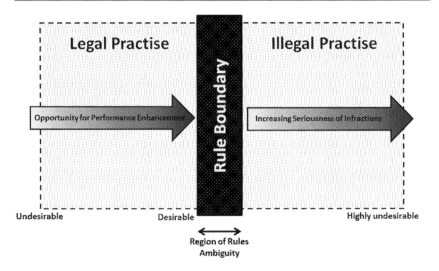

Figure 8.2 The goals of performance enhancement.

Once the boundaries of a rule are crossed, this is the point where an athlete has knowingly or unknowingly cheated. Cheating in sport, with or without the use of technology, is not a new phenomenon (Dyer, 2015). What is interesting is that if individuals participate in competitive sport to demonstrate their physical abilities and skills (Ring & Kavussanu, 2018), e-racing uniquely also offers the ability for someone to undertake it without fear of judgement or reprisal and in relative anonymity. Therefore, the level of temptation or incentive for athletes to cheat in e-racing is likely to increase as the potential rewards, such as prizes or their own achievements, also increase. The scale of rewards has increased to the extent that there is now more attractive prize money (Abanazir, 2019) or opportunities for employment in professional cycling teams (Anon,[2] 2021). This problem is compounded when cheaters either do not recognise that they are doing wrong or utilise their own criteria to morally justify their actions (Ring & Kavussanu, 2018). Ultimately, whilst the majority of e-races could be seen as recreational or of little significance, such corrupt practices create a 'slippery slope' that starts with sport rules being breached, sport ethics being infringed, and the sport integrity itself finally being jeopardised (Andreff, 2018).

Doping has traditionally been associated with the act of illicitly taking performance-enhancing drugs in sport in order to improve an athlete's performance. However, as cheating, doping, or ergogenics have been well established in traditional sports, it is wise to assume that virtual and esports are not immune to similar concerns and issues. Indeed, it has been suggested that cheating in online gaming is 'rampant' (Duh & Chen, 2009). Uniquely, esports has given rise to its own designated style of illicit performance enhancement, which is colloquially known as 'e-doping' (Dyer, 2020), digital doping, or 'cyber doping' (McIlroy et al., 2021). This unfair or illicit behaviour can be described as a user seeking to obtain an advantage over the software or other participants. Whilst it can be challenging to distinguish smart play (e.g. tactics) from cheating, Duh and Chen (2009) offered the following 15-point taxonomy of online games-based cheating:

- Cheating due to misplaced trust.
- Cheating by collusion.
- Cheating by abusing gaming procedures (e.g. leaving a game before a loss or fault is formally recorded).
- Cheating related to virtual assets.
- Cheating due to machine intelligence.
- Cheating via the graphics driver.
- Cheating by denying services to peer players.
- Timing cheating.
- Cheating by compromising passwords.
- Cheating due to lack of secrecy.
- Cheating due to lack of authentication.
- Cheating by exploiting a bug or loophole.
- Cheating by compromising game servers.
- Cheating related to internal misuse.
- Cheating by social engineering.

It has been suggested that cheating behaviour spreads via a social mechanism and that the number of cheater friends of a fair player correlates with the likelihood of the latter also becoming cheaters (Blackburn et al., 2014). These issues are compounded when gaming participants define the act of cheating differently, depending on their own experiences and understanding of the games and their boundaries (Vázquez & Consalvo, 2015). Therefore, it seems clear that if cheating in e-racing is not curtailed or forcibly reduced through the use of objective rules and suitable codes of conduct, e-doping will become more widespread, more ingrained, and more acceptable – thereby further hampering the credibility of e-cycling as a sport in its own right.

To try and prevent riders from cheating, some e-racing apps like Zwift have attempted to construct a series of rules and regulations for riders to adhere to when competing (Anon,[3] 2021). These rules cover guidance related to in-race performance verification, dual power-recording protocols, physical equipment requirements, equipment calibration protocols, pre-race rider checks (weight and height), disputes, participant eligibility, and the sport's overarching governance. However, these are only really applied to prominent events and not the full calendar of activities. The global governance body for cycling, the UCI, has also attempted to define the rules and regulations for cycling-based esports in general. These have a broader overview than those of a single e-racing app and consist of guidance on app provider responsibility, glossary and definitions of terms, participant eligibility, performance verifications, equipment, data management, and the athlete sanctioning process. However, like other forms of sport, athletes and participants may well investigate ways of circumnavigating the rules, exploiting any loopholes, or finding ways of concealing illegal acts (UCI, 2020).

The cyber-dopers

e-cycling has not been any more immune to the temptations of athletes seeking to gain unfair advantages in a digital environment than in everyday reality. This said, the lengths that some athletes who cheat are prepared to go to are quite novel. In 2019, the winner of the inaugural British Cycling eRacing Championships was later disqualified for manipulating their pre-race data (British Cycling, 2019). The rider was then charged with 'unsporting conduct' under clause 5 of its disciplinary code after obtaining an advantageous bicycle avatar on the Zwift e-cycling app. Bicycle avatars are typically awarded by reaching a target of virtual meters 'climbed' in the app. However, the athlete obtained the avatar by using artificially generated means rather than the rides or races they participated in Cyclingnews.com, 2019.

Alternatively, the manipulation of post-ride data has also seen riders formally sanctioned for cheating. In high-quality or high-profile races on Zwift, two methods of power data recording are often required. This typically involves the 'smart' trainer into which the bikes are mounted acting as one source, with an additional power meter acting as another. Both devices are expected to record the same power output of the rider in a defined tolerance level and to submit both files to Zwift for verification on request to ensure the athlete has not cheated. However, in 2020 two riders attempted to cheat by either submitting fabricated files or altering the raw data itself in an attempt to match the two files up (Maker, 2020).

How does an athlete cyber-dope?

So far, a consistent type and diversity of cyber-doping methods have been exposed. These can be summarised as:

- Avatar misrepresentation
- In-game deception
- Data manipulation
- Hardware manipulation

Other examples of cyber-doping methods are weight doping, height doping, post-event data file manipulation, sandbagging, power meter inaccuracy, falsely disclosed functional threshold power, dishonest gender assignment, intentional power miscalibration, dishonest inflation of power output through equipment, sticky watts, and data hacking.

Weight doping

Weight doping is one of the most publicised and criticised acts of e-cycling behaviour. Primarily, most e-racing apps require the user to enter their current bodyweight to help the virtual physics to operate and act on the rider's subsequent simulated riding. A lot of the simulated physics that are applied in a virtual environment are governed by a cyclist's power-to-weight ratio. This calculation is determined by the power being generated at a given moment divided by a rider's body mass (w/kg). As the platform simulates the physics of the outdoor environment, an increase in a rider's power-to-weight ratio means that they will ascend any inclines in the app faster. However, with no obvious way to check, it enables a rider to enter an inaccurate or dishonest value for their body mass. The temptation to do this is arguably high, as a rider's goals or results will ultimately be dictated by what is entered into the app, and the chances of being caught are comparatively low. Another associated issue is that it also depends on how accurate an e-racing platform requires the entered body mass to be in the first place. For example, if it only requires a rider to enter their body mass to the nearest kilogramme, or doesn't constrain *when* this mass is measured, it does not matter if the rider's true mass falls somewhere between two rounded values or accounts for their possible day-to-day variability. The irony is that it may take product solutions based on reality (such as real-time mass measurement) to mitigate the issues created in a simulated environment.

Height doping

Rather like weight doping, height doping is when a rider provides inaccurate or dishonest declarations about their height. In an e-racing app, like body mass, a rider's correct height is important because it influences the avatar's speed. In this case, the height influences their virtual *aerodynamic drag*. In the real world, a rider's drag coefficient is measured as their CdA. This is the relationship between their frontal area and a dimensionless number of their coefficient of aerodynamic drag (Debraux et al., 2011). The e-cycling app provides a generic CdA value based on the rider's entered height and is not individualised (Passfield et al., 2017). Undervaluing the height means that some apps will reduce the rider's virtual CdA to suit and thus reduce their resulting virtual wind resistance acting on an avatar. The result of this will either make an avatar move faster or make it easier to maintain the same speed for less effort than it should be in the simulated environment.

Post-event data file manipulation

When racing conventionally outdoors, riders' results are not primarily assessed on their power output but rather on who crosses the finishing line first. However, in the online environment it is predominantly a rider's power output that coordinates their avatar's behaviour and subsequent performance. This means that if a rider's performance is questioned, the app provider may then request the raw data file that the rider produced in their ride to validate or quality assure their performance. However, if there were any inaccuracies in the rider's physical equipment or if they intentionally cheated, they may decide to manipulate their data before submission to hide such errors.

'Sandbagging'

'Sandbagging' is a self-preservation strategy involving an athlete's feigned demonstration of ability or as a way of gaining a competitive edge over their opponents (Gibson & Sachau, 2000). In the case of e-racing, this is exhibited as a rider intentionally downgrading their ability, either in the selection of the event itself (i.e. choosing a race that is aimed below a rider's current ability) or their behaviour in it (by underperforming until a critical moment is reached). This provides the rider with the means to achieve a superior result in comparison to those they are competing against and who are likely to be unaware of the rider's hidden potential or true ability.

Power meter inaccuracy (accuracy, precision, single-sided PMs)

A power meter is essentially a method of translating a rider's applied physiological effort into a quantifiable value. In essence, a power meter calculates an output (measured in watts) as a result of the angular velocity multiplied by the torque (Passfield et al., 2017). However, whilst the accuracy and precision have been successfully validated against a range of products, there is plenty of scope for inaccuracy due to changes in environmental temperature, technical faults, poor calibration, and limb-to-limb asymmetry, whereas on the bicycle the power output is measured, as well as any relative differences in power output from product to product (Passfield et al., 2017). Some power meters only record the power output from one leg and then double this to determine the rider's power output, even though it is common for riders to have some degree of asymmetry in their leg power output. Again, this creates inaccuracy in a rider's ability. Even if all these issues are addressed, the reported accuracy of values recorded by power meters can still vary hugely from system to system (Gardner et al., 2004; Duc et al., 2007; Pallarés & Lillo-Bevia, 2018; Hoon et al., 2016). Additionally, the apps themselves will typically combine the power output of the rider with their own algorithm to calculate the in-game velocity (Passfield et al., 2017). This could mean that even after performing a self-calibration a cyclist's efforts may be somewhat different to those of others, since the trainers are not standardised in their design, function, or calibration.

All in all, this infers that a rider will use the equipment that is the most favourable to their on-screen avatar's performance, even if it is not the most accurate and reflective of the rider's actual physiological ability. Ultimately though, the main issue is that riding a bicycle outdoors is governed by the laws of physics, which cannot be cheated or negotiated with. However, indoor cycling's 'virtual physics' are governed exclusively by the power meter accuracy and precision – all of which are independent variables of the riders and require total honesty on the part of the athlete. With this in mind, it is not hard to see why cheating or inaccuracy are now issues of concern.

Falsely disclosed functional threshold power

Some e-racing apps categorise their events in terms of a rider's 'functional threshold power' (FTP). FTP is defined as the highest power output a cyclist can maintain in a quasi-steady state for approximately 60 minutes (Borszcz et al., 2018). Several e-racing apps then categorise riders using FTP (measured in watts) per body mass ratio (measured in kilogrammes). However, if a rider is dishonest about this power output, this could contribute to sandbagging or more obvious and overwhelming displays of rider ability.

Dishonest gender assignment

Whilst the designation of gender is the right of the individual, a more dishonest form of gender reassignment is where a male rider who still designates themselves as male in reality opts to be a female rider in the e-cycling app. Akin to sandbagging, their competitors will be unaware and unable to see that the rider they are competing against may have vastly different physical abilities or limitations relating to the physiological differences between sexes. They will appear on one screen as one gender but actually be another in reality.

Poor, drifting, or intentional power miscalibration

All power meters typically require pre-ride calibration or 'zero'ing' to be accurate, precise, and within their operating specifications. Whilst the calibration or zero offset process for power meters should give the user confidence that their equipment is ready for use, the ability of the power meter to do this accurately and with precision can still drift over time. This can be due to changes in ambient temperature, loads or any 'bedding in' taking place of the bicycle's physical components. Some trials have seen the drift due to temperature as high as 8% (Gardner et al., 2004), This would obviously stunt or change the rider's in-game performance over time or later on in a race. Some app users have suggested that a process of 'continuous calibration' would remove many of these errors.

Dishonest inflation of power output through equipment

Along with a rider's physiological metrics, such as height or weight, riders are required to set up their equipment by entering the right user settings into the smart trainer, power meter, or the equipment being used. For example, if a rider intentionally enters a different crank length for their bicycle into a static trainer, this (depending on how the trainer calculates the power output) could lead to an inflation in the calculated power output. Likewise, using a crank-based power meter and non-round chainrings has also been shown to inflate a rider's power output due to recording errors (Anhalt, 2013). Finally, most smart trainers use a 'coast down' procedure to ensure the trainer's operating accuracy. If that process is intervened in any way by the user, it could cause the power readings to be too high or low and affect the in-game avatar performance.

'Sticky watts'

It could be assumed that regardless of which e-racing app a cyclist uses, the basic process of communication between the two remains the same, i.e. the rider obtains a power output, transmits it to the app, the app receives it, and their avatar responds accordingly. However, there have been occasions where transmission lag or reception delay creates an effect colloquially known as 'sticky watts'. This occurs when a power output of a given magnitude continues to be applied to an avatar when the cyclist has stopped applying the same power output in reality. Although this effect could be seen as a glitch or of little consequence, it has been harnessed by e-racers as a way of obtaining a tactical advantage. For example, in the Zwift app, a rider can assume an aerodynamically advantageous downhill riding position known as a 'supertuck'. This is achieved when a certain virtual velocity is reached that allows them to keep up with other riders, thus assuming an advantageous on-screen riding position. If the rider can apply a huge surge in power and then immediately stop pedalling (and does this at a velocity that will allow them to assume this 'supertuck' position), their power output may 'stick' for a few seconds, thereby allowing their avatar to obtain a huge boost in velocity that they did not actually achieve. Ultimately, the quality and type of internet connection can radically affect whether the sticky watt phenomenon can occur. This could also be due to the type of power meter used by the e-racer (Schlange, 2020).

Data hacking

In 2019 it was suggested that the data in e-cycling apps could be 'hacked' or see its app-to-rider transmission intercepted by computer coding, signal analysers, or viral interventions (Yeager, 2019). This would allow a rider to improve their ranking to qualify for higher profile events, obtain unrealistic simulated riding velocities, or win events by manipulating the raw power output data without having to ride the bicycle at all.

Simulation or illustration?

Whilst it has been shown that there are several ways of fraudulently or dishonestly enhancing an e-cyclist's performance, there are also ergogenic effects or technological interventions that could be legally harnessed by the e-racer. As most future improvements in sport are grounded in technology (Balmer et al., 2012), it would seem prudent for athletes to pursue any legal mechanical ergogenic advantages available to them. However, this pursuit raises the question of whether the virtual environment should simulate exactly what is being undertaken by the athlete in reality or not. For example, optimising the core body temperature of an athlete has been shown to be performance enhancing (González-Alonso et al., 1999) by using fans, specific clothing (Davis & Bishop, 2013), or ice vests (Luomala et al., 2012), all of which are not seen or visible in the virtual environment. Furthermore, the avatar does not recognise or illustrate how the power output is actually generated by the athlete in reality, despite the fact that a subtle adjustment in saddle height and position can affect the cyclist's net power production (Peveler, 2008). At which point, whilst arguably disingenuous, there is nothing to stop the cyclist from optimising their physical bicycle geometry to maximise their power production on screen. Their prime concern simply becomes the physical production of power on screen, not how they achieve it in reality. Ultimately, then, the philosophical question that should be addressed is whether an e-cycling app is intended to simulate an athlete actually cycling in reality, or whether it is only concerned with the performance of the avatar in the simulation.

How do we assess performance enhancement?

As virtual bicycle riding and racing is such a new, exciting, and rapidly evolving sporting activity, sports custodians often have to keep up with any unwanted cyber doping once the methods are in circulation. An obvious question to ask here is how any cyber doping could and should be policed when so much of the in-app behaviour relies on the goodwill and honest conduct of its users? Much of this is currently addressed by riders providing evidence of the measurement of both their height and weight and their use of multiple power meters to record their physiological performances. Furthermore, many of the problems relating to the measurement drift of both trainers and power meters could be tackled by some kind of continuous calibration, rather than a singular event of calibration that takes place prior to the athlete starting their ride. However, these will only resolve one-off or short-term occurrences. To create a more long-term solution, this sport may require more extreme measures, such as 'digital performance passports' that in effect replicate the principles of the 'biological passport' already in use in professional cycling (Zorzoli & Rossi, 2010). This 'passport' tracks an athlete's physiological markers over time and can indicate when performance-enhancing drugs are used, thereby providing the means to actually profile an athlete. However, this is logistically demanding for any app platform, with literally thousands of riders now undertaking e-racing. Either way, what this exciting new form of sport has highlighted is that Duh and Chen's framework of digital cheating (2009) should now be expanded with the acknowledgement and addition of the *abuse of physical assets* outside a game or app and not just the digital information. In the end, as with many other sports and technologies, the solution will be one of constant and eternal vigilance. We as a species seem perpetually motivated to be the best that we can be, sometimes at dubious costs. The arenas that we are now willing to do this in have extended from the real world to the virtual domain.

References

Abanazir, C. (2019). Institutionalisation in esports. *Sport, Ethics and Philosophy*, 13(2), 117–131.

Andreff, W. (2018). Different types of manipulation in sport. In M. Breuer & D. Forrest (Eds.), *The Palgrave handbook on the economics of manipulation in sport* (pp. 13–35). Palgrave Macmillan.

Anhalt, T. (2013). *What's up with those funky rings…?* https://bikeblather.blogspot.com/2013/01/whats-up-with-those-funky-rings.html

Anon[1]. (2018). *Chuck Wurster, the man behind RacerMate and CompuTrainer, dies at 86.* https://www.bicycleretailer.com/industry-news/2018/12/23/chuck-wurster-man-behind-racermate-and-computrainer-dies-86#.YK-BKLdKjhc

Anon[2]. (2021). *How to win a WorldTour contract on Zwift.* https://www.cyclingweekly.com/news/latest-news/how-to-win-a-worldtour-contract-on-zwift-495955

Anon[3]. (2021). *Cycling esports rules and regulations.* https://content-cdn.zwift.com/uploads/2021/03/Cycling-Esports-Ruleset-v1.0.6.docx-2.pdf

Balmer, N., Pleasence, P., & Nevill, A. (2012). Evolution and revolution: Gauging the impact of technological and technical innovation on Olympic performance. *Journal of Sports Sciences*, 30(11), 1075–1083.

Blackburn, J., Kourtellis, N., Skvoretz, J., Ripeanu, M., & Iamnitchi, A. (2014). Cheating in online games: A social network perspective. *ACM Transactions on Internet Technology (TOIT)*, 13(3), 1–25.

Borszcz, F., Tramontin, A., Bossi, A., Carminatti, L., & Costa, V. (2018). Functional threshold power in cyclists: Validity of the concept and physiological responses. *International Journal of Sports Medicine*, 39(10), 737–742.

British Cycling. (2019). *British Cycling has upheld a charge of unsporting conduct in the British Cycling eRacing championships, under clause 5 of our disciplinary code.* https://www.britishcycling.org.uk/about/article/20191004-Charge-of-Unsporting-Conduct-in-the-2019-British-Cycling-eRacing-Championships-statement-0

Cyclingnews. (2019). *British eracing champion banned for cheating.* https://www.cyclingnews.com/news/british-eracing-champion-banned-for-cheating/#:~:text=British%20Cycling%20has%20been%20forced,equipment%20in%20the%20Zwift%20platform

Davis, J. K., & Bishop, P. A. (2013). Impact of clothing on exercise in the heat. *Sports Medicine*, 43(8), 695–706.

Debraux, P., Grappe, F., Manolova, A. V., & Bertucci, W. (2011). Aerodynamic drag in cycling: Methods of assessment. *Sports Biomechanics*, 10(3), 197-218. DOI: 10.1080/14763141.2011.592209

Duc, S., Villerius, V., Bertucci, W., & Grappe, F. (2007). Validity and reproducibility of the Ergomo® Pro power meter compared with the SRM and PowerTap power meters. *International Journal of Sports Physiology and Performance*, 2(3), 270–281.

Duh, H. B. L., & Chen, V. H. H. (2009, July). Cheating behaviors in online gaming. In *International conference on online communities and social computing* (pp. 567–573). Springer. https://link.springer.com/chapter/10.1007/978-3-642-02774-1_61

Dyer, B. (2015). The controversy of sports technology: A systematic review. *SpringerPlus*, 4(1), 1–12.

Dyer, B. T. (2020). Cycle E-racing: Simulation or a new frontier in sports technology? *International Journal of Esports*, 1(1). https://www.ijesports.org/article/38/html

Gardner, A. S., Stephens, S., Martin, D. T., Lawton, E., Lee, H., & Jenkins, D. (2004). Accuracy of SRM and power tap power monitoring systems for bicycling. *Medicine and Science in Sports and Exercise*, 36(7), 1252–1258.

Gibson, B., & Sachau, D. (2000). Sandbagging as a self-presentational strategy: Claiming to be less than you are. *Personality and Social Psychology Bulletin*, 26(1), 56–70.

González-Alonso, J., Teller, C., Andersen, S. L., Jensen, F. B., Hyldig, T., & Nielsen, B. (1999). Influence of body temperature on the development of fatigue during prolonged exercise in the heat. *Journal of Applied Physiology*, 86(3), 1032–1039.

Hoon, M. W., Michael, S. W., Patton, R. L., Chapman, P. G., & Areta, J. L. (2016). A comparison of the accuracy and reliability of the wahoo KICKR and SRM power meter. *Journal of Science and Cycling*, 5(3), 11–15.

Luomala, M. J., Oksa, J., Salmi, J. A., Linnamo, V., Holmér, I., Smolander, J., & Dugué, B. (2012). Adding a cooling vest during cycling improves performance in warm and humid conditions. *Journal of Thermal Biology*, 37(1), 47–55.

Macdonald, J. S. (1913). Studies in the heat-production associated with muscular work. (Preliminary communication: Section A.—Methods; section B.—Results.). *Proceedings of the Royal Society of London. Series B, Containing Papers of a Biological Character*, 87(593), 96–112.

Maker, R. (2020). *Zwift bans two pro racers for altering data: An explainer of sorts*. https://www.dcrainmaker.com/2020/11/zwift-bans-two-pro-racers-for-altering-data-an-explainer-of-sorts.html

McIlroy, B., Passfield, L., Holmberg, H. C., & Sperlich, B. (2021). Virtual training of endurance cycling–A summary of strengths, weaknesses, opportunities and threats. *Frontiers in Sports and Active Living*, 3, 31.

Pallarés, J. G., & Lillo-Bevia, J. R. (2018). Validity and reliability of the PowerTap P1 pedals power meter. *Journal of Sports Science & Medicine*, 17(2), 305.

Passfield, L., Hopker, J. G., Jobson, S., Friel, D., & Zabala, M. (2017). Knowledge is power: Issues of measuring training and performance in cycling. *Journal of Sports Sciences*, 35(14), 1426–1434.

Peveler, W. W. (2008). Effects of saddle height on economy in cycling. *The Journal of Strength & Conditioning Research*, 22(4), 1355–1359.

Ring, C., & Kavussanu, M. (2018). The impact of achievement goals on cheating in sport. *Psychology of Sport and Exercise*, 35, 98–103.

Schlange. (2020, Dec 3). *Sticky watts: An introduction*. https://zwiftinsider.com/sticky-watts/

Supriyanto, C., & Liu, B. (2021). Virtual cycling for promoting a healthy lifestyle. *International Journal of Science, Technology & Management*, 2(1), 60–71.

UCI. (2020). *UCI cycling esports regulations*. https://www.uci.org/docs/default-source/rules-and-regulations/11.12-uci-cycling-esports-regulations-en-22.01.2020.pdf

Vázquez, I. S., & Consalvo, M. (2015). Cheating in social network games. *New Media & Society*, 17(6), 829–844.

Wagner, M. G. (2006, June). On the scientific relevance of e-Sports. In *Proceedings of the 2006 International Conference on Internet Computing & Conference on Computer Games Development* (pp. 437–442). CSREA Press.

Yeager, S. (2019). *Zwift hackers expose the next generation of cycling doping.* https://www.bicycling.com/news/a28912281/zwift-hacking/

Zorzoli, M., & Rossi, F. (2010). Implementation of the biological passport: The experience of the international cycling union. *Drug Testing and Analysis, 2*(11–12), 542–547.

Part IV
Diversity and inclusion

Chapter 9

Understanding the potential for esports to support social inclusion agendas

Emily Hayday and Holly Collison

Introduction

Peacekeeping and social development projects utilise *sport* or *play* to attract and engage individuals, targeted populations, and communities through a shared activity in order to achieve wider social, personal, and societal outcomes. The 'Sport for Development and Peace' (SDP) sector has driven this global agenda at the policymaking, advocacy, and practitioner levels for over two decades (Kidd, 2008). Social inclusion has been a pillar of the SDP movement and is embedded in the United Nations Sustainable Development Goals (SDGs), which provides a clear alignment between the strategic use of sport to achieve goals and the capacity of sport to bring vulnerable, marginal, fractured, and diverse groups together.

Social inclusion, and its role in developing social capital, are often outlined as a desirable and overarching outcome of SDP programming, while community sport has been recognised as a way of improving social connection and inclusion for marginalised groups (Coalter, 2007; Dagkas & Armour, 2012). For example, Schulenkorf identified that inter-community sports events can create pathways to social inclusion, act as a catalyst for developing diversified communities, and offer an inclusive environment for social change (2010). Morgan et al. (2019) suggest that participation in community sport enhances social inclusion in multiple ways and provides opportunities to create socially inclusive spaces.

Philip et al.'s recent research on SDP in 'caste ridden India' concludes that soccer facilitated direct intergroup contact opportunities and created meaningful opportunities for social interaction by removing physical barriers in the community (2021). For the SDP sector, sport offers a contextually flexible method for bringing communities together and encourages participation in sport to enhance relationship building, social capital, and the development of soft skills (Van der Veken et al., 2020). However, the critical question remains of whether in today's digitalised world traditional sport is the most suitable or effective 'hook', especially given the popularity and development of online spaces and the video gaming culture (Heere, 2018).

Esports, which can be simply defined as competitive video gaming, is one of the fastest-growing entertainment industries in the world, with audiences

DOI: 10.4324/9781003258650-13

predicted to reach 640 million in 2025 (including occasional viewers and esports enthusiasts). Global esports revenues are anticipated to reach $1.38 billion in 2022 and are forecasted to reach $1.8 billion by 2025 (Tristão, 2022). Esports has become a 'fundamental element in today's digital youth culture' (Wagner, 2006, p. 1) and engagement in esports offers an opportunity for a globally connected space for action through SDP.

Despite a growing body of literature highlighting the potential of sport to support social inclusion goals, Sherry warns that inclusion is a complex outcome to achieve and that there are many challenges and potential social and cultural barriers to overcome (2010). In particular, it is recognised that sport can also perpetuate social exclusion, as access may be restricted for certain groups in society based on, for example, gender, race, religion, and sexual orientation (Bailey, 2005; Spaaij et al., 2014). With this in mind, we suggest an innovative approach to mitigate and counter some of the conditions that threaten social inclusion in physical sport environments.

Esports and social inclusion

In this chapter, we explore how esports, through its unique characteristics and commercial positioning, can act as a new strategy to enhance social inclusion and social development outcomes, especially for youth populations that are often the target of SDP programmes. To do this we apply the social inclusion framework developed by Bailey (2005, 2008), which consists of the following four connected sites of inclusion:

1) Spatial: social inclusion relates to the proximity and the closing of social and economic distances.
2) Relational: social inclusion is defined in terms of a sense of belonging and acceptance.
3) Functional: social inclusion relates to the enhancement of knowledge, skills, and understanding.
4) Power: social inclusion assumes a change in the locus of control.

Bailey's (2005) framework aligns with the ideological foundations of the SDP movement, which aims:

> to bring people together from diverse economic and social backgrounds through a shared activity or interest which is intrinsically valuable (spatial); create or incite a sense of belonging and acceptance of others, irrespective of differences (relational); offer opportunities for the enhancement and development of skills, knowledge, and competencies (functional); and increase social networks, civic pride, and community cohesion to enhance community capital (power).
>
> (Hayday & Collison, 2020, p. 200)

Looking beyond the purist perspective of sport and traditional SDP practices, we examine three key development priorities as suggested sites of esports implementation to enhance social inclusion. Firstly, a unique component of esports is the notion of *space* in the form of a geographically unconstrained global platform at a virtual level for individuals to interact with potential to produce *inclusive environments*. Secondly, esports communities encourage and produce strong social opportunities for interaction, bonding, and *building social capital* (Martončik, 2015; Trepte et al., 2012). Importantly, both the provision of space and social engagement align directly to the *spatial* (closing social and economic distances), *relational* (sense of belonging and acceptance), and *power* (change in the locus of control) dimensions of social inclusion (Bailey, 2005). Finally, we explore the potential for esports in *educational* contexts and its implications for the *functional* (enhancement of skills, knowledge, and understanding) and *power* dimensions of social inclusion. Education is a cornerstone of SDP programming, and individuals who engage in video gaming have been shown to be more computer literate (Appel, 2012). Therefore, a strategic opportunity exists for esports to promote science, technology, engineering, and mathematics (STEM) education and expose individuals to digital careers like animation, sound engineering, video and graphic design, game development, and casting, many of which are fundamental to the successful functioning of the esports industry (Loat, 2021).

Esports community building and inclusive spaces

Esports constructs a global platform and space for youth communities to engage and interact that is not limited by physical or geographical boundaries. This promotes an inclusive environment (*space*), which typically has minimal entry barriers. In contrast to many traditional sports, advances in mobile technology are improving esports accessibility. Creating a space for interaction and social bonding leads to opportunities for social inclusion and the development of social capital over time. Bailey notes that social inclusion 'relates to proximity and closing of social and economic distances' (2008, p. 89). Access and inclusivity are created through the virtual esports *space*, which is removed from real-world stigmas. This makes esports a more inviting environment to many individuals in that competition is blind, thus alleviating some of the physical and social challenges experienced by marginalised populations. From a philosophical perspective, the value and role of *space* and safe environments, both virtual and physical, close the social distance by providing individuals with opportunities for interaction. *Spatial* inclusion is the first step to social inclusion, and once this is achieved there is a potential for other social inclusion dimensions (i.e. *functional*, *relational*, and *power*) to occur (Donnelly & Coakley, 2002).

Safe *spaces* provide meaningful and sustained interactions, which may evolve into the development and formation of communities both within and across multiple contexts. This component of *relational* inclusion provides individuals with a sense of belonging, acknowledgement, and social acceptance (Bailey, 2008).

The notion of community is often used in relation to place, *space*, identity, the establishment of boundaries and difference, or, in more philosophical terms, the symbolic or imagined construction of community extending the fixed, immediate, or shared geographical setting (see Amit & Rapport, 2002; Anderson, 1983; Delanty, 2003).

The community ideal is central to the objective and ethos of the SDP rhetoric. Community is broadly provided as the essential implementation *space*; a goal to achieve for the purpose of local empowerment, sustainability, and peace and an ideal that is assumed to universally connect others in the creation of oneness or nationhood. Sport fits seamlessly into the ideal of community building to achieve non-sporting development goals. This is evident throughout the policy and development discourse. Schulenkorf and colleagues warn 'how the multiple theorizations and interpretations of community found within academic literature are reproduced and literally played out – but also contested, challenged, rejected and reformulated – in the practice of SDP' (2014, p. 385). In esports, the production of communities is highly valued and seen as the centre of esports development. However, the fragmented nature of the industry (genres, formats, playing modes) has resulted in tribal-like tensions between esports communities, which must be accounted for (Hayday et al., 2021).

In the context of *space* and community building, even though current realities, cultures, and limited governance in esports cast doubt on the potential for such online spaces to act as a solution to exclusion, hypermasculinity, and dominance, research has indicated that esports has the 'ideological foundations' to support sport development agendas (Hayday & Collison, 2020, p. 206). Although current tensions exist, esports fundamentally offers a space that can bring people together and provide an inclusive environment, and we suggest that inter-sectoral involvement could be considered as a way of improving the regulatory structures and frameworks, thereby bridging the gap between the ideological and current realties in esports (Hayday & Collison, 2020).

Building social bonds and relational inclusion through esports

The *relational* dimension of social inclusion is also understood as the development and growth of social bonds (Maxwell et al., 2013). An individual's interest in and reasons for participating in esports move beyond competition, with the achievement of individual life goals and relationship building with teammates acknowledged as key motives (Martončik, 2015). Whalen (2013) exposed some remarkable similarities between social opportunities in esports and traditional sport. For example, meeting and interacting with other gamers appeared to be the most significant aspect of a tournament experience. Social engagement is evidenced across all levels of esports (in professional/amateur and online/offline contexts), with participants forming new bonds with peers through the safety and anonymity of the interconnected virtual environment (Trepte et al., 2012,

p. 832). Furthermore, there is some indication that this extends to spectator populations, especially those who are new to the sport. Previous research suggests that audiences are drawn to watching matches together to develop understanding, learning, and social cognition, thus connecting participation and spectating with broader social practices (Rambusch et al., 2017).

Community capital can take many forms: 'sport contributes to social inclusion … to the extent that it increases individuals' sense of control over their lives, as well as "community capital" by extending social networks, increased community cohesion and civic pride' (Bailey, 2008, p. 90). In the esports capital of South Korea, there are esports and gaming cafés known as PC Bangs. These have proved to be social communal hubs in that they allow participants and spectators to manoeuvre between online and offline environments. Therefore, relationships are constructed in multiple forms as individuals move from indirect to direct contact (Chee, 2006; Huhh, 2008). Globally, the physical and virtual community manifestation of esports takes the form of LAN (local area network) parties that can range in size from local to national gatherings and where participants come together motivated by social contact to play both face-to-face and online (Jansz & Martens, 2005). Through the common interest in esports, individuals are attracted to these community gatherings because they provide a sense of belonging and acceptance (*relational*) and at the same time reduce the social and economic distance between groups (*spatial*).

Esports is often regarded as a virtual pursuit, but this common assumption is unfounded. As indicated earlier, the physical spaces of play and spectatorship are equal parts of the esports culture and movement. Physical connections and playing formats heighten the opportunity for social interaction, inclusion, and community building, which in turn provide an environment and opportunity suitable for SDP agendas. In the United Kingdom (UK), the playing format 'Belong' by GAME has 26 venues, all of which create physical spaces for gamers of all abilities to come together to compete and socialise (Belong, 2022).

The implications of this are twofold. Firstly, other industries and sectors are already starting to understand the appeal and opportunities that esports can provide and are responding by diversifying their spaces and products. Secondly, this could indicate a possible shift in the traditional esports culture and mechanisms through which people usually engage. Esports brings individuals together through a shared interest at a *spatial* level, which reduces social and economic distance. More accessible social opportunities for wider audiences help to extend networks, build community capital, and indicate a change in the locus of control (*power* dimension), thus providing an opportunity for esports to be considered as a social development tool through which social inclusion could be achieved for more diverse populations.

When considering the personal and social outcomes associated with esports, there is evidence to suggest that esteem and emotional support are constructed (*functional* dimension) by in-game interactions in a competitive digital context (Freeman & Wohn, 2017). Esports offers a platform through which social bridging and bonding capital can be encouraged and formed, thereby contributing to the *relational* and *power* dimensions of social inclusion (Bailey, 2005; Freiler, 2001). Importantly, the ties that are developed between participants online often continue and extend to offline activities as individuals build global friendships and communities (Trepte et al., 2012). It is this extension beyond the virtual, transitioning from global to local through physical engagement, that provides the rationale and significant potential for application in the SDP landscape.

Functional inclusion: education through esports

The *functional* dimension of social inclusion is closely related to the process of learning and education and assumes that participation allows individuals to develop their competencies and acquire new skills and knowledge (Bailey, 2005, 2008). In the context of SDP, education is perceived as a core element of the role of sport to challenge and raise awareness about social and personal concerns. Aligning to SDG4, 'Ensure Inclusive and Equitable Quality Education and Promote Lifelong Learning Opportunities for All' (UN, n.d., global leaders have developed their agendas to intersect the role of sport with achieving this crucial aim. VanderKlashorst (2018) claims that a central and unique characteristic of sport in development contexts is the involvement of marginalised and often unemployed youth and their access to organisational practices. This suggests a natural and logical fit for esports to be utilised as a new method of engagement in SDP practices.

Esports provides opportunities for youth to develop their *functional* capacities, with research showing league participation resulting in organic learning opportunities, including social-emotional learning, critical analysis, and communication skills (Cho et al., 2019). Hilvoorde and Pot (2016) acknowledge the value of esports under suitable educational supervision as a tool for developing specific elements of digital literacy. Esports is increasingly being used in schools to not only enhance motor skills and tactical and cognitive development but also to reveal possible career pathways (Anderson et al., 2021; Hilvoorde & Pot, 2016).

In the education sector, projects such as the Digital Schoolhouse aim to bridge the gap between industry and education via esports activities and play-based learning. The UK-based project has supported 9,605 teachers, engaged 103,576 students, and involved 52 partner schools. Annually, this programme culminates in a national tournament focused on personal skills development and raising employment aspirations across esports and STEM subjects (Digital Schoolhouse, 2022). Developing the educational competencies of these young people contributes to the *power* and *functional* dimensions of social inclusion. Esports thus enables these populations to broaden their experiences and skills in new areas and to cultivate their sense of individual agency.

In the United States, esports is used to capture the interests of disengaged groups in Southern California through the Orange County High School

Esports League, which consists of 25 schools. In this case esports provides an outlet for young people who are otherwise absent and uninvested in the school environment (Reames, 2018), thus engaging with disempowered individuals to achieve wider educational and *functional* outcomes. Due to esports interventions, these students stay longer in school, participate in educational activities, and socially and educationally engage with the school environment (Reames, 2018). Through esports, a more inclusive environment has been constructed through the *relational* dimension of social inclusion by increasing a specific student population's feeling of acknowledgement and sense of belonging (Bailey, 2008).

Any activity that aims to engage youth populations must consider the parental perspective and their involvement and influence. One esports champion's mother indicated that: 'Parents are struggling with the comparative newness of the digital age and how swiftly everything is changing. But new doesn't have to be bad and technology isn't going to go away' (Carol Bird quoted in British Esports Association, 2018). Increased awareness and education are needed for parents, carers, and educational stakeholders to understand the value, benefits, and associated potential risks of esports (British Esports Association, 2019). In the educational examples given earlier, new theories of change, innovative approaches, and programmes are delivered within traditional practices, institutions, and settings that demonstrate the opportunities and potential of esports.

Reflecting on esports's potential to support social inclusion

The SDP sector consists of organisations tackling a broad range of issues from social inclusion and empowerment to gender equality and education. The contextual flexibility of sport has been critically appraised, yet limited, to sport's adoption of particular issues. For example, in South Africa's Cape Town, surfing is commonplace and makes an appropriate intervention tool in ways that would not be possible in non-coastal areas (Thorpe, 2014). To this end, esports has the potential to change the possibilities in SDP due to its social dexterity, geographical versatility, and physical inclusivity.

Esports approaches the SDP sector with the same development capabilities that have been utilised by Action Sports. To illustrate, we draw on the notable work of Thorpe and her examination of Action Sports for Development and Peacebuilding (2014). Considering new forms of social engagement in the context of SDP, Thorpe explored the transformative potential of transnational (action) sport in relation to its connections, networks, and mobilities. With this in mind, the effects of belonging to a transnational sporting movement or culture, like esports, not only construct global connections and networks but also have the potential to positively impact local community social engagements and future transformations. Thorpe claims that 'virtual and imaginative (im)mobilities are informing contemporary youth's participation in, and consumption of, sport and physical culture, as well as their understandings of place, space, identity and belonging' (2014, p. 265). Action Sport was considered and seen as a way of modernising SDP, staying relevant, and connecting to younger generations (Thorpe & Wheaton, 2011).

Action Sport and esports share several characteristics. For example, they are connected by global shifts in popularity and the engagement of youth, as well as there being tension, resistance, and intrigue as to how and whether they form part of society's 'traditional' view of sport. However, new and innovative approaches (Action Sport or esports) do not necessarily provoke a shift in the diversity, equality, and existing negative cultures that are present in mainstream sport. Traditional sports bring with them culturally embedded stigmas and biases that act as barriers to achieving some of the social outcomes they intend to solve. For example, football is a typically male-dominated sport, which means that a gender empowerment programme through football would naturally have built-in barriers due to the subsequent environmental contexts that interface with the sport (Chawansky, 2011; Saavedra, 2009).

Research suggests that in their infancy, both Action Sport and esports attract narrow participant bases, formed by similar social-cultural attributes (Taylor, 2017; Thorpe & Wheaton, 2011). Wheaton and Thorpe (2018) indicate that Action Sport does not necessarily face the burden of historical and individualised sexism that is seen in other sports, thus potentially offering an alternative for gender relations, which in turn provides encouragement for esports. Furthermore, although esports communities have displayed instances of toxicity, gender misogyny, and discrimination, there is an opportunity to create an inclusive environment through an esports format.

Esports's virtual framing offers a *space* that removes the conditions for discrimination (whether by gender, age, religion, language etc.), as it is characterised by a playing environment that is digitally standardised. This means that an individual's performance is realised through a digital representation (avatars and characters) and is removed from the individual physical self. There are no performance and ability differences between digital characters beyond the aesthetical differences that the characters can assume, so equality is not only assumed but actively realised. This is attractive to individuals and groups who may feel marginalised or excluded from more traditional sporting pursuits and provides an implementation mechanism for SDP programming that can be inclusive in its offering and engagement.

Esports is intrinsically gender neutral due to the reduced physical capabilities approach in the virtual format. Therefore, esports has the potential to operate in the absence of traditional gender stereotypes and disparity, despite real-world gender stigmas having influenced its uptake and the diversity of participation (Hayday et al., 2021; Kim, 2017; Ruvalcaba et al., 2018). There are already signs of female participation initiatives that aim to enhance diversity and female agency and address hypermasculinity in the industry (Any Key, 2022; GirlGamers, 2022; Women in Games, 2022). In this regard, Hayday and Collison (2020) have suggested that esports has the genuine integral foundations to form inclusive practices through its potential to encapsulate the *sport for all* ideal.

Esports faces many of the same challenges and issues that are present in mainstream sport, although its social inclusion dimensions provide its unique function as a genuine pursuit to be considered. Welfare concerns (DiFrancisco-Donoghue et al., 2019; Holden et al., 2018; Macey & Hamari, 2018), development (British Esports Association, 2019; Kim, 2017), and governance (Abarbanel & Johnson, 2018; Abanazir, 2018; Peng et al., 2020) are all acknowledged. These issues need to be recognised and explored if esports is to be adopted as a social development tool. Even though these challenges will evolve as the industry develops and matures, they must be minimised where possible, especially if esports is to be formally endorsed by the global development and sporting community.

Is esports a new bridge between the sports industry and SDP?

As the SDP movement has formalised and become highly institutionalised, a gap remains between the professional sports industry and the SDP sector. However, in recent years professional sports organisations have seen the value of SDP and integrated it into their community-based philanthropic efforts (Qatar Foundation, 2021). The sustainability of SDP and Sport for Development (SfD) spaces is a concern, especially given the volatile global economic climate, which is why SfD hybrids and the integration of SfD across industries (including professional sports organisations) have been proposed as a solution (Raw et al., 2021).

The rise of esports and its growing commercial potential has led to many professional sports teams investing in and creating their own esports teams. COVID-19 accelerated this, in that when live sport was paused many sports organisations looked to digital environments to engage with their audiences during a time of social restriction. Through esports, many sports organisations were able to offer a form of competitive entertainment to fans that was utilised as a form of brand extension (Ke & Wagner, 2020). As sports organisations invest in esports teams or build their own, esports has a chance to evolve beyond its commercial potential and act as a bridge between the professional sports industry and the SDP sector moving forward (as a hybrid model).

Just as traditional sports look to esports to enhance their relevance and engagement with youth audiences, esports could learn from the mainstream sport sector. Esports is at a burgeoning stage of development, with a current focus on stabilising its business models and associated legal and economic infrastructures. Yet, the traditional sport industry has already undergone this transition from amateur to professional and discovered its potential and application to other non-sporting sectors. This means that key insights into areas such as governance, legitimacy, regulation, and corporate social responsibly (CSR) could be utilised by the esports industry.

On the surface, esports as a mechanism for development cannot discriminate, exclude, or judge individuals, and this should be its appeal to the SDP sector. With the understanding that 'in community sport settings social norms may act as barriers to participation' (Maxwell et al., 2013, p. 469), esports is an unrealised opportunity for impact. Critical concerns in the SDP global agenda highlight inclusion, gender empowerment, and education as primary objectives (Kidd, 2008), and we have demonstrated throughout this chapter the potential of esports to act and achieve in these core areas. Esports speaks to the critical analysis and commentary embedded in SDP enquiry and exploration, specifically the distractions and discrimination based on the physical dimension of sport that is pacified by esports's anonymity in the virtual setting. As the esports industry evolves and expands it has the potential to be the cornerstone of a new strand of SDP due to its unique social properties and dimensions.

Social inclusion, esports, and SDP in practice

The versatility of esports is a result of the numerous forms it can take. When factoring in diverse titles, multiple game formats (online, multiplayer offline, competitive tournaments etc.) and different consoles (PC, Xbox, PlayStation, Wii etc.), alongside the growing importance of mobile esports, bespoke interventions can be designed and tailored to the individual needs and social concerns of diverse communities identified by SDP stakeholders and practitioners. To demonstrate the diversity of esports, it is important to understand the consumer (both participant and spectator) dynamics. Individuals who are attracted to esports are drawn to distinct game titles. *FIFA*, *League of Legends*, or *Call of Duty*, to name a few popular game titles, all have distinctly unique fan bases that are extremely loyal to their respective titles. As such, grouping all esports fans together would be short-sighted. The nuance and variety of interest in esports are akin to the differences between individuals interested in golf, rugby, or athletics, and should not be overlooked. It is this variety, and the subsequent difference in game dynamics that each title brings, that forms part of esports's appeal.

This versatility makes esports highly functional in its ability to deliver successful outcomes in both the Global North and the Global South. With vastly differing contextual issues between these communities, only a few sports have been able to successfully intervene across the spectrum and function in the absence of cultural and historical baggage. In the Global North, for example, an esports programme may offer a safe space for youth to address mental health issues, with esports acting as the engagement tool through which social bonding, inclusive interaction, and specialist support could be provided. Conversely, in the Global South, a space to play esports could represent neutral ground to promote social cohesion, inclusion, and integration for youth from conflicting ethnic groups. Presently an esports intervention is more likely to be successful in the Global North because there is a stronger physical, technological, and sociocultural infrastructure to support an esports intervention. However, esports is predicated on the competitive element of video games, and as most games have an offline function the competitive element can still be delivered despite not having online access.

SDP organisations have historically struggled with local capacity issues and short-term economic cycles. Due to the competitive nature of funding, local SDP programmes and organisations have limited abilities and capacities to generate revenue and fundraising (Hambrick et al., 2019; Kidd, 2008; Svensson et al., 2018). This has resulted in the growth and dependence of external partnerships with multiple stakeholder networks across the private and public sectors to overcome these challenges (Coalter, 2010; Giulianotti et al., 2016). This presents a viable opportunity for SDP organisations to utilise and benefit from the growing and economically lucrative esports industry and its emerging CSR agendas.

CSR in esports offering strategic alignment with SDP

Sport has been used as part of CSR strategies for some time and is often seen as a vital source of funding for social change initiatives (Levermore, 2010). Many corporations have a global dimension to their CSR. This is often referred to as corporate global citizenship and encompasses the areas of philanthropy and partnership forming to tackle social issues (Waddock & Smith, 2000). This could provide an opportunity and inevitable CSR rationale for the dynamic and growing global attraction of esports. Whilst global policy adoption and advocacy have continued to strengthen and leverage the use of sport in development contexts, funding is a continual concern, for which CSR may not only offer additional funding streams but provide financial sustainability and security (Rankin, 2017). Esports is surely an attractive innovation for the corporate world to be aligned with in their social obligation mandates.

CSR agendas in esports business models are in their infancy. New partnerships, collaborations, and stakeholder engagement opportunities could focus on revised CSR mandates, thus providing an entry point for esports brands and other commercial entities. For esports publishers, there is a need to consider their CSR strategy in response to inevitable questions about legitimacy, transparency, accountability, and their social obligations. SDP could be the perfect setting for esports CSR activities in terms of not only financial partnerships, but also global marketing, access to resources, networks, skill development, and the sharing of knowledge. Traditional sports organisations consider their development agendas as a source of good as well as a strategy for developing soft power and establishing valuable transnational commercial exposure (Giulianotti et al., 2016). Through partnerships and affiliations with traditional sporting properties, the esports industry has an opportunity to learn from the experiences of those already invested in the sector and fast-track the development of esports organisations and their ethical and philanthropic practices.

Concluding remarks: social inclusion in esports

Arguably, the COVID-19 pandemic has forced a stronger and more sustained narrative on the need to innovate and digitalise the SDP sector. The social effects of the pandemic have strengthened the priority and call to create more inclusive and socially safe environments for communities and vulnerable people. We have argued throughout this chapter that there is a need, justification, and space for esports within the SDP landscape. We have seen an increase in the amount of time spent online, especially on mobile and handheld devices, which has been exacerbated by COVID-19 (Ofcom, 2021). To illustrate, in 2021 a study by Ofcom found that children between the ages of seven and 16 spent nearly four hours a day online, while three-quarters of UK children aged five to 15 played games online. Such figures demonstrate the highly digitalised nature of today's society and the need to better understand and promote the benefits of engaging in esports to achieve wider social, personal, and societal outcomes. Specifically, social inclusion is an ever-present issue in today's dynamic and globally connected society, and esports provides an environment that has the potential to challenge many exclusionary practices that are often seen in community sport settings and beyond.

Esports's primary attraction to SDP is the enhanced opportunities it offers to interact with marginalised populations and those who shy away from traditional sporting spaces. Esports can construct an inclusive bridging mechanism that does not discriminate by virtue of physicality, masculinity, or mainstream sporting cultures. Thus, our understanding of sport and what defines it needs to change in order to connect to the rapidly evolving digital age. Esports elicits the characteristics of a sport and reveals the need for a modernity shift, which accounts for changing cultural trends and social patterns and allows innovative approaches to be used. Evidence via the case studies presented in this chapter suggests that the possibilities for esports are significant and under-utilised, with esports attracting groups that have previously been hard to reach or are absent from SDP playing fields.

When working with youth populations it is important to account for the dangers that can occur within the esports and video gaming sphere. For the participants themselves, concerns around cyberbullying, addiction, and psychological vulnerability must be considered (Bányai, et al., 2018; Burleigh et al., 2019; Zsila et al., 2018). Research has revealed that online gaming can result in multiple negative health effects and that this is why concerns have been aired and questions posed about the potential for gaming disorders and addiction (Kelly & Leung, 2021; Mihara & Higuchi, 2017). However, alongside the negative consequences of esports participation that need to be mitigated against, there is potential for esports to be used to support health, well-being, and social outcomes. Critically, context is important. A recently published study indicates that heavier gaming is likely to result in greater risks to well-being, while moderate gaming displays fewer risks and exhibits some positive benefits (Kelly & Leung, 2021).

More broadly, from both a commercial and organisational perspective there are challenges that still need to be addressed relating to corruption, gambling, and doping in esports (Holden, Kaburakis, & Rodenberg, 2017; Holden, Rodenberg, & Kaburakis, 2017; Peng et al., 2020). These issues need to be investigated further in order to understand the potential risks and possible challenges they could pose at an elite, community, and social intervention level. Ultimately, esports provides many new and, until recently, unimaginable opportunities across multiple development sectors, especially in a community and education context, to support social inclusion agendas. In this chapter, we have introduced the flexibility and opportunities that virtual engagement can bring to traditional SDP methods. As digitalisation dominates daily cultures and forms of engagement, esports can complement and enhance SDP programming by a shift from the football fields to digital spaces. Esports can challenge traditional SDP methodologies and enhance important connections between global and local communities. A call for integration and collaboration has driven recent debates in SDP, and esports may be one opportunity to strengthen the capacity of SDP across development sectors and settings. Further investigations with key stakeholders across SDP and esports would be valuable for exposing additional perspectives and attitudes regarding the potential of esports as a social inclusion tool. In addition, future research would benefit from investigating new forms of CSR and entry points for esports's application and implementation into the SDP landscape.

References

Abanazir, C. (2018). Institutionalisation in e-sports. *Sport, Ethics and Philosophy*, 1–15. https://doi.org/10.1080/17511321.2018.1453538

Abarbanel, B., & Johnson, M. R. (2018). Esports consumer perspectives on match-fixing: Implications for gambling awareness and game integrity. *International Gambling Studies*, 1–16. https://doi.org/10.1080/14459795.2018.1558451

Amit, V., & Rapport, N. (2002). *The trouble with community: Anthropological reflections on movement, identity and collectivity*. Pluto Press.

Anderson, B. (1983). *Imagined communities*. Verso.

Anderson, D., Sweeney, K., Pasquini, E., Estes, B., & Zapalac, R. (2021). An exploration of esports consumer consumption patterns, fandom, and motives. *International Journal of eSports Research (IJER)*, 1(1), 1–18. http://doi.org/10.4018/IJER.20210101.oa3

AnyKey. (2022). AnyKey advocates for diversity and inclusion in gaming. https://anykey.org/

Appel, M. (2012). Are heavy users of computer games and social media more computer literate? *Computers & Education*, 59(4), 1339–1349. https://doi.org/10.1016/j.compedu.2012.06.004

Bailey, R. (2005). Evaluating the relationship between physical education, sport and social inclusion. *Educational Review*, 57(1), 71–90. https://doi.org/10.1080/0013191042000274196

Bailey, R. (2008). Youth sport and social inclusion. In N. Holt (Ed.), *Positive youth development through sport* (pp. 85–96). Routledge.

Bányai, F., Griffiths, M. D., Király, O., & Demetrovics, Z. (2018). The psychology of esports: A systematic literature review. *Journal of Gambling Studies*, 35, 351–365. https://doi.org/10.1007/s10899-018-9763-1

Belong. (2022). Arenas. https://www.belong.gg/arenas/

British Esports Association. (2019, October 22). Esports parents guide: Everything a parent or guardian needs to know about competitive gaming. https://britishesports.org/advice/esports-parents-guide/

British Esports Association. (2018, February 27). What's it like being a parent of an esports player and how can they support their child's interest in gaming? https://britishesports.org/news/whats-it-like-being-a-parent-of-an-esports-player-and-how-can-they-support-their-childs-interest-in-gaming/

Burleigh, T. L., Griffiths, M. D., Sumich, A., Stavropoulos, V., & Kuss, D. J. (2019). A systematic review of the co-occurrence of gaming disorder and other potentially addictive behaviors. *Current Addiction Reports*, 6(4), 383–401. https://doi.org/10.1007/s40429-019-00279-7

Chawansky, M. (2011). New social movements, old gender games?: Locating girls in the sport for development and peace movement. In A. C. Snyder & S. P. Stobbe (Eds.), *Critical aspects of gender in conflict resolution, peacebuilding, and social movements* (pp. 121–134). Emerald Group Publishing Limited.

Chee, F. (2006). The games we play online and offline: Making Wang-tta in Korea. *Popular Communication*, 4(3), 225–239. https://doi.org/10.1207/s15405710pc0403_6

Cho, A., Tsaasan, A. M., & Steinkuehler, C. (2019, August). The building blocks of an educational esports league: Lessons from year one in orange county high schools. In *Proceedings of the 14th international conference on the foundations of digital games* (pp. 1–11). https://dl.acm.org/doi/10.1145/3337722.3337738

Coalter, F. (2007). *A wider social role for sport: Who's keeping the score?* Routledge.

Coalter, F. (2010). The politics of sport-for-development: Limited focus programmes and broad-gauge problems? *International review for the Sociology of Sport*, 45(3), 295–314. https://doi.org/10.1177/1012690210366791

Dagkas, S., & Armour, K. (2012). *Inclusion and exclusion through youth sport*. Routledge.

Delanty, G. (2003). *Community: Key ideas*. Routledge.

Digital Schoolhouse. (2022). *Welcome to digital schoolhouse*. https://www.digitalschoolhouse.org.uk/

DiFrancisco-Donoghue, J., Balentine, J., Schmidt, G., & Zwibel, H. (2019). Managing the health of the esports athlete: An integrated health management model. *BMJ Open Sport & Exercise Medicine*, 5(1), https://doi.org/10.1136/bmjsem-2018-000467

Donnelly, P., & Coakley, J. (2002). *The role of recreation in promoting social inclusion*. Laidlaw Foundation.

Freeman, G., & Wohn, D. Y. (2017, October). Social support in esports: Building emotional and esteem support from instrumental support interactions in a highly competitive environment. In *Proceedings of the annual symposium on computer-human interaction in play* (pp. 435–447). ACM.

Freiler, C. (2001). From experiences of exclusion to a vision of inclusion: What needs to change. Paper presented at the conference A New Way of Thinking: Towards a Vision of Social Inclusion, Ottawa.

Girl Gamers. (2022) *Girl gamers esports festival*. https://girlgamer.gg/

Giulianotti, R., Hognestad, H., & Spaaij, R. (2016). Sport for development and peace: Power, politics, and patronage. *Journal of Global Sport Management*, 1(3–4), 129–141. https://doi.org/10.1080/24704067.2016.1231926

Hambrick, M. E., Svensson, P. G., & Kang, S. (2019). Using social network analysis to investigate interorganizational relationships and capacity building within a sport for development coalition. *Sport Management Review*, 22(5), 708–723. https://doi.org/10.1016/j.smr.2018.12.002

Hayday, E. J., & Collison, H. (2020). Exploring the contested notion of social inclusion and gender inclusivity within esports spaces. *Social Inclusion*, 8(3), 197–208. https://doi.org/10.17645/si.v8i3.2755

Hayday, E. J., Collison, H., & Kohe, G. Z. (2021). Landscapes of tension, tribalism and toxicity: Configuring a spatial politics of esports communities. *Leisure Studies*, 40(2), 139–153. https://doi.org/10.1080/02614367.2020.1808049

Heere, B. (2018). Embracing the sportification of society: Defining e-sports through a polymorphic view on sport. *Sport Management Review*, 21(1), 21–24.

Hilvoorde, I. V., & Pot, N. (2016). Embodiment and fundamental motor skills in esports. *Sport, Ethics and Philosophy*, 10(1), 14–27. https://doi.org/10.1080/17511321.2016.1159246

Holden, J. T., Kaburakis, A., & Rodenberg, R. (2017). The future is now: E-sports policy considerations and potential litigation. *Journal of Legal Aspects of Sport*, 27(1), 46–78. https://doi.org/10.1123/jlas.2016-0018

Holden, J. T., Kaburakis, A., & Rodenberg, R. M. (2018). Esports: Children, stimulants and video-gaming-induced inactivity. *Journal of Paediatrics and Child Health*, 54, 830–831. https://doi.org/10.1111/jpc.13897

Holden, J. T., Rodenberg, R. M., & Kaburakis, A. (2017). Esports corruption: Gambling, doping, and global governance. *Maryland Journal of International Law*, 32, 236.

Huhh, J. S. (2008). Culture and business of PC bangs in Korea. *Games and Culture*, 3(1), 26–37.

Jansz, J., & Martens, L. (2005). Gaming at a LAN event: The social context of playing video games. *New Media & Society*, 7(3), 333–355. https://doi.org/10.1177/1461444805052280

Ke, X., & Wagner, C. (2020). Global pandemic compels sport to move to esports: Understanding from brand extension perspective. *Managing Sport and Leisure*, 1–6. https://doi.org/10.1080/23750472.2020.1792801

Kelly, S., & Leung, J. (2021). The new frontier of esports and gaming: A scoping meta-review of health impacts and research agenda. *Frontiers in Sports and Active Living*, 3, 1–10. https://doi.org/10.3389/fspor.2021.640362

Kidd, B. (2008). A new social movement: Sport for development and peace. *Sport in Society*, 11(4), 370–380. https://doi.org/10.1080/17430430802019268

Kim, S. J. (2017). *Gender inequality in esports participation: Examining league of legends* (Doctoral dissertation).

Levermore, R. (2010). CSR for development through sport: Examining its potential and limitations. *Third World Quarterly*, 31(2), 223–241. https://doi.org/10.1080/01436591003711967

Loat, R. (2021). Levelling up: Opportunities for sport for development to evolve through esports. *Journal of Sport for Development*. 9(1). https://jsfd.org/

Macey, J., & Hamari, J. (2018). Investigating relationships between video gaming, spectating esports, and gambling. *Computers in Human Behavior*, 80, 344–353. https://doi.org/10.1016/j.chb.2017.11.027

Martončik, M. (2015). e-Sports: Playing just for fun or playing to satisfy life goals?. *Computers in Human Behavior*, 48, 208–211. https://doi.org/10.1016/j.chb.2015.01.056

Maxwell, H., Foley, C., Taylor, T., & Burton, C. (2013). Social inclusion in community sport: A case study of Muslim women in Australia. *Journal of Sport Management*, 27(6), 467–481. https://doi.org/10.1123/jsm.27.6.467

Mihara, S., & Higuchi, S. (2017). Cross-sectional and longitudinal epidemiological studies of Internet gaming disorder: A systematic review of the literature. *Psychiatry and clinical neurosciences, 71*(7), 425–444. https://doi.org/10.1111/pcn.12532

Morgan, H., Parker, A., & Roberts, W. (2019). Community sport programmes and social inclusion: What role for positive psychological capital? *Sport in Society 22*(6), 1100–1114. https://doi.org/10.1080/17430437.2019.1565397

Ofcom. (2021). Online nation. https://www.ofcom.org.uk/__data/assets/pdf_file/0013/220414/online-nation-2021-report.pdf

Peng, Q., Dickson, G., Scelles, N., Grix, J., & Brannagan, P. M. (2020). Esports governance: Exploring stakeholder dynamics. *Sustainability, 12*(19), 8270. https://doi.org/10.3390/su12198270

Philip, B., Hoye, R., & Sherry, E. (2021). Sport-for-development and social inclusion in caste-ridden India: Opportunities and challenges. *Soccer & Society*, 1–17. https://doi.org/10.1080/14660970.2021.1993199

Qatar Foundation. (2021). E-Sports FIFA2021. https://www.qf.org.qa/events/e-sports-fifa2021

Rambusch, J., Taylor, A. S. A., & Susi, T. (2017). Cognitive challenges in esports. *Proceedings of the 13th Swecog Conference* 2017, UPPSALA.

Rankin, N. (2017). Sport and corporate social responsibility. https://www.sportanddev.org/en/article/news/sport-and-corporate-social-responsibility

Raw, K., Sherry, E., & Schulenkorf, N. (2021). Managing sport for development: An investigation of tensions and paradox. *Sport Management Review*, 1–28. https://doi.org/10.1016/j.smr.2020.09.002

Reames, M. (2018). Orange county high school esports league combines education, gaming. https://www.sporttechie.com/orange-county-high-school-esports-education-gaming

Ruvalcaba, O., Shulze, J., Kim, A., Berzenski, S. R., & Otten, M. P. (2018). Women's Experiences in esports: Gendered differences in peer and spectator feedback during competitive video game play. *Journal of Sport and Social Issues, 42*(4), 295–311. https://doi.org/10.1177/0193723518773287

Saavedra, M. (2009). Dilemmas and opportunities in gender and sport-in-development. In R. Levermore & A. Beacom *Sport and international development* (pp. 124–155). Palgrave Macmillan.

Schulenkorf, N., Sugden, J., & Burdsey, D. (2014). Sport for development and peace as contested terrain: Place, community, ownership. *International Journal of Sport Policy and Politics, 6*(3), 371–387. https://doi.org/10.1080/19406940.2013.825875

Schulenkorf, N. (2010). Sport events and ethnic reconciliation: Attempting to create social change between Sinhalese, Tamil and Muslim Sportspeople in War-torn Sri Lanka. *International Review for the Sociology of Sport 45*, (3), 273–294. https://doi.org/10.1177/1012690210366789.

Sherry, E. (2010). (Re)engaging marginalized groups through sport: The homeless world cup. *International Review for the Sociology of Sport 45*(1), 59–71. https://doi.org/10.1177/1012690209356988.

Spaaij, R., Magee, J., & Jeanes, R. (2014). *Sport and social exclusion in global society*. Routledge.

Svensson, P. G., Andersson, F. O., & Faulk, L. (2018). A quantitative assessment of organizational capacity and organizational life stages in sport for development and peace. *Journal of Sport Management, 32*(3), 295–313. https://doi.org/10.1123/jsm.2017-0244

Taylor, T. L. (2017). On the fields, in the stands: The future of women in esports [Keynote]. Presented at the UCI esports symposium, University of California, Irvine, May 19.

Thorpe, H. (2014). *Transnational mobilities in action sport cultures* Palgrave Macmillan.

Thorpe, H., & Wheaton, B. (2011). 'Generation X Games', action sports and the Olympic movement: Understanding the cultural politics of incorporation. *Sociology, 45*(5), 830–847.

Trepte, S., Reinecke, L., & Juechems. K. (2012). The social side of gaming: How playing online computer games creates online and offline social support. *Computers in Human Behavior. 28*, 832–839. https://doi.org/10.1016/j.chb.2011.12.003

Tristão, H. (2022, April 19). Esports audience will pass half a billion in 2022 as revenues, engagement, & new segments flourish, Newzoo. https://newzoo.com/insights/articles/the-esports-audience-will-pass-half-a-billion-in-2022-as-revenue-engagement-esports-industry-growth/

U.N. Sustainable Development Goal 4. (n.d.). https://sdgs.un.org/goals/goal4

Van der Klashorst, E. (2018). Exploring the economic, social and cultural rights of youth leaders working in sport for development initiatives at grassroots level in South Africa. *Leisure Studies, 37*(1), 109–116. https://doi.org/10.1080/02614367.2017.1383504

Van der Veken, K., Lauwerier, E., & Willems, S. (2020). "To mean something to someone": Sport-for-development as a lever for social inclusion. *International Journal for Equity in Health, 19*(1), 1–13. https://doi.org/10.1186/s12939-019-1119-7

Waddock, S., & Smith, N. (2000). Relationships: The real challenge of corporate global citizenship. *Business and Society Review, 105*(1), 47–62.

Wagner, M. G. (2006, June). On the scientific relevance of esports. In *International conference on internet computing* (pp. 437–442). https://www.researchgate.net/profile/Michael-Wagner-36/publication/220968200_On_the_Scientific_Relevance_of_eSports/links/00b4952589870231be000000/On-the-Scientific-Relevance-of-eSports.pdf

Whalen, S. J. (2013). *Cyberathletes' lived experience of video game tournaments*. PhD diss., University of Tennessee, MIT Press.

Wheaton, B., & Thorpe, H. (2018). Action sports, the Olympic games, and the opportunities and challenges for gender equity: The cases of surfing and skateboarding. *Journal of Sport and Social Issues, 42*(5), 315–342.

Women in Games. (2022) *Women in games*. https://www.womeningames.org/

Zsila, Á., Orosz, G., Király, O., Urbán, R., Ujheli, A., Jármi, É., Griffiths, M. D., Elekes, Z., & Demetrovics, Z. (2018). Psychoactive substance use and problematic internet use as predictors of bullying and cyberbullying victimization. *International Journal of Mental Health and Addiction, 16*, 466–479. https://doi.org/10.1007/s11469-017-9809-0

Chapter 10

The Olympic Movement and esports governance

Finding the right way of cooperating for diversity, equity, and inclusion

Cem Abanazir

Introduction

The aims to capture the 'youth market' and spread the values identified with the Olympic Games have led the Olympic Movement (OM) to acknowledge the growing popularity and potential of esports (Abanazir, 2021). The 'Olympic Agenda 2020+5: 15 Recommendations' (n.d.) accepted by the International Olympic Committee (IOC) emphasised that young people's interest in video games should move the OM to create new Olympic experiences through sports-themed video games.[1] Accordingly, in the run-up to the 2020 Tokyo Olympic Games, the IOC decided to organise the Olympic Virtual Series – non-medal events consisting of virtual versions of cycling, sailing, motorsports, baseball, and rowing (Olympic Games, 2021a).

The fact that the OM views sports-themed video games as possible medal events at the Olympic Games and has charged international sports federations with the task of organising non-medal events indicates that it has chosen a safer and more familiar path towards cooperating with the esports industry. This chapter explains the OM's view of sports-themed video games and describes the major implications of the interplay between sport, esports, and social issues. Research conducted by Newzoo and Intel (2021) indicates that as 'A significant share of gamers in the U.S. feel game companies should take a stance on societal issues, irrespective of the respondent's race, gender identity, sexual orientation, or having a disability' (p. 4), the focus on social issues is vital.

After looking at how the OM and literature view the place of esports within the OM, the chapter compares the governance and regulatory structures of esports and the OM. The third section explains why the OM opted to charge sports associations in the OM with the task of cooperating with the esports industry. Finally, the comparison of two distinct spheres of activity becomes the basis for exploring the interplay between the OM and esports on social issues.

Finding the right way of cooperating

Disciplines such as the philosophy of sport, sport management, sociology, cognitive science, sport science, business, and law have all considered the emergence

DOI: 10.4324/9781003258650-14

of esports (Parry, 2019; Holden et al., 2017; Darvin et al., 2020; Reitman et al., 2020). These discipline-specific and interdisciplinary investigations have positioned esports in the market, sport, and society. Commentators have also explored esports's position in the OM, with mixed results. Parry (2019) concluded that esports should not become a medal event, whilst Pack and Hedlund (2020) had reservations about certain esports practices (e.g. competitions based on violent video games), but in general, were more open to the integration of esports in the Olympic Games. Miah and Fenton (2021) focused on the commercial opportunities that esports competitions might bring to the OM and concluded that esports would become part of the Olympic and Paralympic programmes. Finally, Pargman and Svensson (2020) and Abanazir (2021) asserted that esports would become part of the Olympic Games as a medal event by the 2030s.

Such ambivalence corresponds to the OM's first tenuous steps in evaluating and exploring esports's place in the movement. The Olympic summits – annual meetings bringing together the OM's prominent stakeholders – have been the OM's primary platform for conveying its views on esports. Since 2017, both the OM's comments on esports and comparisons between the OM and esports have been on the agenda of these summits. The OM has raised questions about the compatibility of Olympic values and video games, the physical and mental health of esports players, and corruption in esports (Abanazir, 2021; Olympic Games, 2017). Conversely, sports-themed video games are a strand in the OM's positive evaluations. This became clear at the Seventh Olympic Summit, when the OM encouraged international sports federations to cooperate with the video game industry and 'explore the potential benefits and applications of the electronic and virtual versions of their sports' (Olympic Games, 2018b, para. 22). In the following two summits, the OM stated that it saw 'great potential' in the cooperation between international sports federations and the video game and esports industries and urged the international sports federations to embrace 'both the physical and non-physical virtual forms of their respective sports' (Olympic Games, 2019, para. 32; Olympic Games, 2020, para. 24). This positive outlook culminated in the 'Olympic Agenda 2020+5: 15 Recommendations' (n.d.), where it was emphasised that '[unique Olympic products] and experiences can fill the gap between virtual sports and the Olympic Games, creating valuable brand associations with [international federations] and their respective virtual sports' (p. 22). Finally, the Tenth Olympic Summit underlined that it deemed the Olympic Virtual Series a success and shared its plans to continue the events annually (Olympic Games, 2021c, para. 12).

In the meantime, one-off esports events have served as testing grounds and PR opportunities. In the lead-up to the 2018 PyeongChang Olympic Games, the IOC organised two video games-based events. First, taking advantage of the popularity of the video game *StarCraft II* in South Korea, a tournament was organised in PyeongChang. In this demonstration event, the IOC collaborated with Intel and the video game's publisher Blizzard Entertainment (Intel, 2018). A few days later, an event based on Ubisoft's officially licensed sports-themed video game

Steep: Road to the Olympics was organised with the IOC's consent. The second event was not realised in PyeongChang but in Katowice, Poland, although it was broadcast in PyeongChang (Olympic Games, 2018a).

There are two interlinked reasons why the OM deemed it necessary to focus on esports competitions based on sports-themed video games and for their governance to be undertaken by international sports federations. First, the governance of esports is, as the Communique of the Seventh Olympic Summit suggests, 'fragmented' (Olympic Games, 2018b, para. 19), and the current landscape is contrary to the OM's dealings. The second reason is that there are certain limits as to which video games may become the bases of esports competitions within the ambit of the Olympic Games. These limits arise from the production and consumption patterns of the Olympic Games themselves. In addition, yet beyond the scope of this chapter, some of these limits are due to the Olympic values, thereby rendering violent video games out of bounds (Pack & Hedlund, 2020). The following two sections concretise these assertions.

Piecing the fragments together

Contemporary sport is based on associativity (Szymanski, 2008). Associational relationships between national, continental, and international sports federations differ, although cooperation towards achieving common goals is the key. Sports federations come into being through the coming together of members. These entities aim to gather the various elements in the production of sport under a single roof in order to organise tournaments, market them if possible, and set norms. This bundle of associational relationships may emerge to the detriment of competing entities, in that sports federations often enjoy monopoly-like powers over sport and its various disciplines (Freeburn, 2018). As witnessed in the short-lived European Super League in football, international and continental sports federations put political and economic pressure on their subjects and possible competitors.

Although the IOC is the 'supreme authority' and leader of the OM (Olympic Charter, Rule 1.1), it delegates and disseminates its power over the Olympic Games, Olympic sports, and disciplines to international and national sports federations and National Olympic Committees. Such power includes the selection of athletes to participate in the Olympic Games (Olympic Charter, Bye-law to Rules 27 and 28 [2.1]), the governance of the sports and disciplines at the Olympic Games (Olympic Charter, Rule 26 [1.5]), and, in some instances, the disciplinary powers enjoyed by the IOC (Olympic Charter, Rule 59 [2.4]).

For the Olympic Games, the importance of international sports federations with monopoly-like powers cannot be understated or underestimated. Here, the IOC designates a single international sports federation as its partner. The partnership is very important, in that in the words of Allison and Tomlinson (2017), the reinstating of the Olympic Games and the founding of international sports federations (2017), 'pirouetted' (pp. 42–43) with the Olympic Games.

The foundation of overarching and monopoly-like organisations was the first step to becoming part of the Olympic programme. In the twentieth century, in order to be counted as an international sport, the activities and an international federation had to be in place in 'a rational-legal structure of regulation, hierarchies and legitimacies' (Allison & Tomlinson, 2017, p. 199).

Concerning the regulation and legitimacy aspects, in view of their associational goals, sports associations have introduced and implemented policies on anti-doping, match fixing, and human rights. In the process, tournament-specific and other regulations both control and standardise the various aspects of the relevant sport and discipline. International sports federations may even require the homologation of certain aspects of a sport, such as sport venues' technical requirements (Loland, 2001), leading to a regulatory landscape that resembles 'a complex pyramid of interlinked regulations' (Beloff, 2012). Thus, international sports federations have to abide by the policies, rules, and moral standpoints of the IOC in the context of the Olympic Games.

Unlike the OM, esports competitions are not organised under the auspices or with the consent of an overarching international esports federation or national and continental esports federations that are members of an umbrella organisation. Institutions like the International Esports Federation (IESF) and the World Esports Association (WESA) are not the highest authorities of esports that enjoy the regulatory powers akin to international sports federations and they do not have a monopoly-like position in the esports industry.

The OM's contention that there is 'tough competition between commercial operators' (Olympic Games, 2018b, para. 19) is perceptive. There are at least three aspects to this competition. At one level, there is competition between enterprises that are not developers/publishers. Enterprises such as ESL (Electronic Sports League) aim to secure the most popular video games from the developers/publishers and become the dominant force in the market (Jenny et al., 2016). At another level, video game developers/publishers compete with each other, thereby rendering certain video game genres crucial. When a video game or genre (a fluid term due to the possibility of mixing the elements of various genres in a single video game or series) proves to be very popular with players and spectators, the developers/publishers can develop and publish their takes on the genre in order to take a share of the market (Abanazir, 2021). The third level of competition is when developers/publishers compete with non-developer enterprises and developers/publishers in the organisation of esports competitions. The income and popularity that competitions might generate can even result in developers/publishers acquiring non-developer enterprises to increase coverage (Abanazir, 2019).

The role of esports competition organisers further deviates from international sport governance and the Olympic Games in that some genres and titles could become the bases of esports competitions. A video game genre consists of many different games, and each and every video game could even be called a discipline for the purposes of esports (Adamus, 2012). Disciplines lead to further differences in the rules of esports competitions arising from these video games (Witkowski, 2012), which should be seen as another barrier to a cumulative approach. Finally, as esports competitions have fewer written rules, the regulatory landscape does not resemble a 'complex pyramid'. However, the organisers could still engender the moral aspirations undergirding sport, especially those of the OM. For instance, the World Cyber Games (WCG) aimed to promote harmony in humankind through esports (Summerley, 2020).

To summarise, the lack of a monopoly-like international esports federation that brings stakeholders together has moved the OM to find a tenable way of interacting with different esports actors. Concordantly, the OM had two choices: either to wait for an umbrella organisation and a coherent hierarchy of esports to be formed, or to charge its stakeholders with addressing this issue. International sports federations are already part of the OM, which satisfies the necessary monopolies and hierarchies in the organisation of esports competitions. The OM thus trod a safer and quicker path by going for a less complicated option. Nonetheless, these are not the only reasons for this approach.

Controlling the means of production

As already indicated, the second reason for the IOC's position was the limits presented by the production and consumption patterns in esports. The various actors in the OM and the IOC have fruitful relationships with the video game and esports industries. Sports-themed video games like the *FIFA Series*, Ubisoft's *Steep: Road to the Olympics*, and Sega's *Olympic Games Tokyo 2020* and *London 2012* have acted as bridges between the IOC and the video game industry. Likewise, international sports federations and video game developers/publishers have collaborated in the design and development of sports-themed video games and the organisation of esports tournaments (Miah & Fenton, 2021).

Despite strategic collaboration with the esports industry, undue influence and interference from the latter would be anathema for the OM. The underlying reason for this is that autonomy has a place in the Fundamental Principles of Olympism in the Olympic Charter. Here, it is stated that '[Sport organisations within the Olympic Movement] have the rights and obligations of autonomy, which include freely establishing and controlling the rules of sport, determining the structure and governance of their organisations' (art. 5). The OM's defence of autonomy is so strict that a Taiwanese IOC member's recourse to ordinary courts of law in a sporting case is credited as the triggering event for the creation of the Court of Arbitration for Sport (Duval, 2018), which has exclusive jurisdiction over any dispute arising from or in relation to the Olympic Games (Olympic Charter, Rule 61). In this regard, the OM's encouragement of international sports federations to first 'ensur[e] they gain or retain appropriate control over the electronic/virtual versions of their sports' (Olympic Games, 2018b, para. 22) and later 'to consider how to govern electronic and virtual forms of their sport and explore opportunities with game publishers' (Olympic Games, 2019, para. 32) should come as no surprise.

The esports industry's intervention in the OM through esports competitions is a distinct possibility. The terms 'executive ownership' and 'executive owner', introduced by Karhulahti (2017), give a clue to this. Karhulahti points out that there would need to be a video game available – a commercial product – in order to participate in an esports competition. 'Executive ownership' gives developers/publishers a wide range of options for marketing, selling, and even discontinuing a video game if it is deemed unprofitable. Depending on its intellectual property rights, each video game developer/publisher, depending on its intellectual property rights, is an executive owner that 'literally (re)writes the rules of its game, supplies the essential technology, and ultimately decides on the existence of the sport as a whole' (p. 46).

The prevalence of executive ownership could undermine the IOC's claim to be the supreme authority and leader of the OM. Executive ownership leads to the creation of regulatory and adjudicatory regimes that could pander to the interests of the executive owner. At a meta-level, the OM (Duval, 2018) and the developers/publishers (Busch et al., 2016) have regulatory and dispute resolution powers over their respective stakeholders and clients. To increase the efficacy of the production and consumption processes of their games and tournaments, the OM and the esports industry have introduced norms and procedures to resolve any dispute that might result. The crux of the matter is that the regulatory and dispute resolution powers presuppose the presence of separate 'private regimes' with a global reach (Fischer-Lescano & Teubner, 2004). These regimes and powers do not normally have any contact with each other because they regulate separate spheres of activity. However, if esports competitions become medal events, the participants would potentially be covered by the overlapping governance regimes of the OM and the developer/publisher. That is, an esports player who takes part in a virtual medal event at the Olympic Games would be bound by the rules and regulations of the OM, the entity that developed/published the video game, and the organiser of the esports competition in question. In this scenario there would be a multitude of rules with roots in different entities, which could affect how social issues are regulated at the Olympic Games.

Conflict and harmony, exclusion and inclusion

As highlighted earlier, international sports federations and the IOC enact policies and norms to reach their associational goals. The position of the OM as the keeper of the Olympic Games and the leadership of the IOC together undergird the terms of interaction with different spheres of society and business. As international sports federations and elements of esports have different interests, goals, policies, and norms, there can be 'conflict' or 'harmony' between their private (i.e. not related to states) regimes at the macro and micro levels (Wai, 2014).

This could lead to two possible scenarios in the interaction between the OM and esports regimes concerning social issues:

a) The stance of the OM and the elements of esports may be in conflict on some social issues.
b) The stance of the OM and the elements of esports may be in harmony on some social issues.

The following sub-sections present an overview of the scenarios and concretise the assertion of harmony and conflict by analysing inclusion and exclusion in the OM and esports.

Scenario (a): conflict

Despite recent efforts to achieve gender balance, sport's track record on athlete participation is less than perfect, in that the OM can still present barriers for women. As Patel (2015) has shown, in one way or another, sports as diverse as running, ski jumping, boxing, canoeing, and golf have excluded women from certain competitions. As late as 2007, the IOC president boldly asserted that the addition of women's ski jumping would 'dilute and water down' Olympic medals (Young, 2010, p. 96).

Exclusionary policies are not only rooted in sport and society's misogynistic, masculinist, and ableist tendencies (Darvin et al., 2020), but also in the resulting narrative that men and women should compete separately. The segregation of men and women is based on the idea that women are physically 'inferior' and that competing together with men would not be 'fair'. Two of the different strands of justification point out (the others being the argument from traditional gender roles and the argument from defeminisation) that if it was not for segregation there would be health risks for female competitors and the competitive balance in sports competitions would be disrupted (Pérez Triviño, 2011; Patel, 2015). Although mixed teams are permitted in curling, tennis, and relay races, the fact that the same number of men and women athletes are allowed in the team supports the idea that competitive balance and 'physical inferiority' are still at the forefront. Finally, the positive steps that the OM has taken to ensure equal participation for athletes in the Olympic Games do not change the fact that segregation is still in place.

Despite a recent change in course by the IOC in its 'Framework on Fairness, Inclusion and Non-Discrimination on the Basis of Gender Identity and Sex Variations' (IOC, 2021) emphasising that physical appearance, transgender status, and sex variations should not result in the presumption of unfair advantage, both hyperandrogenous and transgender athletes face exclusion from sport due to the specific regulations of sports federations. Here, the IOC defers to the international sports federations as to 'how an athlete may be at a disproportionate advantage against their peers, taking into consideration of the nature of each sport'

(IOC, 2021, p. 1). Thus, the policies and practices at the Olympic Games can perpetuate the binary view of sex (Adlwarth, 2022). Due to their higher testosterone levels, hyperandrogenous and transwomen athletes, and especially those who have confirmed their gender as female after puberty, face an uphill struggle. As in the case of gender segregation, although the health argument is an issue in contact sports, the competitive balance argument asserts that, due to their development, hyperandrogenous and transwomen athletes have an 'unfair advantage' over their competitors. For instance, World Rugby, the international federation recognised by the IOC, does not allow 'Transgender women who transitioned post-puberty and have experienced the biological effects of testosterone during puberty and adolescence' to compete in women's rugby (World Rugby, n.d.). As in the case of South African runner Caster Semenya, similar regulations by the World Athletics (formerly IAAF) force athletes to undergo 'gender verification' processes. On the other hand, even though changes have been made to the eligibility norms of certain sports federations, athletes who have confirmed their gender as female have to overcome institutional and societal prejudice (Patel, 2015). The moral panic that ensued following transgender weightlifter Laurel Hubbard's inclusion in the New Zealand Olympic Team for the 2020 Tokyo Olympic Games demonstrates the global public's view of the subject.

As esports organisers have not introduced regulatory prohibitions concerning the participation of esports players (Darvin et al., 2021), esports may appear to be more inclusive than the OM. Furthermore, despite questions about their legitimacy and efficacy, developers/publishers have laid down strict norms for ethical conduct for the gamers themselves (Busch et al., 2016). Concordantly, the exclusionary normative practices of the OM and the lack of them in esports could create conflict between the parties. As presented in the previous sections, this conflict would involve the two forces trying to maintain as much control as possible over their products, the Olympics Games and video games.

Nevertheless, bearing in mind T. L. Taylor's (2012) warning that analyses of computer gaming are 'tricky to pull off' due to the variety of game cultures (p. 111), the dark side of esports should be included in any debate about a possible conflict between the OM and the esports industry. Esports suffers from well-documented issues such as marginalisation, hostility, discrimination, harassment, heteronormativity, male-orientation, and stereotyping prevalent in the video games industry and esports (Darvin et al., 2020; Kruthika, 2020; Taylor, 2012; Tjønndal & Skauge, 2021). The absence of segregationary and exclusionary regulations is offset by 'gender-zoning', which 'refers to the use of treatment discrimination and harassment by male gamers to push women and girls away from participating in specific games or game genres and in online communities' (Darvin et al. 2021, p. 492). Whilst regulatory practices are not exclusionary, institutional practices such as 'booth babes' and masculinist consumption patterns are (Witkowski, 2018, p. 189). The inequality in non-sports-themed action games for women (Ratan et al., 2015) is exacerbated by what Taylor and Stout (2020) have called 'toxic meritocracy', in that at higher levels of competition participation is invariably male-dominated and masculinised, to the exclusion of 'others' (p. 453). Despite the inclusion of transgender players and the presence of mixed and all-women teams, sexist and transphobic harassment has not disappeared. The late Maria 'Remilia' Creveling, the first woman and transgender esports player in the *LoL* Championship Series (LCS), cited the toxic atmosphere as a reason for taking a break from professional esports (Seiner, 2019). Similarly, Siutila and Havaste's (2019) research into Reddit posts concerning all-women esports teams shows that meritocracy undergirds strict and exclusionary interpretations of skill exhibition and that there are contentions about the futility of all-women teams, the necessity to create mixed teams in their place, hiding one's sex and gender (themes noted before by Taylor [2012, pp. 123–128]), and staying silent in the face of harassment.

Due to these social views and contentions, women remain underrepresented in college and professional esports (Darvin et al., 2021). Even though it would be a step towards convergence with the practices of traditional sports, the viability of women-only events is one of the points of debate (BBC, 2021; Siutila & Havaste, 2019). The Girl Gamer Challenge (n.d.) has taken sides in the debate by adopting a competition rule stating that 'Each player must be women-identifying'. Hence, the demographics of high-level competitions suggest that diversity would suffer if eligibility rules about engendered participation were not embraced at the Olympic Games. The challenge in that regard is the IOC's desire to accept sports and disciplines that can provide the 'best athletes' in the Olympic Games (Abanazir, 2021). When coupled with the obsession with meritocracy, the OM could be an obstacle to equity, diversity, and inclusion. This would naturally create further conflict between the OM and the elements of esports.

Scenario (b): harmony

The OM has recommended that 'the sports movement should focus on players and gamers rather than on specific games. This focus on individuals should promote the participation in sport' (Olympic Games, 2019, para. 32). The OM's stance is a well-rounded summary of what is at stake, given that executive owners and video game developers/publishers can easily create barriers to participation. If esports becomes part of the Olympic programme, and if the practice of sport is perceived as a human right by the OM (Olympic Charter, Fundamental Principles of Olympism, art. 4), then any barriers to participation that are erected by entities with power over their products would be anathema to the OM.

The crucial aspect of the OM's (previously) strict contentions regarding competitive balance and the health of competitors as presented in the previous section is that they were ignored in the organisation of esports events under the IOC's auspices. Simply put, the OM's practices moved closer to those of esports. Sasha 'Scarlett' Hostyn, a transgender woman, won the *StarCraft II* tournament in the run-up to the 2018 PyeongChang Olympic Games (Intel, 2018, para. 2). Likewise, for the Olympic Virtual Series, the five sports and their disciplines had neither separate competitions for men and women nor specific regulations for hyperandrogenous and transgender athletes (Palar, 2021). The Olympic Virtual Series 'Chase Race' on the virtual trainer Zwift included both male and female cycling greats (Zwift, 2021).

Consequently, by collaborating in a mixed event that includes esports players, the OM has shown that harmony between the policies and norms of the OM and the elements of esports is possible. While a lack of obstacles to participation in these events does not automatically ensure inclusion, bringing down regulatory barriers is an essential first step towards it. Such events would also show that the inclusion of transgender players in esports at the Olympic Games is an achievable goal.

Nonetheless, contrary to the OM's justified focus on participation, the OM and esports could both impede participation. For instance, the eligibility rules of the *eBaseball Powerful Pro Baseball 2020* competition organised in the Olympic Virtual Series stated that a competitor must live in Japan, Korea, or Taiwan ('Chinese Taipei' at the Olympic Games) and 'own' *eBaseball Powerful Pro Baseball 2020*. Furthermore, the only available platforms for the competitions were PlayStation 4 and Nintendo Switch (Olympic Games, 2021b). This created a twofold problem. First, participation in the tournament was not universal but was confined to carefully drawn geographical boundaries. If Olympism and the values associated with it should be and are universal (Parry, 2006), then these self-introduced barriers go against this goal. Second, the fact that owning the video game and a specific console was compulsory to attendance should also be considered as a barrier to participation. If, in the words of the OM, the 'focus on individuals should promote the participation in sport' (Olympic Games, 2019, para. 32), then a prospective player should be able to participate in the tournament from an esports café or a video gaming centre without having to buy the console and the game. In this case, the OM and the video game industry's interests were in harmony to the point that owning a commercial product became a prerequisite for participation. The video game itself and the norms of the OM thus turned out to be exclusionary forces.

Conclusion

This chapter has explored the underlying reasons for the OM's steps towards incorporating sports-themed video games into the Olympic Games. Despite certain advantages, such as efficiency and ease of supervision, this way of governing and regulating esports does not lessen the inherent problems within the OM and the esports industry.

First, in a regulatory and adjudicatory landscape where the powers of the OM, and especially those of the IOC, are vehemently guarded against external interference (Duval, 2018), pressure from the elements of esports on these powers is a tangible concern for the OM. To prevent that, cooperation between the parties in which the international sports federations or the IOC would have the last say – or at least a meaningful say – in the governance of esports competitions is advantageous to the OM. Second, if cooperation is to be permanent, social issues such as exclusion, discrimination, and inequality will need to be addressed. On the one hand, in line with the idea of harmony between the regimes, cooperation between the OM and the elements of esports could mitigate the problem of exclusion within the OM and the esports industry. Events like the *StarCraft II* competition in PyeongChang, whose winner was a transgender woman, show that cooperation can breed diversity, equity, and inclusion. On the other hand, conflicts between the parties may result in the failure to take full advantage of a relationship that could increase the participation of disadvantaged persons, such as women, hyperandrogenous women, and transwomen.

To prevent and address exclusion and discrimination of any kind, clear and specially crafted processes against harassment, discrimination, and exclusion must be in place. In this regard, the OM (the dominant institution for the Olympic Games) can put its regulatory and moral aspirations to good use (Witkowski, 2018, p. 192). Considering the OM's aversion to intervention from the outside and the video game developers'/publishers' power over their products thanks to 'executive ownership', the two parties will need to find common ground and goals. If this is not done, the goals of inclusion, non-discrimination, and diversity will suffer at the hands of both the OM and the esports industry.

This chapter has underlined the positive steps, such as lifting the regulatory restrictions for the Olympic Virtual Series. Nevertheless, two outstanding issues will need to be considered in future research. First, the inclusive structuring of the Olympic Virtual Series should not be prematurely celebrated because as it consists of non-medal events it is not part of the Olympic programme. The arguments that justify exclusion could be revived when the stakes are high and moral panic is nigh. The reaction against Laurel Hubbard's participation as a woman in the 2020 Tokyo Olympic Games shows that inclusive society, the OM, and the esports industry need to be vigilant and determined in their approach to social issues, especially in the context of the Olympic Games. Second, there is a paradox about inclusion in the Olympic Games. Whilst the goal of having non-male esports players at the Olympic Games comes to the forefront in the context of esports competitions, the practice of gender segregation at the Olympic Games, as criticised earlier, could be seen as a way of creating inclusionary and diverse practices. This chapter is neutral with regard to this paradox (but see Witkowski, 2018, pp. 197–199), although it should be asserted that at the very least, policies addressing social issues will need to be properly justified. In short, the exclusionary justifications concerning the segregation of men and women and the exclusion of transgender women should not be part of the discourse on esports at the Olympic Games.

Note

1 Following Crawford (2015), this chapter uses the term 'sports-themed video games' rather than 'sports video games' or 'sports simulations'. There are two reasons for

choosing the term to depict video games such as the *FIFA Series* and the *Madden Series*. First, the term would make it seem that these types of video games are indeed sports. Second, the term 'sports simulation' would not be fitting, because these video games omit certain rules and aspects of the sports that they are simulating. Moreover, in some cases they do not even aim to simulate the source sport (Crawford, 2015, p. 575).

References

Abanazir, C. (2019). Institutionalisation in e-sports. *Sport, Ethics and Philosophy*, 13(2), 117–131. https://doi.org/10.1080/17511321.2018.1453538

Abanazir, C. (2021). Of values and commercialisation: An exploration of esportss' place within the Olympic movement. *Sport, Ethics and Philosophy*. https://doi.org/10.1080/17511321.2021.1945669

Adamus, T. (2012). Playing computer games as electronic sport: In search of a theoretical framework for a new research field. In J. Fromme & A. Unger (Eds.), *Computer games and new media cultures: A handbook of digital games studies* (pp. 477–490). Springer.

Adlwarth, A. (2022). Sex testing in sport mega-events: Fairness and the illusive promise of inclusive policies – Situating inter* and trans*athletes in elite sport. In K. Dashper (Ed.), *Sport, gender and mega-events* (pp. 33–55). Emerald Publishing.

Allison, L. & Tomlinson, A. (2017). *Understanding international sport organisations: Principles, power and possibilities*. Routledge.

BBC. (2021, September 7). 'Esportss: Why are there so few professional women gamers?' Retrieved February 15, 2022 from https://www.bbc.com/news/av/technology-58466374

Beloff, M. J. (2012). 'Is there a *Lex Sportiva*?' In R. C. R., Siekmann & J. Soek (Eds.), *Lex Sportiva: What is sports law* (pp. 69–90). TMC Asser Press.

Busch, T., Boudreau, K., & Consalvo, M. (2016). Toxic gamer culture, corporate regulation, and standards of behavior among players of online games. In S. Conway & de J. Winter (Eds.), *Video game policy: Production, distribution, and consumption* (pp. 176–190). Routledge.

Crawford, G. (2015). Is it in the game? Reconsidering play spaces, game definitions, theming, and sports videogames. *Games and Culture*, 10(6), 571–592. https://doi.org/10.1177/1555412014566235

Darvin, L. Holden, J., Wells, J., & Baker, T. (2021). Breaking the glass monitor: Examining the underrepresentation of women in esportss environments. *Sport Management Review*, 24(3), 475–499. https://doi.org/10.1080/14413523.2021.1891746

Darvin, L., Vooris, R., & Mahoney, T. (2020). The playing experiences of esports participants: An analysis of treatment discrimination and hostility in esports environments. *Journal of Athlete Development and Experience*, 2(1), 36–50. https://doi.org/10.25035/jade.02.01.03

Duval, A. (2018). The Olympic charter: A transnational constitution without a state? *Journal of Law and Society*, 45(S1), S245–S269. https://doi.org/10.1111/jols.12112

Fischer-Lescano, A., & Teubner, G. (2004). Regime-collisions: The vain search for legal unity in the fragmentation of global law. *Michigan Journal of International Law*, 25, 999–1045.

Freeburn, L. (2018). *Regulating international sport: Power, authority and legitimacy*. Brill.

Girl Gamer Challenge. (n.d.). Rules. Retrieved February 15, 2022, from https://girlgamer.gg/rules/

Holden, J. T., Rodenberg, R. M., & Kaburakis, A. (2017). Esportss corruption: Gambling, doping and global governance. *Maryland Journal of International Law, 32*, 236–273.

Intel. (2018, February 7). *Intel Extreme Masters PyeongChang: Stunning finale concludes historic esportss event ahead of the Olympic Winter Games 2018*. Retrieved January 7, 2022, from https://newsroom.intel.com/news/intel-extreme-masters-pyeongchang-stunning-finale-concludes-historic-esportss-event-ahead-olympic-winter-games-2018/

IOC. (2021). Framework on fairness, inclusion and non-discrimination on the basis of gender identity and sex variations. Retrieved July 30, 2022, from https://stillmed.olympics.com/media/Documents/News/2021/11/IOC-Framework-Fairness-Inclusion-Non-discrimination-2021.pdf?_ga=2.122267721.39657954.1659194226-1436268667.1656603907

Jenny, S. E., Manning, R. D., Keiper, M. C., & Olrich, T. W. (2016). Virtual(ly) athletes: Where esportss fit within the definition of 'sport'. *Quest, 69*(1), 1–18. http://doi.org/10.1080/00336297.2016.1144517

Karhulahti, V.-M. (2017). Reconsidering esports: Economics and executive ownership. *Physical Culture and Sport, 74*(1), 43–53. http://doi.org/10.1515/pcssr-2017-0010

Kruthika, N. S. (2020). Esportss and its reinforcement of gender divides. *Marquette Sports Law Review, 30*(2), 347–370.

Loland, S. (2001). The logic of progress and the art of moderation in competitive sports. In T. Tännsjö & C. Tamburrini (Eds.), *Values in sport: Elitism, nationalism, gender equality and the scientific manufacture of winners* (pp. 39–56). E & FN Spon.

Miah, A., & Fenton, A. (2021). Esportss in the Olympic and Paralympic Games: The business case for integration. In D. Chatziefstathiou, B. García, & B. Séguin (Eds.), *Routledge handbook of the Olympic and Paralympic Games* (pp. 160–170). Routledge.

Newzoo & Intel. (2021). *Diversity and inclusion in gaming: Insights and opportunities*. https://newzoo.com/insights/trend-reports/diversity-inclusion-report-intel-newzooo

Olympic Agenda 2020+5: 15 Recommendations. (n.d.). Retrieved January 7, 2022, from https://stillmedab.olympic.org/media/Document%20Library/OlympicOrg/IOC/What-We-Do/Olympic-agenda/Olympic-Agenda-2020-5-15-recommendations.pdf#_ga=2.109055877.1262524182.1617693851-616753925.1575537379

Olympic Games. (2017, October 28). *Communique of the Olympic summit*. https://www.olympic.org/news/communique-of-the-olympic-summit

Olympic Games. (2018a, February 9). *Steep road to the Olympics grand finals brings esports fans together ahead of the games*. https://www.olympic.org/news/steep-road-to-the-olympics-grand-finals-brings-esports-fans-together-ahead-of-the-games

Olympic Games. (2018b, December 8) *Communique of the 7th Olympic summit*. https://www.olympic.org/news/communique-of-the-7th-olympic-summit

Olympic Games. (2019, December 7). *Declaration of the 8th Olympic summit*. https://www.olympic.org/news/declaration-of-the-8th-olympic-summit

Olympic Games. (2020, December 12). *Declaration of the 9th Olympic summit*. https://www.olympic.org/news/declaration-of-the-9th-olympic-summit

Olympic Games. (2021a, April 22). *International Olympic committee makes landmark move into virtual sports by announcing first-ever Olympic virtual series*. https://olympics.com/ioc/news/international-olympic-committee-makes-landmark-move-into-virtual-sports-by-announcing-first-ever-olympic-virtual-series

Olympic Games. (2021b, May 13). *Join us at the ballpark for the first-ever Olympic virtual series baseball event!* https://olympics.com/en/news/join-us-at-the-ballpark-for-the-first-ever-olympic-virtual-series-baseball-event

Olympic Games. (2021c, December 11). *Declaration of the 10th Olympic summit.* https://olympics.com/ioc/news/declaration-of-the-10th-olympic-summit

Pack, S. M., & Hedlund, D. P. (2020). Inclusion of electronic sports in the Olympic games for the right (or wrong) reasons. *International Journal of Sport Policy and Politics, 12*(3), 485–495. http://doi.org/10.1080/19406940.2020.1801796

Palar, S. (2021, June 21). *Olympic virtual series.* Olympic Games. https://olympics.com/en/featured-news/olympic-virtual-series-everything-you-need-to-know

Pargman, D., & Svensson, D. (2020). Play as work: On the sportification of computer games. *Digital Culture & Society, 5*(2), 15–40. http://doi.org/10.14361/dcs-2019-0203

Parry, J. (2006). Sport and Olympism: Universals and multiculturalism. *Journal of the Philosophy of Sport, 33*(2), 188–204. http://doi.org/10.1080/00948705.2006.9714701

Parry, J. (2019). E-sports are not sports. *Sport, Ethics and Philosophy, 13*(1), 3–18. https://doi.org/10.1080/17511321.2018.1489419

Patel, S. (2015). *Inclusion and exclusion in competitive sport: Socio-legal and regulatory perspectives.* Routledge.

Pérez Triviño, J. L. (2011). *Ética y deporte.* Desclée de Brouwer.

Ratan, R. A., Taylor, N., Hogan, J., Kennedy, T., & Williams, D. (2015). Stand by your man: An examination of gender disparity in league of legends. *Games and Culture, 10*(5), 438–462. http://doi.org/10.1177/1555412014567228

Reitman, J. G., Anderson-Coto, M. J., Wu, M., Lee, J. S., & Steinkuehler, C. (2020). Esportss research: A literature review. *Games and Culture, 15*(1), 32–50. https://doi.org/10.1177/1555412019840892

Seiner, J. (2019, January 3). 'The second they realize I'm a woman, I no longer have power': Navigating toxicity, harassment in esportss. *Chicago Tribune Website.* https://www.chicagotribune.com/lifestyles/ct-life-women-esportss-20190103-story.html

Siutila, M., & Havaste, E. (2019). A pure meritocracy blind to identity: Exploring the online responses to all-female esportss teams in reddit. *Transactions of the Digital Games Research Association, 4*(3), 43–75.

Summerley, R. (2020). The development of sports: A comparative analysis of the early institutionalization of traditional sports and e-sports. *Games and Culture, 15*(1), 51–72. http://doi.org/10.1177/1555412019838094

Szymanski, S. (2008). A theory of the evolution of modern sport. *Journal of Sport History, 35*(1), 1–32.

Taylor, N., & Stout, B. (2020). Gender and the two-tiered system of collegiate esportss. *Critical Studies in Media Communication, 37*(5), 451–465. http://doi.org/10.1080/15295036.2020.1813901

Taylor, T. L. (2012). *Raising the stakes: E-sports and the professionalization of computer gaming.* The MIT Press.

Tjønndal, A., & Skauge, M. (2021). Youth sport 2.0? The development of esportss in Norway from 2016 to 2019. *Qualitative Research in Sport, Exercise and Health, 13*(1), 166–183. http://doi.org/10.1080/2159676X.2020.1836509

Wai, R. (2014). Private v Private: Transnational private law and contestation in global economic governance. In H. M. Watt & D. P. F. Arroyo (Eds.), *Private international and global governance* (pp. 34–53). Cambridge University Press.

Witkowski, E. (2018). Doing/undoing gender with the girl gamer in high-performance play. In K. L. Gray, G. Voorhees, & E. Vossen (Eds.), *Feminism in play* (pp. 185–203). Palgrave Macmillan.

Witkowski, E. (2012). On the digital playing field: How we "do sport" with networked computer games. *Games and Culture*, 7(5), 349–374. http://doi.org/10.1177/1555412012454222

World Rugby. (n.d.). Transgender women guidelines. Retrieved February 15, 2022, from https://www.world.rugby/the-game/player-welfare/guidelines/transgender/women

Young, M. (2010). The IOC made me do it: Women's ski jumping, VANOC, and the 2010 Winter Olympics. *Constitutional Forum*, 18, 95–107.

Zwift. (2021, May 27). Be a part of sporting history: Event schedule for olympic virtual series cycling events revealed. https://news.zwift.com/en-WW/199426-be-a-part-of-sporting-history-event-schedule-for-olympic-virtual-series-cycling-events-revealed

Part V

Conclusion

Chapter 11

Conclusion

Moving forward in research on social issues in esports

Anne Tjønndal

The contributions in this book have demonstrated that there is both a need and justification for research into social issues in esports. The development of sport is greatly impacted by technology and digitalisation, and a key example of this is the emergence of esports. This is visible through the fact that many international and national sports organisations now include esports in their activities. This developmental trend, which has been further exacerbated by the COVID-19 pandemic, is likely to continue in the years to come. The ongoing convergence of sports and gaming through esports also disrupts traditional definitions and perspectives of what sport is and should be (Parry, 2019, 2021; Naraine, 2021; Tjønndal, 2020). Studying social issues in esports is important for ensuring that these novel digital sporting spaces are inclusive and safe for the people who participate in them. It could be argued that this is especially important in esports, given the age range of many of the players and fans.

There are many directions in esports studies, and social issues are one among them (Reitman et al., 2020; Riatti & Thiel, 2021). The research presented in this book examines several social issues relating to esports. The aim has been to highlight the need for continued research on social issues in esports by disseminating knowledge from a collection of early research contributions on the topic, with a view to inspiring and encouraging students and researchers to complete research projects that expand our knowledge about social issues in esports. Based on the contributions in this book, in this chapter, I synthesise the key findings from the included chapters and suggest some potential paths for moving forward in this research field.

Key findings from the research presented in the book

The research presented in this book provides novel insights into social issues in esports related to gender, mental health, doping, cheating, diversity, and inclusion. Regarding gendered social issues in esports, the research contributions demonstrate how women are often marginalised and subjected to harassment, both as players and leaders in esports organisations. Specifically, there are four main findings from the chapters included in Part II, entitled 'Gender'. Firstly, the

DOI: 10.4324/9781003258650-16

empirical data presented in Chapters 3–5 collectively illustrates how women are underrepresented at all levels and positions in esports organisations, including as players and leaders. This concurs with previous research on gendered social issues in esports (Darvin et al., 2021a; Darvin et al., 2020; Taylor & Stout, 2020; Rogstad, 2021). The second finding is that women esports players who excel in international tournaments are portrayed in gender-stereotypical ways in the media and their gender is questioned when they win (Chapter 3). The third is that the informal recruitment processes of managers and leaders produce gender inequality in esports organisations (Chapter 4). Such processes are problematic, in that male-dominated networks appear to be highly influential as to who is given the opportunity to lead esports organisations. The fourth and last main finding is that women esports players have clearer and stronger opinions about the representation of female characters in games than men. Women players also highlight that they experience female character options as limited and that being able to play female characters is important to them (Chapter 5). Scarce and marginalised representations of women in games, gender-stereotypical presentations of women players, and informal recruitment processes for leadership positions that privilege men over women all contribute to a cycle in which girls and women are discouraged from participating in esports. Thus, gender continues to be the basis of substantial social issues in esports.

From Part III, 'Mental Health and Integrity Issues', the editor highlights three main findings. In terms of mental health, esports athletes frequently experience stressors related to teammates and performance. Although coping with stress is an inherent part of elite sport, Poulus and Polman (Chapter 6) find that stressors in esports athletes are often related to communication issues, anti-social behaviour, making mistakes, and high self-expectations. Such stressors could significantly impact the mental health of esports athletes. However, in their chapter Poulus and Polman also emphasise that at present no research has been conducted on potential gender or age differences in e-athletes' stress and coping mechanisms. Knowledge about such differences is needed if coaches and esports support staff are to be able to effectively support esports athletes in their efforts to cope with their stressors or the negative emotions caused by them. Two of the chapters included in Part III focus on integrity issues in esports, mainly doping and cheating. Chapter 8 describes doping issues in esports and demonstrates how the widespread use of cognition-enhancing stimulants like Adderall and Vyvanse is a social issue that threatens both the integrity of esports competitions and the health of athletes who have no illness-related need for these drugs. A key issue highlighted in this chapter is the recognition that much of the integrity-related focus on esports has been on high-profile match-fixing scandals, thereby leaving the eradication of doping relatively uncharted. Lastly, an important finding from Chapter 8 is that the digital technologies that facilitate esports enable novel forms of cheating and dishonesty as ways of gaining competitive advantages over opponents. Using e-Cycling as an empirical example, Bryce Dyer frames these new ways of cheating as 'cyber doping' and presents four common online cheating types, including avatar misrepresentation, in-game deception, data manipulation, and hardware manipulation.

Part IV, 'Diversity and Inclusion', includes two chapters (9 and 10) with knowledge contributions on social issues in esports and examinations of the potential of esports to contribute to social inclusion and diversity in sport. The main argument in Chapter 9 is the capacity of esports to interact with marginalised populations and those who shy away from traditional sporting spaces. The chapter highlights that esports can construct an inclusive bridging mechanism that does not discriminate by virtue of physicality or mainstream sporting cultures. Similar to the findings from Part II, on 'Gender', the arguments by Hayday and Collison are also spotlighted in previous research on social issues in esports (Tjønndal & Skauge, 2021). Finally, Chapter 10 analyses the potential and pitfalls of the possible inclusion of esports in the Olympic Movement (OM) in the near future. A take-home message from author Abanazir is that regulatory and organisational issues need to be overcome if esports is to be included in the OM. How the IOC and esports industry handle these issues could either create conflict or harmony, particularly when it comes to the inclusion of marginalised athlete groups.

Moving forward in research on social issues in esports

Combating social issues will need to become a paramount objective as esports continues to grow in popularity globally. For now, and as indicated in the book, research on social issues in esports is limited. These limitations include methods and samples, theory, topics, and geosocial contexts.

Research on social issues in sport has covered topics such as (1) participation and dropout patterns in sport, (2) integrity, ethics, and moral behaviour, (3) race and ethnicity, (4) gender, (5) social class, (6) disability, (7) religion, (8) health, (9) fandom and commercialism, (10) governance and politics, and (11) doping and violence (Sleap, 1998; Kew, 1997). When it comes to the relatively novel sports phenomenon of esports, the majority of these issues lack scholarly investigation. As is often the case, research lags behind the developmental trends in society and practice. The two social issues in esports that appear to have been given the most attention to date are gender and mental health (see Chapter 2). Current research in these areas suggests that esports faces similar challenges as traditional sports when it comes to social issues. It is therefore clear that further empirical research is needed on gendered issues and discrimination in esports, as well as on mental health issues in esports.

The current lack of social issues in esports research appears to be due to the paucity of empirical investigations, theoretical diversity, and contextual diversity in study design and samples. The latter is also connected to methodological limitations in esports research on social issues. Methodologically, much of the current esports research consists of descriptive and exploratory work (Reitman et al., 2020). In terms of specific approaches, conceptual papers, document analyses, and surveys appear to be common, especially in esports research in the fields of psychology, business, and management (Jang et al., 2021; Trotter et al., 2020; Hamari & Sjöblom, 2017). However, as Reitman et al. (2020) point out, the representativeness of the samples is often difficult to assess in these studies. This is hardly surprising, given that generalisable quantitative samples require substantial economic and human resources. The lack of resources for rigorous, long-term research projects is an apparent weakness in this field. Due to the novelty of social issues in esports research and the limitations of current research spanning topics, theory, and methods, it is not feasible to provide any thematic or theoretical guidelines for future academic work on social issues in esports. At least three overarching directions are needed in order for research on social issues in esports to move forward. These are: (1) the need for further empirical investigations, (2) the need for sociological inquiries, and (3) the need for contextualisation and diversity of esports contexts.

The need for empirical investigations into social issues in esports

Many of the key research texts on esports have been conceptual and theoretical (Jenny et al., 2017; Thiel & John, 2018; Hallmann & Giel, 2018; Parry, 2021; 2019; Naraine, 2021; Abanazir, 2019; Hayday et al., 2022). Conceptual work is often necessary and useful in novel research fields within the social sciences. It takes time to design and conduct good empirical research projects, and early theoretical contributions to an emerging field will often help to inform the empirical research that follows. Many scholars believe that the time is now right for research to move forward with empirical investigations into a wide variety of social issues, such as race and ethnicity, disability, religion, gender, health, fandom and commercialism, governance and politics, doping, ethics, and integrity. The research presented in this book, together with the literature review in Chapter 2, suggests that social issues related to race and ethnicity, disability, religion, fandom and commercialism, governance, and politics are imperative directions for future research.

The need for critical and sociological inquiries into social issues in esports

The chapters in this book represent an early attempt to collate and synthesise the current and emerging trends in social issues in esports research. The chapters consist of empirical and theoretical contributions, many of which aim to critically examine various social issues at different levels and in esports contexts. However, a shortcoming in esports research on social issues is the lack of critical perspectives applied to studies of esports practices. The reason for this deficiency could be connected to the limited sociological research on esports. For instance, at the time of writing (May 2022), only three peer-reviewed articles on 'esports' have been published in the top three international sociology of sport journals – *International Review for the Sociology of Sport* (IRSS), *Sociology of Sport*, and *European Journal for Sport and Society* (EJSS). The same search in five of the top international sociology journals yielded no publications at all on the topic (see Table 11.1).

As critical analyses of social issues are key to sociology in general and sociology of sport in particular, promoting sociological work on esports would more than likely contribute to advancements in this research field.

The need for contextualisation and diversity of esports contexts

In terms of methodological directions for future research, there is a need for empirical studies of different contexts in order to move forward in research on social issues in esports. By different contexts I mean (a) different parts of the world geographically, (b) different types of esports game genres and organisations, and (c) different groups of people who are engaging in esports. While Chapter 2 identifies that the geographical origins of research on social issues in esports are refreshingly broad compared to many other novel research fields in sport, the novelty of the field implies that research on social issues in esports in different parts of the world is still needed. Neither sport nor esports is a singular field. Sociology of sport has contributed to sports-specific knowledge about a variety of sporting activities and organisations. This diversity of contexts is also needed if research on social issues in esports is to move forward. Some examples in this book are Chapter 3 (on *Hearthstone*), Chapter 8 (on e-Cycling), Chapter 5 (on SVGs), and Chapter 4 (on private and voluntary esports organisations). In order to move forward in research on social issues in esports, there is a need for further studies into specific esports contexts related to geography, esports game genres, esports organisation, and different sociodemographic groups of people engaged in esports.

Table 11.1 Sociological work on esports

Journal	Published articles on esports (search conducted in May 2022)
EJSS	• Rogstad (2021) • Thiel & John (2018)
Sociology of Sport Journal	None
IRSS	• McLeod et al. (2021)
Annual Review of Sociology	None
American Sociological Review	None
American Journal of Sociology	None
Sociology (the journal of the British Sociological Association)	None
Sociological Theory	None

Concluding remarks

First and foremost, the contributions in this book should be read as furthering esports research on social issues. In this concluding chapter, I have pointed to key findings from the research presented in the book. Based on these contributions, I have also suggested possible paths for moving forward in this research field, such as carrying out qualitative and quantitative studies of social issues in esports related to topics like race and ethnicity, disability, religion, gender, health, fandom and commercialism, governance and politics, doping, ethics, and integrity. In addition, there is a need for critical and sociological investigations into social issues in esports, more and different study contexts, and a sensitivity to the geographical and socio-cultural context of the framework in which social issues arise and the esports context. To summarise, the social issues studied in this book highlight the need for deeper empirical explorations of the different game genres and social issues found in esports. In today's rapidly paced, changing, and global society, social issues remain a recurring and persistent challenge. Decades of research on the sociology of sport have demonstrated how such issues impact people involved in sports organisations. Now, as sport becomes increasingly digitalised in a multitude of ways, sport sociologists need to turn their attention to examining exclusionary practices and social issues in esports.

References

Abanazir, C. (2019). Institutionalisation in e-sports. *Sport, Ethics and Philosophy*, 13(2), 117–131. https://doi.org/10.1080/17511321.2018.1453538

Darvin, L., Holden, J., Wells, J., & Baker, T. (2021a). Breaking the glass monitor: Examining the underrepresentation of women in esports environments. *Sport Management Review*, 24(3), 475–499. https://doi.org/10.1080/14413523.2021.1891746

Darvin, L., Vooris, R., & Mahoney, T. (2020). The playing experiences of esports participants: An analysis of treatment discrimination and hostility in esports environments, *Journal of Athlete Development and Experience*, 2(1), Article 3. https://doi.org/10.25035/jade.02.01.03

Hallmann, K., & Giel, T. (2018). eSports – Competitive sports or recreational activity? *Sport Management Review*, 21(1), 14–20. https://doi.org/10.1016/j.smr.2017.07.011

Hamari, J., & Sjöblom, M. (2017). What is eSports and why do people watch it? *Internet Research*, 27(2), 211–232. https://doi.org/10.1108/IntR-04-2016-0085

Hayday, E., Collison-Randall, H. & Kelly, S. (2022). *Esports insights*. Routledge Focus.

Jenny, S. E., Manning, R. D., Keiper, M. C., & Olrich, T. W. (2017). Virtual(ly) athletes: Where eSports fit within the definition of "Sport". *Quest*, 69(1), 1–18. https://doi.org/10.1080/00336297.2016.1144517

Jang, W. W., Byon, K. K., Baker III, T. A., & Tsuji, Y. (2021). Mediating effect of esports content live streaming in the relationship between esports recreational gameplay and esports event broadcast. *Sport, Business and Management*, 11(1), 89–108. https://doi.org/10.1108/SBM-10-2019-0087

Kew, F. (1997). *Sport: Social problems and issues*. Routledge.

McLeod, C. M., Xue, H., & Newman, J. I. (2021). Opportunity and inequality in the emerging esports labor market. *International Review for the Sociology of Sport*. https://doi.org/10.1177/10126902211064093

Naraine, M. L. (2021). Actually, esports is sport: A response to Parry's (2019) misguided view. *Sports Innovation Journal*, *2021*(2), 33–44. https://doi.org/10.18060/24812.

Parry, J. (2019). E-sports are not sports. *Sport, Ethics and Philosophy*, *13*(1), 3–18. https://doi.org/10.1080/17511321.2018.1489419

Parry, J. (2021). Esports will not be at the Olympics. *Journal of Olympic Studies*, *2*(2), 1–13. https://doi.org/10.5406/jofolympstud.2.2.0001

Reitman, J. G., Anderson-Coto, M. J., Wu, M., Lee, J. S., & Steinkuehler, C. (2020). Esports research: A literature review. *Games and Culture*, *15*(1), 32–50. https://journals.sagepub.com/doi/pdf/10.1177/1555412019840892

Riatti, P., & Thiel, A. (2021). The societal impact of electronic sport: A scoping review. *German Journal of Exercise and Sport Research*, 1–24. https://doi.org/10.1007/s12662-021-00784-w

Rogstad, E. (2021). Gender in esports research: A literature review. *European Journal for Sport and Society*. https://doi.org/10.1080/16138171.2021.1930941

Sleap, M. (1998). *Social issues in sport*. Palgrave Macmillan.

Taylor, N., & Stout, B. (2020). Gender and the two-tiered system of collegiate esports. *Critical Studies in Media Communication*. https://doi.org/10.1080/15295036.2020.1813901

Thiel, A., & John, J. M. (2018). Is eSport a 'real' sport? Reflections on the spread of virtual competitions. *European Journal for Sport and Society*, *15*(4), 311–315. https://doi.org/10.1080/16138171.2018.1559019

Tjønndal, A., & Skauge, M. (2021). Social innovation and virtual sport: A case of esports in Norway. In A. Tjønndal (Ed.), *Social innovation in sport* (pp. 135–168). Palgrave Macmillan.

Tjønndal, A. (2020). "What's next? Calling beer-drinking a sport?!": Virtual resistance to considering eSport as sport. *Sport, Business and Management*, *11*(1), 1–17. https://doi.org/10.1108/SBM-10-2019-0085

Trotter, M. G., Coulter, T. J., Davis, P. A., Poulus, D. R., & Polman, R. (2020). The association between esports participation, health and physical activity behaviour. *International Journal of Environmental Research and Public Health*, *17*(19), 7329. https://doi.org/10.3390/ijerph17197329

Index

Abanazir, C. 149
Abarbanel, B. 14
Abbiss 66
AC *see* avoidance coping
Acker, J. 46–47, 50–51, 59–62
Action Sports for Development and Peacebuilding 137–138
Adderall 7, 105–108
Allison, L. 150
amphetamines 102
analytical design and strategy 69
anomie theory 103
anti-doping policies 102
appraisals of stress 90–91
associativity 150–151
athlete cyber-dope 120; data hacking 124; dishonest gender assignment 123; dishonest inflation of power output through equipment 123–124, falsely disclosed functional threshold power 123; height doping 121; poor, drifting or intentional power miscalibration 123; post-event data file manipulation 121–122; power meter inaccuracy (accuracy, precision, single-sided pms) 122–123; sandbagging 122; sticky watts 124; weight doping 121
athletes and aggressive behaviour 16
attention-deficit hyperactivity disorder (ADHD) 107
audience and social media stressors 90
avoidance coping (AC) 84, 91–94

Bahrke, M. S. 102
Bailey, R. 132, 133
Bascón-Seda, A. 15
Behnke, M. 90
Blizzard Entertainment 32
Blondin, J.-P. 85

Brock, T. 14
building social bonds and relational inclusion 134–136
Butler, J. 67, 73, 74
Butovskaya, M. L. 16

caste ridden India 131
CdA 121
CET *see* coping effectiveness training
Chan, D. 19
Chargaziya, L. D. 16
cheating 101–102
Choi, C. 17, 18
CMRT *see* cognitive-motivational-relational theory
cognition-enhancing drugs 106
cognitive-motivational-relational theory (CMRT) 83–84, 84, 86
Cohen, L. J. 84
Collison, H. 8, 138–139
combating social issues 4, 167
community 134
community capital 132, 135
competitive e-athletes 95
components of, inequality regimes 51
conflict 154–156
controlling means of production 152–153
convergence of esports and traditional sport 65–66
coping 7, 84; classifications 85; effectiveness 85–86, 91–94; response 91–94; strategies 17, 84–85, 92–93
coping effectiveness training (CET) 95
corporate social responsibly (CSR) 139, 141
CounterStrike: Global Offensive (CS:GO) 48, 86
COVID-19 pandemic 101, 115–116, 142
Cross-Roads Innvitational 38, 40

CSR *see* corporate social responsibly
CSR strategic alignment, SDP 141
current and emerging trends 21–22
cyber-dopers 120

Darvin, L. 20–21, 47–48
data and methods: analytical design and strategy 69; participant recruitment 68; variables and descriptive statistics 68–69
data hacking 124
Defense of the Ancients 2 (DOTA 2) 14, 83
descriptive statistics: of dependent variables **70**; of explanatory variables and respondents' locations **71**; and variables 68–69
detection of doping 109
developers/publisher 151–153, 156
digital interviews, esports leaders 51
digitalisation 3–4
Digital Schoolhouse 136
disciplines 148–149
dishonest gender assignment 123
dishonest inflation of, power output through equipment 123–124
doping 107; to cyber doping 117–120; functions 107–108; history of 104–106; overview of, traditional sports: the history of, doping and anti-doping 102–103; recommendations 108–109; synopsis 109–110; therapeutic use exemptions (TUEs) 104; WADA Code and drug classes 103–104
Dreiskämper, D. 109
drug classes 103–104
dumb trainers 117

Eason, L. 41
e-athlete 85–86; sources of stress experienced 86–90; *see also* e-cycling
eBaseball Powerful Pro Baseball 2020 competition 157
e-cycling *116*; app 117; equipment 117; history of 115–116; performance, simulation/illustration 124–125
edoping, esports 12–13
education 133, 136–137
Electronic Sports League (ESL) 105, 151
elite e-athletes 87, 90
elite LoL e-athletes 87
Elling, A. 53
Elling, J. 53
emotion-focused coping (EFC) 84

empirical studies, stigmas 15
enterprises 151
environmental constraints stressors 90
e-racing 118
ESL *see* Electronic Sports League
esports: community building and inclusive spaces 133–134; governance *see* Olympic Movement (OM); and social inclusion 132–133; *see also individual entries*
Esports Federation of India 13
Esports Integrity Coalition (ESIC) 13, 105, 109
esports organisations 6
Esports World Championships in 2020 116
exclusion and inclusion, OM 153–154; conflict 154–156; harmony 156–157
executive ownership/owner 153

falsely disclosed functional threshold power 123
female character options 72–74
female character representations 74; positive and non-sexualised representations 75
female characters, importance: analytical design and strategy 69; game content and gendered media representations 67; gender, identity and esports 66–67; gendered character representations and player motivation 74–76; limitations 76–77; options 72–74; overview 65–66; participant recruitment 68; results 69–72; variables and descriptive statistics 68–69
female representation 65, 67; *see also* women representation
Fenton, A. 149
Fiskaali, A. 16
Folkman, S. 84
four statements, gendered character representations 68
franchises game 65
Freitas, B. D. A. 13–15
functional dimension 136
functional threshold power (FTP) 123

game content 67
game genre 65
gaming addiction: coping strategies and motivations 17; lower score, mental health measurements 17; risk of 16

gaming frequency 68–69
Gaudreau, P. 85
gender 6
gender, identity and esports research 66–67
gender and esports 20
gendered character representations 74–76
gendered media representations 67
gender equity leadership 51
gender-inclusive sporting spaces 46–47
gender inequity: control over systems 56–58; recruitment, organising process that produces 54–56; shape and degree 53–54; visibility and legitimacy 58–61
gender-related controversy 31
gender-swapping 32
gender topics 20
global esports revenues 132
Global North and Global South 140
global platform 133
Grandmaster league format 36–37
Gray, K. L. 19
growing commercial potential 139
Gupta, D. 13

Hamilton, B. R. 38
harmony 156–157
Havaste, E. 156
Hayday, E. 8
Hayday, E. J. 138–139
HCT competitive system 33
HCT system open qualifiers 33
Hearthstone 6; Blizzard Entertainment 32; first transgender woman in HCT2, Luna Eason 37–38; first woman at official event, Rumay Wang 38; first woman Grandmaster, Pathra Cadness 36–37; first woman in HCT2, Xinyu Wang 34–35; first woman world champion, Xiaomeng Li 36; lawsuit, invitational events 38–40; synopsis 40–41; tournament structure 33; world championship tiers 33
Hearthstone Championship Tour (HCT) 33
Hearthstone's HCT2 34–35
Hearthstone World Championship 2019 36, 37
Hedlund, D. P. 149
height doping 121
Hilvoorde, I. V. 136
Himmelstein, D. 86
history of doping: evolution of doping regulations in esports 104–105; key to success? why professional esports players dope 105–106
Holden, J. T. 6, 7
Hovden, J. 54

identity performances 67
IESF *see* International Esports Federation
independent national esports actors 49
inequality regimes 50
integrity issues, esports 12
interaction and social bonding 133
internal evaluation stressors 90
International Esports Federation (IESF) 31, 105, 151; controversy 31–32
International Olympic Committee (IOC) 148, 150; adoption, anti-doping policies 102

Johnson, M. R. 14

Kanter, R. 56
Karhulahti, V.-M. 153
Kelly, S. 17
Kim, C.-H. 34

lawsuit and representation of women, *Hearthstone* 38–40
Lazarus, R. S. 83, 84
leadership and gender inclusion: findings and discussion 51; synopsis 61–62
League of Legends Championship Series (LCS) 105, 156
Leis, O. 87
limitations 76–77
limited and stereotypical representations of women 65
logistic regressions **72, 73, 75, 76**

Macey, J. 17
Macías, G. R. 15
Madden 65
male gamer stereotype 66–67
Massanari, A. 66
match-fixing and gambling, esports: *Defence of the Ancients 2* (DOTA 2) 14; legal ramifications and regulations 14; media and public debate 14; socioeconomic and cultural backgrounds 14; threat, growth and legitimacy 13–14
Mavromoustakos-Blom, P. 34
McLeod, C. M. 18
media representations 67

mental health 7; and well-being 17–18
mental toughness (MT) 94–95
mental well-being 16
Miah, A. 149
mindfulness-acceptance-commitment training (MAC) 95
moderators and mediators stress 94–95
Morgan, H. 131
moving forward, social issues 165, 167–168; contextualisation and diversity 169; critical and sociological inquiries 168–169; empirical investigations 168; key findings 165–167; synopsis 170
multiplayer online battle arenas (MOBA) 49

National Basketball Association (NBA) 105–106
negative mental health outcomes 17
negative perception of, videogames 15
new bridge, sports industry vs. SDP 139–140
Newzoo and Intel 148
Nicholls, A. 85
Norwegian Centre for Research Data 68
Norwegian Olympic and Paralympic Committee and Confederation of Sports (NIF) 48–49, 57

official *Hearthstone* event 38
Ohno, S. 16
Olympic and Paralympic programmes 149
Olympic Movement (OM) 8, 148; address exclusion and discrimination 158; conflict 154–156; controlling production 152–153; cooperation 158; exclusion and inclusion 153–154; finding way, cooperating 148–150; harmony 156–157; international sports federations and IOC 153–154; piecing fragments together 150–152; regulatory and adjudicatory landscape 157; synopsis 157–158
Olympic Virtual Series 148, 156–158
online-based cycling 115
online collective card game 32–33; *see also Hearthstone*
organisation of esports, Norway 48–49
organisations doping policy 105
Orlando, A. 48

Paaßen, B. 66
Pack, S. M. 149

Palanichamy, T. 17
Pargman, D. 149
Parry, J. 149
Parshakov, P. 18
participant recruitment 68
participants description **52**
Patel, S. 154
peacekeeping and social development projects 131
performance enhancement, virtual bicycle 125–126
performance enhancement goals *118*
performance-enhancing drugs (PEDs) 12–13, 101, 103
performance-enhancing stimulants 107
performance expectation stressors 87, 90
performance-related stressors 87
Peter, S. C. 15
PFC and EFC strategies 95–96
Philip, B. 131
piecing the fragments together 150–152
Piggott, L. 6
player motivation 74–76
Polman, R. 7
poor, drifting/intentional power miscalibration 123
portrayals of, female characters 74
positive and non-sexualised representations 75
post-event data file manipulation 121–122
Pot, N. 136
potential understanding, social inclusion agendas 131–132; community building and inclusive spaces 133–134; CSR strategic alignment, SDP 141; esports and social inclusion 132–133; functional inclusion, education 136–137; reflecting potential 137–139; social bonds and relational inclusion 134–136; social inclusion, esports and SDP in practice 140–141; sports industry vs. SDP, bridge 139–140; synopsis 142–143
Poulus, D. 87, 90
Poulus, D. R. 7
power meter inaccuracy 122–123
precarity 67–68
primary appraisal 83
problem-focused coping (PFC) 84
psychological impacts 66
PyeongChang Olympic Games 149–150

quantitative approach 13

Index

racism and ethnicity 19–20
Rainbow Six: Siege (R6) 85–86
reflecting potential, social inclusion 137–139
regulating challenges, doping 107; functions 107–108; recommendations 108–109
Reitman, J. G. 168
relational dimension 134
representation and proliferation, female characters 65
research, gender, identity and esports 66–67
research papers **21**
revenue 101
Riatti, P. 5, 19, 46, 48
right way of cooperating 148–150
Rogstad, E. 7, 48
Rogstad, E. T. 20
Rosenthal, R. 13
Rosenthal, R.R. 7
Røsten, S. 6
Roth, S. 84

safe spaces 133
Salmons, J. 51
sandbagging 122
Schelfhout, S. 34
scholarship 6
Schulenkorf, N. 131, 134
science, technology, engineering and mathematics (STEM) 133
scientific knowledge 4
SDP programmes 8
secondary appraisals 83–84
selection criteria leadership 51
self-preservation strategy 122
sexualisation of characters 74
Shaw, A. 67, 73, 74
Shen, C. 67
Sherry, E. 132
Shulze, J. 17, 20
Siutila, M. 156
six thematic parts 12
Sjoberg, E. 6
Skauge, M. 7
smart bikes 117
smart trainers 117
Smith, M. 86
social engagement 134
social inclusion 131, 142–143; dimensions of 133; esports, and SDP in practice 140–141; framework 132

social inequality 18, 21–22; earnings and youth participation 18–19
social issues: common topics 11; current knowledge and research trends 11; current lack 167–168; databases 11–12; empirical and theoretical explorations 4; esports 4–5; maltreatment and bullying 4; moving forward *see* moving forward, social issues; overview 5–8; perspective 96–97; research papers **21**; sport impact digitally 3; systematic literature review 12; technology and digitalisation 3; themes 12; topics 167; *see also individual entries*
sociological work on esports **169**
South Africa's Cape Town 137
Sport for Development and Peace (SDP) 8, 131–132, 131–136; CSR strategies 141; practice 140–141; and sports industry 139–140
sport leadership and governance 46
sport organisations 4
sports-themed video games 149–150
sports video games (SVGs) 7, 48, 65–66
StarCraft II 149
sticky watts 124
stigmas associated, esports participation 15–16
Stout, B. 21, 47, 155
Straub, B. 109
stress and coping 83–86; coping response and effectiveness 91–94; e-athletes experience 86–90, **88–89**; moderators and mediators 94–95; practical implications 95–96; research directions 96–97; stress appraisals 90–91
stressors categorised 87, 90
stressors identified study 86
strong social opportunities 133
Svensson, D. 149
SVGs *see* sports video games

taxonomy of, online games-based cheating 119
Taylor, N. 21, 47, 155
Taylor, T. L. 155, 156
team issues stressors 90
teammate stressors 87, 95
technology 117
Tempo/Storm 31–32
theoretical framework, gender regimes in organisations 50–51
Thiel, A. 5, 19, 46, 48

Thorpe, H. 137, 138
Titanar *Hearthstone* Elite Invitational in 2018 35
Tjønndal, A. 6
Tomlinson, A. 150
traditional sports 65–66, 86–87, 92–96, 138–139; doping *see* doping
Trotter, M. G. 96
Tweedie, J. W. 7
2017 Summer Championship 34

United Kingdom (UK) 135
United Nations Sustainable Development Goals (SDGs) 131
United States, esports 136–137
USA poverty threshold 18

Van der Klashorst, E. 136
variables and descriptive statistics 68–69
Vermeulen, L. 35
violence and stigma, esports 15
virtually cycling 7, 115; assess performance enhancement 125–126; athlete cyber-dope 120–124; simulation or illustration 124–125; *see also* e-cycling
Voorhees, G. 48

The WADA Code 103–104
Wågan, F. A. 6
WCG *see* World Cyber Games
weight doping 121

WESA *see* World Esports Association
Westmattelmann, D. 109
Wheaton, B. 138
wheel on 117
Williams, D. 74
Wilner, R. 6
women and non-playing roles 20–21
women banned 31
women leadership: gender diversity 47; literature review 48; researchers findings 47
women representation: first Grandmaster, Pathra Cadness 36–37; first in HCT2, Xinyu Wang 34–35; first official event, Rumay Wang 38; first transgender in HCT2, Luna Eason 37–38; first world champion, Xiaomeng Li 36; lawsuit, invitational events 38–40; *see also* female characters
World Anti-Doping Agency (WADA) 103
World Cyber Games (WCG) 152
World Esports Association (WESA) 105, 151
Wreyford, N. 56

Yesalis, C. E. 102
Yu, B. 21

Zhao, Y. 15
Zhu, Y. 15